As the Puck Turns

As the Puck Turns

A PERSONAL JOURNEY THROUGH THE WORLD OF HOCKEY

BRIAN CONACHER

John Wiley & Sons Canada, Ltd.

National Library of Canada Cataloguing in Publication Data

Conacher, Brian, 1941-
    As the puck turns / Brian Conacher.
Includes index.
ISBN 978-0-470-15295-9
    1. Conacher, Brian, 1941-. 2. Hockey. 3. Hockey—Biography.
I. Title.
GV848.5.C65A3 2007   796.962092   C2007-904384-4

Production Credits
Cover and interior design: Jason Vandenberg
Interior text layout: Tegan Wallace
Front cover photo: Graphic Artists/Hockey Hall of Fame
Wiley Bicentennial Logo: Richard J. Pacifico
Printer: Tri-Graphic Printing Ltd.

John Wiley & Sons Canada, Ltd.
6045 Freemont Blvd.
Mississauga, Ontario
L5R 4J3

This book is printed with biodegradable vegetable-based inks. Text pages are printed on 60lb. 100% PCW using TG ECO100 by Tri-Graphic Printing, Ltd., an FSC certified printer.

Printed in Canada
1 2 3 4 5 TRI 11 10 09 08 07

To the spirit, tradition, history and
future of the great game of hockey

Table of Contents

Preface

LIONEL CONACHER, my father, was named Canada's Athlete of the First Half Century (1900–1950). He was the oldest son of Ben and Elizabeth Conacher of Toronto and one of ten children (five boys and five girls). Of these siblings and their offspring, six Conachers have played in the National Hockey League (NHL): Lionel and his brothers Charlie and Roy, my cousins Peter and Murray Conacher Henderson, and me. Combined, we played on six Stanley Cup championship teams between 1932 and 1967. Lionel, Charlie and Roy are the only three brothers inducted into the Hockey Hall of Fame.

With this rich hockey family tradition, I've been involved in and around all aspects of the game and the business of hockey for most of my life. I've played at all levels: minor hockey, public school, high school, major junior, university, Canada's National and Olympic teams, minor professional (American Hockey League, Central Hockey League), NHL, World Hockey Association (WHA), and adult recreational hockey. Off the ice, I've coached and managed minor hockey, high school hockey, minor professional, and the WHA Indianapolis Racers and Edmonton Oilers. And most recently, I was president of the NHL Alumni Association, an organization that represents the interests of all former NHL players and preserves the spirit, tradition and history of the great game of hockey.

In 1970, I wrote *Hockey In Canada: The way it is!*, one of the first sports books written by a professional athlete. I tried to articulate a realistic account of the Canadian and international hockey environments at both amateur and professional levels in the 1950s and 1960s.

Some thirty-seven years later, I am again motivated to express my thoughts about what I think is the best team sport: ice hockey, a game that has occupied my interest and imagination for more than fifty-five years. Recounting some of my experiences in the world of hockey might contribute to solutions to the many complex issues and challenges facing the game and business of hockey. My hope for this book is that it gives some insight into and direction for the game of hockey, which I feel has lost its way, and help make it great once again.

The NHL is at the top of the hockey hierarchy, and has an intrusive and pervasive influence, not only on all Canadian hockey players but also on all Canadians. The world of hockey plays as true fiction and has become the great Canadian soap opera; thus, *As the Puck Turns*.

This book continues my unique personal journey through the world of hockey beginning in the late 1960s.

Acknowledgements

AS I was a hockey player, I am a journeyman writer, certainly not a natural one. Consequently, I sought the capable assistance of those who could help me better tell this story. Special thanks is owed to Ron Edwards and Edna Barker, as well as Karen Milner and Elizabeth McCurdy of Wiley for their much needed assistance to better organize my often rambling recollections into a tighter and more articulate story. I hope the result has made this book an informative and enjoyable read. Also I'm indebted to Kevin Shea, an experienced writer who was my sounding board for the many drafts, as well as my guide through the world of publishing. And last, I'm thankful for my life's experiences without which there would be no story to tell, and to these famous words that sent me in the right direction:

Two roads diverged in a wood, and I—

I took the one less traveled by,

And that has made all the difference.

Robert Frost

Prologue

FEBRUARY 17, 2007, forty years almost to the day since the Toronto Maple Leafs won their eleventh Stanley Cup championship in 1967. I'm standing at centre ice in the Air Canada Centre in Toronto, joined by my teammates from that winning team. All the players are here save for the departed Tim Horton and Terry Sawchuk, as well as coaches George "Punch" Imlach and Francis "King" Clancy. The Leafs organization is paying tribute to our achievement. It was a special team at a special time. The average age of the team was the oldest to win the Stanley Cup; we won against our archrivals, the Montreal Canadiens; it was the last year of the Original Six era of the NHL; ten players would go on to become members of the Hockey Hall of Fame; and it was Canada's centennial year. It was a time for great celebration. It was also a time of great expectations: we assumed a twelfth Stanley Cup victory would follow in the not too distant future. And yet in 2007, I—along with every loyal Leafs fan—was asking myself why the Leafs haven't won the Stanley Cup in the interim. Why has it been so elusive?

In the seasons since 1967, the Leafs have had many good and some great players. But in the 1967–68 season, Punch Imlach—partly out of spite and vindictiveness against players who joined the fledgling NHL Players' Association (NHLPA) and partly because of the NHL expansion—started dismantling the winning team, and the organization has never fully recovered. And there has been the irresponsible, impulsive,

1

interfering and tyrannical leadership of Harold Ballard and those who followed him. Combined with some questionable management and coaching over the years, the Leafs have become a team and organization still trying to find their way out of the hockey wilderness.

The lack of on-ice success can be traced to ownership and the boardroom. Most successful professional sports franchises are well led at the top. No matter how good the players, weak and unsettled leadership somehow makes its way onto the playing surface. Some observers think for years the Leafs organization has been one of the most misguided and poorly led professional sports franchises in North America. The ownership and the board have continually failed to provide the direction and leadership necessary to produce a winner on the ice. As leaders and giants in other fields, they have cast a small shadow in the world of NHL hockey.

And with each passing year, it has become more difficult to win the Stanley Cup. Why? In no way to diminish the achievement of the 1967 Leafs of which I'm proud to have been a member, but the playoff format at the time was such that if you were one of four teams to make the playoffs, you needed only four wins in the semi-finals to play in the Stanley Cup final.

In the 1966–67 season, the Leafs struggled in the regular season, but went into the playoffs playing our best hockey of the season. In six games, we upset the regular season champions, the Chicago Black Hawks. And then on to meet the Montreal Canadiens for the Stanley Cup. In six games, the Leafs became Stanley Cup champions for the third time in four years. Who would have thought at the time that at least forty years of futility would follow?

Winning the Stanley Cup isn't easy. You need good players, good team chemistry, good leadership to play your best hockey in the play-offs—and some luck. But in 1967 the Leafs had to peak only for at most fourteen games, in two best-of-seven series.

Today a team has to win three best-of-seven series just to get to the final. In my opinion, it's much more difficult to win the Stanley Cup now, not only physically but also mathematically. A perfect example is the 1993 playoffs. In some of their most exciting playoff hockey in years, the Leafs played twenty-one games (five went into overtime) only to lose in a seventh game against the Los Angeles Kings, led by Wayne Gretzky. So close to the Holy Grail of hockey, and yet so far! Had the Leafs won, they would have played the Canadiens for the Stanley Cup in a classic rematch of the 1967 series. It was not to be, and it will never happen again under the current playoff format, which for many fans leaves a lot to be desired. If the two best teams in the league are in the same conference, and with conference champions determined before the final, they can never get to play for the Stanley Cup. And too many times in recent years, the two best teams haven't had the opportunity to play for the Stanley Cup—regrettable for both the fans and the NHL. A rethink of the playoff format with the fans uppermost in mind might be a good idea.

As I stood in the Air Canada Centre, memories of my hockey journey flooded back. I realized that I hadn't seen and experienced the world of hockey as many other people have, but it was always interesting and at times bizarre, filled with many twists, turns and bounces along the way.

Return to Hockey

IN THE fall of 1965, I became a professional hockey player with the Toronto Maple Leafs organization. Before that I was a member of Canada's first National Hockey Team (Nats). The Nats were envisioned and coached by Father David Bauer, one of the truly original and inspirational thinkers in the Canadian hockey landscape at a time when the NHL strived for total domination. I represented Canada in the 1964 Olympic Winter Games in Innsbruck, Austria, and again at the 1965 World Hockey Championships (WHC) in Finland. The Nats established a pinnacle for young hockey players as an alternative to the NHL.

Father Bauer's concept for a national hockey team was idealistic and conflicted with the NHL's desire to control or influence all levels of hockey development in Canada. He believed that a national team of select top amateurs could successfully represent Canada in international hockey and at the same time enable aspiring players to combine and balance their educational needs with the pursuit of hockey excellence.

In my two roller-coaster years under Punch Imlach, the Leafs went from winning the Stanley Cup in 1967 to missing the playoffs the next season. In the spring of 1968 I was left unprotected, and my playing rights were acquired by the Detroit Red Wings. I was a journeyman NHLer and decided I would be better off to get on with my life outside hockey rather than be traded around the league every few years and live my life as a hockey gypsy. In the fall of 1968 I retired as an NHL player. My first post-hockey job was with a commercial real estate company in Toronto.

In early 1969, Johnny Esaw, the sports director for the CTV Network and for CFTO-TV, the network's flagship station in Toronto, invited me to be part of his broadcast team as the colour commentator for the WHC in Stockholm, Sweden. I had no broadcasting experience, but I took the job.

In Stockholm, Canada recorded its weakest showing in international hockey. It bothered me to watch my former team continually overmatched by the best players the Soviet Union, Czechoslovakia and Sweden had to offer. In spite of the best efforts of all the players, the reality was that teams made up of Canada's best "true amateurs," while coming close on several occasions, could not defeat the best "sham amateurs" of the Soviet Union and Europe. The players from the Soviet Union, particularly, were clearly professionals by any reasonable definition.

Consequently, Hockey Canada, the independent Crown corporation set up to represent and oversee Canada's participation in international hockey along with the Canadian Amateur Hockey Association (CAHA) made their first attempt to gradually change the WHC into a truly open tournament where Canada's best could play against the best of the Soviet and top European teams on a level sheet of ice.

Bunny Ahearne, the president of the International Ice Hockey Federation (IIHF), was no friend to Canadian hockey. He manipulated and controlled the international game, and took every opportunity to restrict and compromise Canada's chances to compete on equal terms with the top teams.

I have an all too vivid and painful memory of how Canada's Olympic hockey team was duped out of a medal at the 1964 Olympic Winter Games. In our final game, a victory over the Soviets would have given us the gold medal. With a loss, Canada, Sweden and Czechoslovakia would be tied for second place and a silver medal. But between the second and third periods, Ahearne, in conjunction with the International Olympic Congress (IOC) headed by Avery Brundage, decided arbitrarily to break the possible tie based on goals for and against.

That decision caused our team to be demoted to fourth place, and we were out of the medals. Marshall Johnston, one of our players, aptly summed up our Olympic experience when he said to Father Bauer: "The shepherd and his flock have been fleeced!"

Ahearne's power base was aligned with the Soviet bloc, not with Canada, and his every move was calculated to maintain the support of the Soviets. He was arrogant and bold and even suggested that the IIHF had jurisdiction over the NHL. Bunny Ahearne saw himself as the international czar of hockey around the world. However, he knew that without the high-spirited and rugged Canadians being at least competitive, IIHF tournaments would make for bad box office. So, in the summer of 1969, with a strong push from Canada, the IIHF made a major change to its rules: Canada could reinstate as amateurs up to nine former professional players, excluding current NHLers.

I was no longer actively involved with the Nats program, but I still followed it and kept in touch with Father Bauer. When I heard Canada was finally going to be permitted to use reinstated professionals in international competition, I was optimistic. At long last, Canada would have a legitimate chance to reclaim its place at the top of international hockey. I felt from experience that the Nats were only one or two experienced and skilled players away from capturing the coveted gold medal that had eluded Canada since 1952.

And after years of lobbying to get the WHC, Canada would host the tournament for the first time, in Winnipeg, in February 1970. It was very important to Hockey Canada, the CAHA, the Nats program and Canadian pride that Canada's team was competitive.

Most hockey fans in Canada were preoccupied with the NHL and either oblivious or apathetic to Canada's futile efforts in international hockey, generally considering it second-rate competition. Canada's recent involvement in international hockey was generally unknown and unappreciated, more a national embarrassment than a source of national pride. However, international competition stirs deep emotions in all Canadians, no matter what the sport, and none more than hockey. It galled Canadians that even our second-best hockey teams couldn't beat any other team in the world. Canadians had always felt that Canada was the best hockey nation in the world, for it had the

NHL, stocked primarily by Canadian talent. After all, hockey was "our game"!

In the fall of 1969, Hockey Canada began to assemble a Nats team whose goal was to restore Canada's pride and status as the premiere hockey power in the world. And what better place to do it than on a home rink in Winnipeg? Father Bauer contacted me for a third time about joining the Nats. I hadn't contemplated playing hockey again, but the hope of being on a winning Nats team got my interest and my commitment. With the tournament in Canada and the apparent unified support of all hockey bodies, Canadians hoped it would be the year Canada pulled its face out of the mud in international hockey.

Although they could have used nine former professionals, the Nats headed to the Izvestia Tournament in Moscow in December with only five players added to the lineup. They came from the NHL and the American Hockey League (AHL). The five were: myself (Toronto, NHL), Billy Harris (Toronto, NHL), Bobby Le Page (Montreal, AHL), Michel Poirier (Montreal, AHL) and Barry MacKenzie (Minnesota, NHL). Only MacKenzie and I had played with the Nats before.

The team was made up of players who were part of the Nats program, such as Ken Dryden, Fran Huck, Terry O'Malley and Chuck Lefley. Most players on the team were highly regarded NHL prospects; there were also some top senior-level players. We all knew we were not the best players Canada had to offer, only the best available at the time and under the circumstances.

We were a motley ragtag crew as we headed to the Izvestia Tournament. Our team included players of many ages from many different organizations and systems, and we had varying degrees of skill and experience. We were even required to use hand-me-down equipment. But unity and focus were our common bonds as we pursued our goal: to redeem Canada's place at the top of the international hockey world. The chemistry was right, and we were a team.

We all knew the Izvestia Tournament would show whether using pros made the Nats more competitive. We defeated East Germany 5–4, trounced Finland 10–1, convincingly dumped Sweden 5–2, tied the Soviet Union 2–2 and lost our only game to Czechoslovakia 4–0.

The Nats had won the Centennial Tournament in Winnipeg in 1967; that win and our second-place finish in the Izvestia Tournament were Canada's best showings in international hockey since 1962. Overnight, Canada was back in the running for a gold medal. The Nats returned to Canada with renewed enthusiasm. Our confidence grew with success, but unknown to us, things were again brewing in the backrooms of the international hockey world.

It was probably the tie with the Soviet Union that set off Bunny Ahearne's alarm bells. The IOC also got involved. Ahearne and Brundage probably felt that permitting Canada to use some former pros would make the Nats more competitive, but not likely improved enough to win the WHC or Olympics. But with the Nats dramatically improved performance in Moscow using only a few pros, Ahearne and Brundage likely feared a threat to their power base if Canada restored itself as the top international hockey power. It appeared that neither the IIHF nor the IOC wanted Canada to rise again to the top of the international hockey world.

While the Nats were touring Canada with the Czechoslovakian national team in late December 1969 and early January 1970, preparing for the upcoming WHC, the IIHF and the IOC once again cooked up a deal to kick the feet out from under Canada's bid to stand tall in international hockey. In collusion with Ahearne and prodded on by the Soviet bloc, the IOC threatened that players would be ineligible for the Olympics if amateur and professional players competed together in official tournaments. As had happened so often before, yet again, to preserve their self-interests, the IIHF and IOC were trying to cheat Canada out of a chance to compete fairly.

Then, on January 5, 1970, after our game with the Czechoslovakian national team in the Ottawa Civic Centre, John Munro, the federal minister responsible for sports, walked into our dressing room, accompanied by Gordon Juckes, the chairman of the CAHA, and Father Bauer. Munro explained the position of the IIHF and IOC: Canada's current Nats, a mixed amateur-professional team, would contaminate and jeopardize the eligibility of amateur players for the Olympics if play continued against each other. So despite efforts made, plans laid and hopes raised, and as a matter of national principle and pride, Munro announced Canada's withdrawal from international hockey competition. In a state of shocked disbelief, all the players sat in stunned silence.

Was it the right decision? After I got over the extreme personal disappointment, I agreed it was not only the right decision at the time, but probably the only one Canada could have made. However, our withdrawal from international hockey created more questions and challenges than it answered, as it was made without any real plan for how to proceed. And regrettably, it almost certainly meant the end of the Nats program envisioned and nurtured by Father Bauer. And it left Canada on the outside of the international and Olympic hockey worlds.

To most hockey fans in Canada, withdrawal from hypocritical and frustrating international hockey was no big deal and seemed to go mostly unnoticed. Canadian hockey fans still had their NHL to follow where it was felt the best players played the best hockey. International hockey went on the back burner for the Canadian hockey fan after our unceremonious withdrawal.

Could the Nats have won the 1970 WHC in Winnipeg with its ad hoc team of amateurs and pros? We'll never know. How strong were the Nats teams from their inception in 1963–64 to their temporary demise in 1970? Obviously not strong enough to win gold for Canada in the six world competitions in which they competed. But, as the future would show, the Nats teams were a lot better than most Canadian hockey people—particularly the NHL—gave them credit for. Most Canadians looked upon the Nats as a second-rate team and completely underestimated the calibre of top international hockey. Consequently, Canada slipped into an international hockey void, which wouldn't change until September 1972.

Shortly after the Nats team was disbanded, I wrote *Hockey in Canada: The way it is!* My primary focus was to document the brief existence of the Nats and to acknowledge the contribution of Father Bauer to the program, which was a worthwhile chapter in Canada's hockey history.

At the same time, I began working for CFTO-TV, an opportunity created by Johnny Esaw. Sports broadcasting seemed like an ideal post-hockey career. Shortly after I began, the CBC and CTV networks entered into a joint venture with CKLW-TV in Windsor, Ontario. Their plan was to revitalize the station and try to better penetrate the adjacent Detroit market. CFTO-TV was pleased with my on-air development, and I was offered the position of sports director in Windsor. It was a great opportunity for me to build a sports broad-casting career. On July 1, 1970, my wife, Susan, and our son, Sean, who was born June 26, headed out to a new career in a new city.

As the sports director for CKLW-TV, I covered the Detroit Red Wings. In the summer of 1971, Ned Harkness, the general manager of the Wings, approached me about making a comeback. Detroit still had my playing rights, and I was only thirty years old, healthy and still fit. While I enjoyed my job as a sports broadcaster, I got itchy feet to try to play again.

My comeback was less than successful. The Red Wings were a team in real transition at the time, struggling for a winning combina-tion. I was a utility forward who could fit in almost anywhere, which had some value. But about halfway through the season, Johnny Wil-son, the coach, took me aside after practice one day. Apparently, Bruce Norris, the team owner, didn't like the way I skated, and told Wilson to park me on the bench. He offered no explanation of what it was about my skating he didn't like: style, speed or what? Norris just didn't like it, and it was his team. I started to realize my worst fears about making a comeback.

In early January 1972, Harkness wanted to send me down to play with the Fort Worth Wings of the Central Hockey League (CHL). The Detroit organization owned three professional teams at the time. Neither the NHL Red Wings nor the AHL Tidewater Wings ap-peared headed for the playoffs. Fort Worth was Detroit's development team, and the organization wanted to move a few veteran players there to try to get at least one team into post-season play. Billy Hicke and Tom Martin joined me as veteran players brought in to bolster the team in the push for the playoffs.

I knew my NHL career was finished, but I wasn't prepared to walk away from my contract, which went to the end of the season. Detroit might have thought I wouldn't go down to Fort Worth since I still maintained a part-time relationship with CKLW-TV. But CKLW-TV generously said I could have a leave of absence and return when the season was over.

Susan and I packed up enough for a few months, bundled Sean, who was about eighteen months old, into our car, and headed south to Fort Worth, Texas. Our trip from Windsor to Fort Worth in early January 1972 was memorable: bad weather, icy roads, our first visit to McDonald's and Don McLean on every radio station singing "American Pie."

When we got to Fort Worth the team was out of the playoff picture with half the regular season remaining. The second half of the 1971–72 season was fun! The Wings went from being the doormat of the CHL to being a contender. We qualified for the playoffs. Even though it was the minors, I was determined to make the best of the situation. Also, I was playing regularly, and that always solved a lot of problems for a player. If you liked watching from the bench, then you were in the wrong business. I was only in Fort Worth for about four months, but I thoroughly enjoyed playing there. The team lost out in the second round of the playoffs, but we had salvaged what earlier in the season had been a possible disaster.

Susan had gone to college in the US. By coincidence, one of her roommates lived in Fort Worth. As a result, we had an enjoyable time off the ice as well. When the season ended in April, Susan, Sean and I made our way home to Windsor. I returned to my position as sports director at CKLW-TV. My professional hockey playing days were behind me forever, or so I thought.

The Canada–Soviet
Hockey Series

IN THE two years following Canada's withdrawal from international hockey, Hockey Canada and the CAHA worked behind the scenes with the NHL and with Alan Eagleson, the head of the NHLPA, to get Canada back into international hockey.

After months of complex international negotiations, they came up with a scheme that would see our best players face the best of the Soviet Union, the dominant international hockey power at the time. On April 23, 1972, they reached an agreement: there would be an eight-game exhibition series between September 2 and 28, in which a team of Canadian NHL all-stars would face-off against the Soviet national team. The Canada-Soviet Hockey Series (Series) would start with four games in Canada (Montreal, Toronto, Winnipeg and Vancouver); the final four games would be played in Moscow.

Finally, Canada would have a chance on a level playing field to establish that it was the supreme hockey nation in the world. Or so the media and most hockey people and fans naively thought. While the games were to be strictly exhibition games, everyone knew they would be of utmost importance. Canada's national pride was at stake. The Soviets had prepared for years for the opportunity to prove they could play against the best in the world, and also win. How presumptuous of those upstart Soviets! Canadians were confident the NHL and Canadian hockey were undisputedly superior.

After a hiatus of almost two and a half years, the Series put international hockey in the spotlight in Canada. However, most Canadians were ignorant about how good international hockey really was. They perceived it as second-tier at best, played by second-rate players, and a long way from the NHL level. That perception was certainly going to change!

—◊—

How did I get involved in the Series? It was early August 1972, and I was working at CKLW-TV in Windsor when Johnny Esaw called. CTV had been locked out of hockey coverage almost completely: NHL broadcasts were exclusively the domain of the CBC's Hockey Night in Canada. But Esaw obtained the rights to international hockey for CTV. While there was much less interest in the Olympics and WHCs than in NHL coverage, international rights were the best that was available at the time. And then along came the first Series. I'm sure Esaw felt the Series would have good ratings, but I think no one dreamt it would become the all-time best Canadian sports series.

Johnny called to talk about the Series and his challenge to find staff for broadcasting it. Because it was international hockey, Johnny preferred not to use current Hockey Night in Canada broadcasters, who were identified with the CBC. The Series was historic, so he wanted Foster Hewitt. Even though Foster had been retired for a few years, who better to do the play-by-play than the dean of hockey broadcasters? And because I had played international hockey against the Soviets as recently as 1969, had played on a Stanley Cup team in 1967 with the Leafs, had done colour commentary on international hockey and was in sports broadcasting, Johnny chose me to work with Foster as colour commentator. In fact, there was no one in sports broadcasting at the time with my wide range of first-hand experience. The opportunity was a real plum in the sports broadcasting profession, and while excited and anxious, I felt well qualified and capable of doing the job.

About a week after Esaw's first call, I got another one. Awkwardly, Johnny informed me that the NHL didn't want me to be the colour commentator, and while Eagleson apparently had no objection, he wasn't prepared to insist on me. I was stunned and devastated. Johnny told me I was his strong recommendation and the most qualified person available, but he wasn't prepared to insist on me, either. So from an emotional high, I plummeted. When I hung up from that brief and abrupt call, I sat at my desk, numbed by what I'd just heard. Here I was trying to get a sports broadcasting career started with the hope that hockey coverage would be a big part of it, and my career was over before it began.

Why had the NHL objected to my involvement? Since I wrote *Hockey in Canada: The way it is!*, I had been persona non grata with the NHL. My criticism of the way the league controlled and manipulated the game and its players, and of the league's continual undermining of the efforts and success of the Nats program as envisioned by Father Bauer, irked the NHL bosses big time. The NHL wanted nothing happening in hockey in Canada, and in particular the NHL, which they didn't control. And they definitely didn't control me. They were probably concerned about what I might say as the colour commentator. It seemed that I was off the Series with no apparent recourse.

Then fate intervened. I was in Toronto, as was Father Bauer, and I dropped by for a visit. He was still involved with Hockey Canada, and Hockey Canada was one of the partners in the deal for the Series. With him that day was Father Athol Murray, the legendary head of Notre Dame School at Wilcox, Saskatchewan. "Père" Murray, as he was known, was a great developer of men, a great philosopher and a man of God. I had met him several times; he was a great friend of Father Bauer's and a great supporter of the Nats program. Père Murray believed in the importance of having an alternative and balanced hockey system in Canada, and not one that was predominately professionally controlled or orientated.

They had heard I'd been chosen to be the colour commentator on the Series, but they hadn't heard I'd been dropped. They were shocked. Père Murray was a great admirer of my father, Lionel, and appreciated my involvement in the formative years of the Nats program. He simply said, "This isn't right!" I certainly agreed, but what could be done? Père Murray said he would call his friend John. I assumed he meant Johnny Esaw. No, he meant his friend John Bassett, Sr., the head of Baton Broadcasting, owner of CFTO-TV and the CTV Network. He promptly dialed Mr. Bassett's home phone. It must have been fate, because in the late afternoon on a weekday, John Bassett answered the phone. Père Murray said, "John, this Conacher lad is a fine young man and he deserves and is qualified to do this job…and the decision to drop him isn't right."

Well, Bassett was incensed. Even though I was a few feet away from the phone, I could tell that neither the NHL nor anyone else was going to tell him who to use on a broadcast where CTV had paid a considerable price for the broadcast rights. As far as he was concerned, CTV owned the rights to the Series and would staff and produce the games as they saw fit. Through Père Murray, Bassett told me to show up at CFTO-TV the next day, and said I was back on the Series. I was most appreciative for this somewhat divine intervention, and to the day they died, every time I bumped into Père Murray or John Bassett, Sr., I thanked them for helping me.

I was nervous about the reception I would get when I showed up at the CFTO-TV production meeting. I sensed everyone was aware of my situation, but I decided not to discuss it; I would just do the most professional job I could. Johnny Esaw might have been in an awkward position as the executive producer, but I never discussed it with him. I didn't know what John Bassett said to him, or whether Johnny was happy to have me back on the broadcast team. All I knew was that I was well qualified and grateful to be on the job.

Although Johnny Esaw negotiated the broadcast rights for CTV, he shared the broadcasts with the CBC. Because of the magnitude of production and interest in the Series, CBC and CTV negotiated which network would broadcast which games. Esaw was insistent that CTV broadcast the historic first game. CTV would produce games one, three, five and seven; the CBC would produce games two, four, six and eight. Esaw gambled that the Series would be decided long before Game Eight. How wrong he was.

By this time, the first game was just around the corner. The broadcast and production teams made their way to Montreal. Before we knew it, the Series was ready to begin.

—⟋⟍—

On August 30, the Soviet team arrived in Montreal, led by the coaching tandem of Vsevolod Bobrov, once a legendary Soviet player, and Boris Kulagin. Most Canadians knew the names of only a few star players, and no one had ever heard of a young goalie named Tretiak.

When the Soviets stepped onto the ice at the Montreal Forum on August 31 to practice, Foster and I were among the few permitted to watch. I couldn't help but be impressed with their fitness, speed, agility and puck skills; they were focused, disciplined and ready to take on the world. The Soviet hockey development system was structured to promote the very best players towards the Soviet national team, and the single most important goal of the national team was winning the gold medal at the Olympic Winter Games, which had been the pinnacle of opportunity until 1972.

Soviet national teams were built on four-year cycles, culminating with the Olympics; after the Games, some of the veteran players were replaced by younger players ready, willing and able to fill the spots. In the middle, there was a core of experienced international players. I had the opportunity to play against a few of these players at the 1969 Izvestia Tournament. The Soviet team that travelled to Montreal was a carefully selected collection of players who had skill, balance, depth, discipline and their trademark superb conditioning. It was truly a finely tuned team of all-stars.

Canada's general manager and head coach, Harry Sinden, had a much more challenging job in assembling Team Canada. Finding talented players wasn't the biggest challenge; putting together a real all-star team was. The Soviets had been doing it for years; now the NHL had to do it for its first international series. Sinden had been a defenceman with the gold-medal-winning Whitby Dunlops in 1958, when Canada was still a winning power in international hockey, and he coached the NHL Boston Bruins to a Stanley Cup in 1972. He certainly seemed to be the most logical choice to assemble and lead Team Canada. But he would soon learn that a lot had changed in international hockey since he had been involved.

While many of the thirty-five Team Canada players selected were some of the most talented and marquee players in the NHL at the time, among them Bobby Orr, Phil Esposito, Yvan Cournoyer, Stan

Mikita, Frank Mahovlich, Rod Gilbert, Pat Stapleton, Bobby Clarke, Ron Ellis, Serge Savard, Ken Dryden and Tony Esposito, many questioned selections like Dale Tallon, Jean-Paul Parise, Wayne Cashman, Bill Goldsworthy, Jocelyn Guevremont, Rod Seiling, Brian Glennie, Red Berenson and even a guy named Paul Henderson. But Sinden knew he needed a blend of skaters, checkers, goal scorers, skill players, journeymen role players, youth, experience and, where possible, players who had some international experience (for example Seiling, Dryden and Berenson). As with every all-star team, some people thought certain players should have been selected over others.

And Sinden wasn't free to recruit just anyone: Team Canada came exclusively from the NHL. Because of this pettiness, players like Bobby Hull, Gerry Cheevers and J.C. Tremblay were not eligible for Team Canada because they had jumped to the WHA, which was readying for its inaugural season. The Series was a deal exclusively between Hockey Canada, the CAHA and the NHL, brokered by Eagleson, who headed the NHLPA. Some people even thought being one of Eagleson's clients enhanced a player's chances of being one of the thirty-five players Sinden and assistant coach John Ferguson selected.

The Team Canada training camp started August 13 in Toronto's Maple Leaf Gardens. Sinden and Ferguson had only three weeks to get their collection of players from many different organizations and systems rounded into a unified team, then pared down to the most suitable eighteen or twenty players who could meet the challenge. It was a tall order at the best of times. As well, they had to worry about who was going to play with whom, deal with all the egos and also had to try to get the right chemistry, to make the team work.

One of the first issues they dealt with was the status of Bobby Orr. It became evident immediately, that due to knee problems, Bobby wasn't fit to play. However, with or without Orr and some other players hockey fans thought suitable choices for Team Canada, the general feeling was there was plenty of talent and firepower to beat the Soviets.

As soon as the Series was announced, Canadian sports media speculated about whether an NHL all-star team would be invincible against the best team the Soviets could assemble. I was amazed by the naivety, ignorance and brash arrogance of players, team management and NHL executives in general.

The NHL, the media and most Canadian hockey fans grossly underestimated the calibre of international hockey. The Soviets were the top international team in recent years, but Czechoslovakia, Sweden and Finland were also very competitive and capable of playing against or even beating professional teams right up to the NHL. International hockey had expanded and improved significantly in the 1960s, but Canada still believed the NHL was the undisputed leader of the hockey world and had the best players. When the Soviets stepped onto the ice in the Montreal Forum on August 31 for their first practice, there probably weren't more than a handful of Canadians who thought the Soviets were any better than a good Canadian minor professional team.

Predictions were everywhere in the media right up to the eve of the first game. The overwhelming consensus was that Team Canada would win the Series handily, and the Soviets would be lucky to win a game. One of the few dissenters was John Robertson of the *Montreal Star*, who predicted the Soviets would win six of the eight games. He had valid reasons for his prediction, but his reasons seemed too sensible to be credible, and no one believed him.

It was heresy to suggest the Soviets might have developed to the NHL level. Billy Harris, who played in the 1969 Izvestia Tournament with me, had coached the Swedish national team for the 1972 Olympic Winter Games, when Sweden tied the Soviets 3–3. Harris warned that the Soviets would be considerably better than most Canadians expected. He also predicted the Soviets would win the Series. He based his prediction primarily on their superb conditioning and the goaltending of Vladislav Tretiak. He was dismissed as a negative and eccentric critic. The only acceptable doctrine was the gospel according to the NHL: the Soviets might be good, but certainly not good enough to beat a team of NHL players. Even Johnny Esaw, who hired me for the Series, predicted the Soviets would win only two games, one in Canada and one in Moscow. I didn't let myself get drawn into the speculation; there would be plenty of opportunity for my comments during the games. I knew the NHL was in for a big surprise, but I didn't know for sure how close to the NHL the Soviets would be competitively. I was sure it would be a lot closer than most everyone thought.

I wasn't even convinced the current Soviet national team was necessarily the best team the Soviets had produced in the previous ten years. The 1968 and 1972 Soviet Olympic teams, coached by the tyrannical but knowledgeable Anatoly Tarasov, were exceptionally strong, with talented players like Anatoly Firsov, the Mayorov brothers, Vitaly Davidov, Viacheslav Starshinov, Konstantin Loktev and Veniamin Alexandrov. For whatever reasons, none were on the team the Soviets sent to Canada. Firsov, who had been a Soviet superstar for more than ten years, was missing from the lineup reportedly because of knee problems. However, both teams had deep rosters and neither planned to use the players who couldn't be in the lineups as an excuse.

—⁓—

September 2 was hot and steamy in Montreal, one of those torrid late-summer days. Foster and I made our way up to the broadcast gondola in the Montreal Forum, which must have been close to one hundred degrees Fahrenheit. During the warm-up, the ice was already sweating, and there was a light mist hovering over the surface. It was going to be a hot, sweaty grind on that sheet of ice. Looking down from above, the crowd was a restless sea of motion, and there was an energy and electricity in the building that came from the anticipation of being part of something historic.

As was the tradition in international hockey, there were opening ceremonies and the exchange of token gifts between the players. Most players on Team Canada had never experienced such ceremonies, which caused a delay the players could have done without. All they wanted was to get on with the game.

At 8:29 p.m., Phil Esposito faced off against Vladimir Petrov at centre ice, beginning what many hockey fans think was the most exciting, dramatic, intense hockey series of all time.

This was no ordinary hockey series. Canada was looking for vindication for all the years of futility and frustration endured in international hockey. The Soviets were looking for world recognition as the supreme hockey power. And exhibition series or not, it would be a real test of different systems, both on and off the ice, their system of communism and socialism against Canada's democracy and capitalism. It was them against us!

Team Canada lost possession on the opening faceoff, but regained it quickly, and after only thirty seconds Phil Esposito scored the first of his seven goals in the Series. The fans erupted, almost blowing the roof off the Forum. Neither Foster nor I could hear through our headsets. It was certainly the start all Canadians had dreamt of and prayed for; some thought the Series was over with that first goal. It was, "I told you we'd blow these guys away!" It was all the proof the fans needed to confirm that Canadian hockey truly was supreme and Canada's NHL players were clearly the best in the world.

And to reconfirm our supremacy, minutes later Paul Henderson scored to give Team Canada what seemed to be a commanding lead. (Henderson would also score seven goals in the Series.) Again the Forum crowd erupted in ecstatic joy. Canada was the best! (It was prophetic that Team Canada's first two goals were scored by Esposito and Henderson.)

I knew that, though they may have been rattled by two quick goals and a fast start by Team Canada, the Soviets would not collapse. Midway through the period they were over their early-game jitters; they found their skating legs and got on the scoreboard to make it 2–1. And then, on a short-handed goal, they tied the game at 2–2 to end the period.

Drenched with sweat, fatigued, deflated and clearly shaken, Team Canada sat in their dressing room in a state of shock, trying to cope with the reality they had just experienced. All thirty-five Team Canada players, whether on the ice or in the stands, realized the Series was going to be quite different from what they thought when they agreed to play. It wasn't going to be a leisurely holiday trip to Moscow with some hockey thrown in; it would be gut-wrenching, exhausting work just to survive and succeed.

The Soviets were ready for the Series; Team Canada was not. It was difficult, after having most of the summer off, to catch up quickly to a team that kept fit and that trained all year.

And nothing could have prepared Team Canada for its lack of experience in international competition. After only one period, every player on the team and every hockey fan in Canada were forced to realize that the Soviets were very, very good. Team Canada needed a crash course on how to play against the Soviets, who could all skate like the wind, handle and pass the puck, make creative plays, shoot accurately and hard, were strong on the puck offensively and defensively—and they were tough. They had four balanced lines, so it wouldn't be enough to shut down their top line—they had four top lines, plus depth on their bench. And their trademark was their superb conditioning. They could skate flat out for sixty minutes of every game. A most formidable opponent!

The second period was barely underway when Valery Kharlamov made his presence known with an explosive play and scored to give the Soviets a 3–2 lead. And to confirm it was no fluke, he scored a second goal in a spectacular solo effort, giving the Soviets a two-goal lead with half the game left to play. From the broadcast booth it seemed that Team Canada couldn't keep up to the Soviets who were in mid-season form. Team Canada was in trouble. At the end of the second period the Soviets headed to their dressing room in apparent control.

Foster and I could see the fans were shocked and disbelieving. There were many realities to be grasped about these formidable opponents. Their style and pattern of game weren't what NHLers were used to. From the vantage point of the broadcast booth, we observed constant motion, lots of circling, short, quick passes and a pace and tempo of play that only the most fit could keep up with. And no amount of checking, holding, clutching, grabbing, slashing or punching seemed to bother the Soviets. In their stoic manner, they shrugged off every attempt to intimidate them. Their discipline and control were extraordinary. They wouldn't be intimidated even by the toughest NHLers.

Team Canada gamely started the third period, trying to get back into the game. Bobby Clarke scored Team Canada's first goal in forty-two minutes and closed the gap to 4–3, but then the flood gates began to open when Boris Mikhailov restored the Soviets' two-goal lead.

Team Canada had run out of gas. Sensing their helplessness, the Soviets went for the jugular. I commented that they had never been known to let up when they had an opponent down. I knew they were going to play flat out right to the end, and if running up the score was the result, so be it.

The NHL was going to have some egg on its face, but I was not upset. Those of us who had known for years how very, very good the Soviets were finally felt some vindication. But I certainly didn't want Team Canada to lose the Series and had real empathy for the players on the ice, as I had been in their skates many times myself. But I also knew it was possible the Soviets could win, particularly with the conditioning edge they had, even against a team of NHL all-stars.

Losing this first historic international game would be bad enough, but to be embarrassed and humiliated by the Soviets would be unbearable. When the score got to 7–3, I was praying for the game to be over before the Soviets ran up the score. The Soviets had always been great front-runners, and they never quit until the end, no matter what the score. Game One wasn't over one second too soon. Foster and I had watched the Forum crowd ride an emotional roller coaster from an ecstatic high early in the game to a state of shocked despair by the middle. Though disappointed, the fans were prepared to acknowledge the effort and skill of the Soviets. Team Canada had been humiliated, and their acts of frustration late in the game only made them look more inadequate. It was a tough experience to swallow, not only for Team Canada and the NHL but for all Canadians. As the Team Canada players made their way off the ice at game's end, heads down in exhaustion; they staggered to the dressing room through a fog that hung over the ice like a surreal shroud.

The Soviets had beaten many good teams over the years by simply skating their opposition into exhaustion, then striking for several late goals to ensure victory. In Game One, Team Canada had fallen victim to the standard Soviet trap. Team Canada was just another hapless victim!

The Canadian players developed instant respect for their opponents, who were skilled and competitive hockey players. The devastated crowd filed out of the Montreal Forum in numbed silence;

television watchers stared blankly at their sets, and the media scrambled to get a new slant on the Series.

The end of Game One was a real watershed in hockey history. On that hot humid night, NHL hockey, professional hockey, international hockey—in fact wherever the game was played—hockey was about to change forever. It didn't take eight games to prove the Soviets could play with the best. The myth of NHL invincibility had been shattered and dispelled forever, and a new era for hockey was about to begin.

The summer of 1972 was not a good one for the NHL. First the upstart WHA changed the whole economics and salary structure of major-league professional hockey in North America; then the damn Soviets came into one of Canada's hockey shrines and humiliated a team of NHL all-stars at "our game." What next?

—⁓—

Broadcasting Game One was a unique experience. I knew what could happen, but chose not to discuss my insights until the Series began. Some of my comments and observations may have seemed slanted towards the Soviets, but my first-hand experience qualified me to make those comments. I also knew what it was like to play against the Soviets and lose. And I knew what was needed to beat them. I called it the way I saw it.

Foster and I were a good fit as a broadcast team. I knew Foster Hewitt from my years with the Leafs. He was primarily a radio man. When he did the original play-by-play for Hockey Night in Canada, covering the Leafs games on television in the 1950s, his descriptions sometimes lagged behind the play, and thus didn't always match the pictures. Foster never seemed really comfortable as a television play-by-play caller and eventually stepped aside to be replaced on Hockey Night in Canada by his capable son Bill. Foster returned to radio, his first love. He knew the NHL players like the back of his hand, but was nervous about pronouncing the names of the Soviet players. I was familiar with many of the Soviet players; I anglicized many of their names and in general didn't worry about getting their names right. I said in jest to Foster: "Just put an 'ov' or 'ev' on the end of each name and you'll be all right." Throughout the Series, Foster called Tretiak

Tret-tree-ak, and even Team Canada's Yvan Cournoyer got branded once as Corn-oy-eh. Once Foster got the rust out of his voice and the adrenalin going, he left his indelible mark on the games with his unique style. It was a thrill to work beside this broadcast legend.

The Team Canada road show moved to Toronto's Maple Leaf Gardens. Their dream had quickly become a nightmare. To a player, they had been embarrassed and humiliated in their own country. The national slap in the face by the impertinent Soviets turned the indifference felt by most Canadians before Game One into concerned interest. The hockey war was on. And the Soviets had won the first battle. In just sixty minutes of play in Montreal, the Series had gone from casual exhibition game to intense struggle, with national pride and world bragging rights as the ultimate prize.

Everything changed after the first game. And everyone was anxious to know how Team Canada was going to respond to the unforeseen Soviet challenge in Game Two. Canadians were scared at the thought of losing the Series to the Soviets.

The media had been on the Team Canada bandwagon right up to the start of the Series; they almost broke their collective legs jumping off after Game One. They barraged Team Canada players and management for an explanation of the unexpected loss in Montreal. But Game Two was scheduled for September 4, and the team had little time to fret over the loss. They needed to go back to the drawing board and quickly figure out a formula to beat the Soviets. Everyone associated with Team Canada was anxious, defensive, irritable and in a foul mood. Players and management withdrew and avoided the media and public wherever possible. As it turned out, that was the conception of Team Canada as a real team. However, the actual birth was to be several painful games away.

After a review of the Game One tapes by the coaching staff, John Ferguson then confronted me outside the team's dressing room. He accused me of being a "Commie lover" and said if I liked them so much why didn't I go live in Russia. I was surprised, but told him that all I was doing was reporting what happened on the ice. I said I wasn't about to apologize for any comments or observations I made. I wanted to be objective and fair, but I was going to call it the way I saw it.

I might have said: "I told you so!" If only the NHL had asked people who had played against the Soviets, they might have been better prepared. But the NHL and Team Canada were set on doing it their way, and paid the agonizing and painful price. The NHL had made its own bed, but there was the possibility that all Canadians might have to lie in it if Team Canada lost the Series.

In 1972 the NHL bosses seldom thought about what was best for the game or its players; it was almost always about what was best for the business of hockey. For example, they effectively shelved the Nats program in 1970 because they thought it was not good for business—based on financial costs. They saw that a well-educated, more mature player entering professional hockey in his early twenties would initially cost an NHL owner more than an eighteen-year-old, poorly educated player with little or no business experience or opportunity. This mindset and arrogance contributed to the formation of the upstart WHA.

And the NHL was now faced with yet another serious challenge from international hockey. All in one summer: the NHL was confronted with major challenges from the WHA as a competitor major professional league and potentially a greater challenge for supremacy over all of hockey. Yet at the time, the NHL was very much in an expansion mode, anxious to meet wealthy people who might want to own an expansion team.

During my season with the CHL Fort Worth Wings, through Susan's college friend, we met Buzz Kimbell at a party. As it turned out, Buzz was a good friend of Lamar Hunt, the Texas billionaire who owned the Kansas City Chiefs (American Football League). Both were in Toronto in September and I was able to get them tickets to Game Two. Before the game, Buzz invited Susan and me over to their hotel. We got on the elevator with Buzz and Lamar; as the doors were closing, NHL president Clarence Campbell got on the elevator with us. Since 1970, when my book was published, Campbell was no fan of mine. After some awkward but polite acknowledgements, I introduced Buzz and Lamar. Well, Campbell's mouth just about dropped to the floor when the name Lamar Hunt registered. He was like a panting puppy dog, drooling at the prospect of Lamar as an NHL owner.

I thought Campbell was going to whack the Stop button so he could make a pitch to Lamar. But we arrived at our floor and said our good-byes, leaving Campbell on the elevator alone. I'm sure he was asking himself how I had come to know Lamar Hunt. In reality, I didn't know Lamar Hunt any better than he did, but I got a real chuckle watching Campbell's normal stuffed-shirt personality completely disintegrate on that elevator ride.

—⚬—

Sinden had to get Team Canada ready for Game Two. His first challenge was to choose eighteen to twenty players from his roster of thirty-five. He had to find the right combination to meet the challenge from the talented, superbly conditioned and powerful Soviet team. The loss in Montreal was a big blow to many players' egos and really shook the team's confidence, which was suddenly fragile. At least now Sinden and his players knew what they were up against.

For Game Two, the second edition of Team Canada took to the ice with eight player changes. Ken Dryden, who struggled in goal in Game One, was replaced by Tony Esposito. Sinden needed a stronger defensive effort, so he looked for a combination of personnel and style of play that would slow down the Soviet dynamo. Harry had a deep bench and it was early in the Series; he still didn't know which group of players were the right ones to be part of the team this Series so strongly demanded.

Game Two started with every Canadian tuned in, hockey fan or not. The country was in a state of high anxiety and panic that Team Canada might actually lose the Series. It was very much them against us, both on and off the ice. The fans in Maple Leaf Gardens were traditionally quiet, but for this game their quietness seemed more concern than tradition. There certainly wasn't the electricity and excitement there had been in the Montreal Forum at the start of Game One.

From the opening faceoff it was evident Team Canada was focused on the challenge before them. Sinden used all his coaching strategies, for example last line change and matching lines, to make sure he had the players he wanted on the ice at all times. These games were no longer just exhibition games; they were the real thing.

The game plan was to stop the Soviets from getting anything start-ed. Team Canada used tenacious and rugged checking to disrupt the Soviets' precise and crisp playmaking. They slowed down the tempo of play. It was traditional NHL style hockey, and it required the play-ers to be in top condition. Team Canada wasn't there yet. But, using sheer guts and determination, they neutralized the Soviet offence in the first half of the game.

Stopping the Soviets was only part of the challenge. While playing their punishing and rough defensive style, Team Canada also needed to generate some offence. Well into the second period, Phil Esposito scored the first goal of the game. He was knocked down behind the Soviet goal and got back up just as the puck came to him. He stepped out in front of the goal and beat a surprised Tretiak with a lightning-quick deft move. The goal confirmed that Team Canada could gener-ate offence as well as stop the Soviets.

The score remained at 1–0 until early in the third period. On a Team Canada power play, Yvan Cournoyer came down the right wing, took a perfect pass in full stride from Brad Park and showed the So-viets an explosive burst of Canadian speed unseen to that point. He skated past the Soviet defence as if they were pylons, then ripped a shot that beat Tretiak cleanly. The Gardens crowd finally got off its hands and erupted in a state of ecstasy for the first time since the first period of Game One.

The joy was short-lived: Alexander Yakushev scored on a Soviet power play to make the score 2–1. The crowd again hushed in fear that it could be a repeat of Game One. Foster and I could feel the tension is the crowd.

And then came the turning point of the game. Team Canada was serving another penalty, and the Soviets pressed to tie the game. They were set up in the Team Canada zone when Phil Esposito intercept-ed a pass and cleared the puck out of the Team Canada end along the boards. Peter Mahovlich pounced on the puck and headed up ice with only one Soviet defenceman to beat. Mahovlich froze the Soviet with a fake slapshot, stepped around him, collected the puck and headed for the goal. With a combination of moves not seen be-fore or since, Peter turned Tretiak inside out with a series of dekes and somehow got the puck in the goal, then stood triumphantly, like a giant redwood tree, over a sprawling Tretiak. That goal was one of the most spectacular of the Series. To make sure there would be no comeback that night, big brother Frank Mahovlich nailed the coffin shut to close out the scoring at 4–1. The only goals in the Series for the Mahovlich brothers couldn't have come at a more crucial time. Team Canada was back in the Series! The Soviets were human, and they could be beaten. Hockey fans could breathe again. But everyone knew that the Series was a long way from over.

—⚓—

Game Three was in Winnipeg and presented a new set of challenges for Team Canada. They had gotten the monkey off their back in Toronto, but Sinden still had to find the best lineup to continue their success. Conditioning, while improving, was still an issue. And playing the rugged and demanding physical and defensive style was exhausting. The big question was whether Team Canada could keep up the style of play that was successful against the Soviets.

The make-up and style of play of Team Canada One and Team Canada Two were quite different. Sinden still wasn't sure which team was the right team. As well, Sinden had promised to get all the players into the lineup for at least a game. However, the idea of the NHL using the Series to showcase its best players was over. Team Canada could no longer afford to keep that promise. There was too much at stake. Sinden was still trying to put together the best team and everyone knew that only the best team was going to be good enough. And maybe not good enough! Instead of being a coach's dream, having thirty-five of the best players in hockey to choose from was turning into a nightmare. Sinden didn't need thirty-five players; he needed the right eighteen to twenty players to play against their most formidable opponent. At least he knew which style of play would contain the Soviets: close checking, heavy hitting and not letting the Soviets get anything started. Did Team Canada have the legs and stamina to play this way?

For Game Three, Sinden went with the same lineup as for Game Two, with Tony Esposito in goal again.

Meanwhile, to everyone's surprise, Vsevolod Bobrov and Boris Kulagin made five changes to the Soviet team, inserting youth and more speed. The line of Alexander Bodunov and Yuri Lebedev, centred by Viascheslav Anisin, I later dubbed "the Headache Line," as that was what they became for Team Canada.

Sinden knew goal scorers were not enough. Team Canada also needed strong, rugged defensive players who, while not necessarily stars in the NHL, were the type of players every team needed to win. The puck had no sooner been dropped in Game Three when two of these foot soldiers demonstrated their roles. Some people had wondered why Jean-Paul Parise and Wayne Cashman were selected for Team Canada. They knew only one style of play, rough and tough: grinding and mucking along the boards and in the corners, whacking and hacking at every opportunity with reckless abandon. This style of play reduced the game to its most base elements. It wasn't pretty, but it seemed to be the only way to throw the Soviets from their patented and disciplined style of play.

The Soviets thought they had seen typically rugged Canadian-style hockey in international competition over the years, and they thought they were well prepared for it. But they had never experienced the aggressiveness of the likes of Cashman, Parise, Bobby Clarke and company. And from Foster's and my vantage point in the broadcast booth, it truly seemed to be a war on ice, with Team Canada using every tactic they could get away with to throw the Soviets off their standard game plan. Get the Soviets looking, which in turn slowed them down and disrupted their precision plays. That was the strategy.

Team Canada put the Soviets off balance right from the opening faceoff, and Parise scored for a quick lead. The Soviets bounced right back and showed they were dangerous even short-handed, when Vladimir Petrov got a breakaway and tied the game. A late goal by Jean Ratelle gave Team Canada a 2–1 lead as the period ended.

In the second period, Team Canada continued with its 'Big Bad Bruins' style of play. Cashman and Parise continued their work along the boards and in the corners, working the puck to the triggerman, Phil Esposito. When Phil got a pass in the high slot, he did what he did best and drilled home his third goal of the Series, making it 3–1.

For a while, it seemed Team Canada was in control. But I commented that a 3–1 lead was very fragile against a team like the Soviets.

For the second time in the game, Team Canada had a power play and pressed the Soviets in their end. The Soviets sprung Valery Kharlamov loose, and he raced in to score, closing the gap to 3–2. Team Canada had learned another lesson about playing the Soviets: they had to keep up their defence even when they had the man advantage. Less than a minute later, Paul Henderson showed that he too had a hot stick, and he re-established Team Canada's two-goal lead. It was his second goal of the Series.

Then the Headache Line started to live up to its nickname. The Soviets confirmed that they wouldn't go away. Lebedev closed the gap to 4–3, and then Bodunov tied it up to end the second period.

I knew Team Canada was disappointed to have let a two-goal lead slip by, but there was still a period to win the pivotal game of the Series. The third period was barely underway when Sinden got the answer to the critical question: did Team Canada have the conditioning and stamina to keep up their style of play? And the answer was, no they didn't. Team Canada hit the wall as their conditioning left them gasping. Was it going to be another Game One collapse?

On sheer guts and determination, Team Canada toughed it out for twenty minutes, desperately trying to avoid a loss. Both teams had good chances to win the game, but neither could get the decisive goal. For Team Canada it was a disappointing tie; they let the game slip through their hands, one that got away. To their credit, they played the Soviets to a stalemate for twenty minutes and prevented them from scoring when they had Team Canada on the run, as they had done in Game One. This would augur well for the future. The Series was all tied up, with a win, a loss and a tie each. It was shaping up to be a long, tough Series.

Everyone now knew the Soviets weren't one-game wonders; they would be in the Series right to the end. In the post-game media scrum, which Foster and I attended, everyone was surprised when Sinden and Ferguson acknowledged publicly for the first time that the Soviets were not only good, but as good as the best in the NHL. And further, there might be something to learn by studying the Soviets' unique development system and style of play. These were huge admissions from men associated with the NHL. Only a week earlier, Canadians thought that we had some divine right over hockey. This illusion was certainly gone forever.

—⚏—

On to Vancouver. Game Four presented another challenge for Sinden: Team Canada was almost out of time in the Canadian segment of the Series. They had only one game to establish their control and dominance before they headed to the unknown of Moscow. Every game became more and more important. It was another must game for Team Canada. Game Four was the fourth game in seven days. While Team Canada's conditioning was improving with each game, it came at a price: fatigue. The players paid a huge physical price to keep up with the Soviets for sixty minutes.

Considering the fatigue factor, both physically and emotionally, combined with some injuries and the pressure of still trying to formulate a winning lineup, Sinden made eight changes in the lineup. And after agonizing, he also gambled on Dryden again in goal.

Foster and I were stunned when, during the warm-up, there was booing. We assumed it was poor sportsmanship, that the Canadian fans were booing the Soviets. Then in utter astonishment, we realized the fans were actually booing Team Canada. Players generally say they don't hear the crowd, but I was sure every Team Canada player heard the boos and was most distressed by them. The Vancouver fans were clearly expressing their frustration and disappointment in the team's performance to date. It was a bad omen.

From the opening faceoff, Team Canada continued their aggressive and intimidating style of play, the only style they really knew. Good old Canadian hockey. But was it any longer good enough against a team that had dismantled and neutralized our basic physical approach to the game by mastery over the fundamentals of the game: skating, puck handling, passing, playmaking, shooting, all developed to a high skill level, packaged in a strong team concept and played at high speed?

Early in the game Team Canada took a penalty for a vicious cross-check. The Soviets made Team Canada pay once again when Boris

Mikhailov scored on the power play. It was the first time the Soviets had scored the first goal in a game. A bad start! A few minutes later Team Canada was again penalized, and again Mikhailov scored, his second power-play goal of the game. The crowd was clearly unhappy with Team Canada, and the booing was more noticeable.

With the game less than six minutes old, the Dryden gamble began to backfire. I played with Ken at the 1969 Izvestia Tournament, which was his first exposure to international competition. The Soviets and other top international teams moved the puck quickly across the scoring zone with crisp pinpoint passing, a tactic which caused Ken problems in 1969 and again in 1972. He would go on to become a Hockey Hall of Fame goalie, but his best performances were not in international competition.

Team Canada contained the scoring damage to just two goals in the first period, giving the Soviets a 2–0 lead, but not a commanding one. Early in the second period, Gilbert Perreault scored on an end-to-end rush, getting Team Canada into the game and closing the gap.

And then we started to see the wheels fall off for Team Canada. A questionable goal, which would have tied the game at 2–2, was disallowed, and the team started to slide into a black hole. The Soviets stretched their lead to 4–1 midway through the period. Team Canada could make nothing go right. And we noticed the crowd had become unmerciful and ugly, booing every mistake. Even the Soviets looked surprised at this turn of events. Team Canada was being booed in their own arena. What next?

Down but not out and dumbfounded by the reaction of the home fans, Phil Esposito, who was emerging as Team Canada's leader, tried desperately in the third period to get them back into the game: he set up a goal, which brought the score to 4–2. But Shadrin slammed the door on any hope of pulling it out when he scored to make it 5–2. Even a late goal by Dennis Hull on another Esposito setup, which made it 5–3, did nothing to appease the fans. Team Canada lost another must game.

Both players' and fans' emotions boiled over. The Vancouver fans were in a vocal and ugly mood. They weren't happy with Team Canada's performance in the four Canadian games, and they let the team know it. It showed the intense level of frustration felt by all Canadians as a result of seeing our hockey heritage and assumed hockey supremacy so blatantly assaulted by the Soviet team. The Soviets, who were an enemy to our way of life off the ice, had become our enemy on the ice as well.

At game's end, every player on Team Canada was physically and emotionally spent. And none more so than Phil Esposito. He was selected as Team Canada's player-of-the-game. After Esposito accepted his award, Johnny Esaw interviewed him on the ice. And Phil let it all hang out. Everyone, Esaw, the fans in the stands and everyone watching on television witnessed one of the most emotional and heartfelt post-game interviews ever given. It wasn't really even an interview; it was more an outburst and rant. And while it might have seemed like excuse making or sour grapes by any other player, coming from Esposito it said volumes about his heart and soul and intense desire to win, not for himself, but for Canada. From our broadcast position, Foster and I listened and watched in stunned silence to this unbelievable end to an unbelievable game.

Playing for your country is like no other experience in sport and can only truly be understood and appreciated by those who have done it. The Soviets initially had a huge advantage over Team Canada, as many on their team were veteran international players. After four games, all the players on Team Canada realized the overpowering emotional pressure of wearing the Maple Leaf on their sweaters. Such pressure could crush you, particularly if your team lost. Not even playing in a Stanley Cup final is like playing for your country. It's bad enough to let yourself or your team down, but to let your country down is an overwhelming burden. And no one can teach you this experience. Team Canada needed instant experience in international hockey, but it was taking them several games to acquire it. Their learning curve was almost vertical.

What cost Team Canada in the Canadian portion of the Series was that they ran out of gas, physically and also emotionally. To be successful in international competition in any sport, competitors must be in both top physical and emotional condition. They need composure, mental toughness, self-discipline and focus. Many players on Team Canada had more trouble dealing with their emotions than with the

Soviets' skills and speed. It could be very frustrating to play against the Soviets. Their style and quality of play were very demanding, and when things didn't go well, frustration often boiled over, composure eroded on the ice, and the trouble began. The Soviets quickly exploited these situations.

If Team Canada was going to win the Series, players had to learn to control their emotions and frustration. They had to maintain composure on the ice and on the bench. Some players would not achieve this during the Series, but Team Canada would eventually make their emotions work for them. In sport, emotion can be a positive or negative force, and there is a fine line between the two.

When Phil Esposito left the ice after his emotional outburst, Team Canada was lower than a skunk at a garden party. With a record of only one win, two losses and a tie in the easiest part of the Series, things seemed very ominous as the team headed for Moscow. Only Ken Dryden and Rod Seiling had any real idea of what it was like to play in Moscow. With four games to go in the Series, Team Canada could certainly still win, but it was going to take a Herculean effort.

The intense battles of the first four games had occurred in just seven days. The second four games began in Moscow on September 22. The two weeks in between were anything but relaxing. No group of Canadian hockey players had ever felt more alienated or alone, not just from hockey fans, but from a whole country, than did Team Canada during that period. It seemed like the country had turned its back on the team. For different reasons—frustration, embarrassment or anger at the so-called NHL all-stars—Team Canada took a terrible beating in the media between the two parts of the Series. Emotionally, the players were very fragile and sensitive as they tried to rationalize and get a grip on the situation they found themselves in. For some players, getting their egos onside was the biggest challenge they faced between games. And where was the fun?

On to Moscow

ON SEPTEMBER 12, Team Canada reunited in Toronto. Virtually deserted by their fans, they were treated more like Team Shame than Team Canada at the airport as they prepared to fly to Sweden on their way to Moscow.

It was planned to use the Swedish excursion to acclimatize Team Canada to Europe, the time change, the larger ice surface they would be playing on for the first time, playing in a totally unfamiliar setting, and most important, European officiating. Foster Hewitt and I did not join Team Canada on the Stockholm trip, but followed it closely, then went directly to Moscow to resume our broadcasts.

Unfortunately, the trials and tribulations for Team Canada didn't end when they arrived in Sweden to play two "friendly" exhibition games against the Swedish national team as a tune-up for part two of the Series in Moscow, which started on September 22. The two games in Sweden occurred during the fiftieth anniversary of Swedish hockey, and became a showcase of how far Swedish hockey had progressed over the years. While the Swedes played a different style of hockey than the Soviets, they too were much more accomplished than Team Canada expected.

Sinden wasn't concerned about the stiff competition the Swedish team provided, but he was upset about the hostile and antagonistic reception Team Canada had received, fanned by the sensationalism of the media. Team Canada seemed to be adrift, without a country and unwelcome wherever it went. They won the first game in Sweden 4–1 and salvaged a draw in the second. But the players still didn't have their emotions in check, and European officiating was a whole new experience.

Team Canada got its first exposure to that officiating in the form of two West Germans, Josef Kompalla and Franz Baader. Both had been senior officials for major IIHF and Olympic games for years. IIHF hockey had developed and improved dramatically in recent years, but its officiating had lagged badly behind. It seemed that IIHF officials thought they, and not the players, were the most important part of the game. I had experienced their influence on games when I played international hockey, and realized it was just one more obstacle Team Canada had to overcome to win. Just to play against these top international teams was difficult enough; now the team also had to contend with what appeared to be partial and incompetent officiating.

Team Canada came to Europe with a reputation that even Sinden's Whitby Dunlops had a part in forming. Teams from Canada were known for playing a very rough and crude style of hockey based on aggressive and intimidating physical play. The top international hockey nations of the IIHF didn't like the Canadian style, so they controlled and neutralized it by penalizing the Canadians at every opportunity. All Canadian teams that played in IIHF or Olympic competitions had to deal with the penalties. It was a blessing in disguise that at least Team Canada experienced IIHF officiating before they played in Moscow. Bad officiating was just one more hurdle Team Canada had to deal with on its rocky road to success.

With only a few days left before the Moscow games were to begin, Sinden didn't have his Moscow lineup resolved. He was still looking for the right eighteen to twenty players to meet the monumental challenge before them. But first, he had to deal with a brewing mutiny. Team Canada was still a team in name only. The thirty-five players were not a close group. NHL players on different teams rarely fraternized, and over the years they had developed a lot of deep-rooted grudges and bad blood. In Sweden, however, they were all orphans, driven together by their common isolation from home and country. Or most of them were driven together. There were several discontented players. Sinden consulted Al Eagelson, and they realized they had to confront and deal with the malcontents or the Moscow games could be a disaster. In a closed-door team meeting, both players and management got their concerns off their chests.

By the end of the meeting, everyone agreed that Team Canada could only win the Series if everyone pulled together. Self-interest, ego and player status had to go. So, out of the adversity that Team Canada dealt with in Stockholm, and after a very painful labour, the real Team Canada was born. It would carry Canadians' hopes to Moscow. From that time on, no outsiders got close to Team Canada; they retreated into themselves. Their sense of team and strength came in their emerging close-knit camaraderie, and outsiders, including Foster and me, were not welcome.

—∭—

On to Moscow!

Team Canada players had travelled a lot around North America, but few had been to Europe, let alone the Soviet Union. And in 1972, Moscow was a severe cultural shock for even the most experienced traveller. A week in Moscow would be an experience of a lifetime, even without the hockey games. It was very much a city of the Cold War. The Series would have been an important event at any time, but in 1972 it was truly historic.

Some people hoped the Series would bring a thawing of relations between the democratic West and the communistic East through the medium of international sport. The Soviet Union had for years used excellence in sport to promote and showcase the communist way of life. So far in the Series, there had been no thawing on either side: it was still war on ice, us against them and everything the Soviets represented.

I'd been to Moscow twice before. My first trip was in early 1964 as a member of Canada's Olympic hockey team, for some exhibition games before the Winter Games in Innsbruck, Austria. Then, in December 1969, I was a member of the Nats team that competed in the Izvestia Tournament. That Nats team was the last Canadian team to play the Soviets. On the trip with Team Canada, I noticed that living

conditions were still spartan in Moscow, compared to Canadian standards, but there were improvement since my first two visits.

The accommodations were another thing added to the ever growing list of things Team Canada had to adjust to while in Moscow.
The Intourist Hotel was a relatively new modern high-rise, reserved
primarily for foreign visitors. While it was light years better than the
Metropole Hotel, where I had stayed before, it was still a long way
from hotels in North America. Most rooms were very small. The beds
were narrow and short, and gave a new meaning to the word "firm,"
not at all what NHL players were used to. The beds made for some
restless nights. Another big issue for Team Canada was food. Meals
in the hotel were lavish by Soviet standards, but very different from
what most of the players were accustomed to. Team Canada brought
a lot of food with them, to supplement the hotel food, but the food
remained another thing to get used to in this strange land.

The Soviet hosts also played mind games. It was quite common to be
awakened by the strange ring of the telephone in the middle of the night
to find no one on the line. The players thought they were in the Soviet
Union of the James Bond movies; they worried about eavesdropping in
the rooms and wondered if they were constantly under surveillance. I recognized one of the team chaperons from 1969, a huge hulk of a man who
seemed to be more bodyguard than chaperon. His job was to make sure
no one got close to us and that none of us got too close to any Mosco-
vites. Everybody was watching somebody in Moscow. And there was the
legendary story of some players finding a strange bump under the carpet
in their room. Thinking it was an eavesdropping device, they unscrewed
it, only to hear a huge crash. They had unscrewed the chandelier in the
room below. Whether real or imagined, the Soviet hosts definitely played
mind games with their Canadian visitors. Just more distractions to keep
the players from focusing on the enormous challenge that lay ahead.

All four games in Moscow would be played in the Luzhniki Sports
Palace, an eleven-thousand-seat arena in the Lenin Sports Complex,
which was in the middle of Moscow. Compared to NHL venues, the
arena was substandard: the ice surface wasn't maintained nearly as

well; there was wire-mesh netting around each end instead of Plexi-glas; there were several small dressing rooms instead of one large one. Team Canada needed to get used to all these things, and quickly.

The Canadian players took to the ice for a practice the day before Game Five. As if they didn't have enough to deal with in getting ready for the game the next day, Sinden and Ferguson were faced with yet another crisis in what seemed to be a never-ending string of them. The players who weren't in the lineup for the game worked out after the regulars. Their job was to keep themselves ready in case they were needed. Not a glamorous role, and some of these NHL superstars weren't used to being left out of the starting lineup. Vic Hadfield was one; he'd had enough of watching. If he wasn't good enough to play, then why bother practicing?

The first rule a hockey player learns is: don't back the coach into a corner. Sinden and John Ferguson were trying to get the team ready for an important game, and Vic Hadfield decided to mutiny. And the Soviet team was watching. Sinden's reaction to this horrific situation might well have been as important as any action he took as the coach of Team Canada. He ordered Hadfield off the ice and onto the first plane home. Before the day was over, Richard Martin and Jocelyn Guevremount, malcontents who shared Hadfield's view were also headed home. The nightmare of handling thirty-five of the top NHLers had come to a climax. Sinden realized early into the Series that having thirty-five players on his roster was a mixed blessing and could be a logistical nightmare once it was determined that winning against the Soviets was going to be such a major test. He couldn't afford to play favourites or be diplomatic and try to keep everyone happy. The task at hand was so urgent he only had room for the eighteen to twenty players who made up the very best Team Canada possible. And hopefully it would be good enough. The silver lining in the situation was it was one more step in the making of the real Team Canada, which was being slowly molded, forged under fire and tested under adversity.

The Series resumed on the evening of September 22. The setup for broadcasting from Moscow had its own formidable hurdles. I could tell that producing these games so there would be a picture on the millions of television screens in Canada was a major challenge. The Series was the first television show ever produced in the Soviet Union that was televised to the West. While certainly not of the historic magnitude of the hockey games, from a television perspective, the production of the games was a significant technical achievement.

Broadcasting from the booth in Moscow was a unique experience, even for a veteran like Foster Hewitt. The arena had about twenty rows of seats, which went all the away around. Our ad hoc broadcast booth was in the back row near centre ice. It was cramped and congested, full of people and equipment. Foster and I, with our microphones and monitors, were squeezed into a very tight space. It was cozy, to say the least. It was also very hot, as hot as the Montreal Forum had been. In North America, broadcasters were above the crowd; in Moscow, we were surrounded by fans. And they were Soviet fans, not Canadian. Television wires and cables ran from God knows where, through the arena, under the seats and people's feet, to get to our booth. I was sure the production people sweated every moment of the broadcasts, fearing that someone would unplug us—intentionally or unintentionally.

Soviet broadcast techniques were much simpler and less commercial than what we were used to. Nikolai Ozerov, the Foster Hewitt of the Soviet Union, did his play-by-play call (broadcast over the state-controlled television system) from rinkside near the Soviet team bench. His style was low-key and minimalist in comparison to the Canadian way.

A few rows below us was a bunker similar to Harold Ballard's in Maple Leaf Gardens. There the top Soviet government officials sat when in attendance. There was an obvious police or military presence near the bunker. At ice level, a walkway went from the first row of seats to the team benches. This area was also policed and had a lot of people with the look of security about them.

The Soviet crowd was a drab one in comparison to those in Canada. People were generally well dressed—this was a major event in Moscow—but looked like they were going to a funeral with their sombre faces and their grey and dark-coloured suits or military uniforms. I wondered if the crowd was hand-picked for political purposes, or were these real Soviet hockey fans who frequented the arena to see the Moscow Dynamo and the Central Red Army teams play in the Soviet Elite League?

—⁂—

After fourteen days of hell since the last game in Canada, Game Five was set to go. The Team Canada players laced up their skates, got their final directives from the coaching staff, took a collective deep breath and headed to the rink. And if the adrenalin wasn't already pumping, it kicked into overdrive when they stepped onto the ice to a thunderous roar from the crowd. How could it be? This was Moscow. But there they were, some three thousand Canadian fans, waving flags and banners, wearing Team Cananda T-shirts and jerseys, ringing bells and rattling noisemakers of all shapes and sizes in boisterous support of their team. It was the best thing Team Canada had heard or seen since the Series began, which seemed to be an eon ago. In a strange land and in a strange rink, the fans helped them feel at home when they were away from home. The fans' important role in the Series had just begun. The fans who ventured on this unique trip to Moscow came from every part of Canada and from all walks of life. Their common interest was hockey, and they were loyal, diehard fans. They sat in a group across the rink from our broadcast booth, behind the penalty boxes. They stood out like red vests at a funeral, drowning out their Soviet counterparts, who were probably stunned at the enthusiastic support for Team Canada. (In a society where obscurity was the norm, Soviet fans had difficulty letting their enthusiasm show for their team as outwardly as the Canadians.) Before the Series was over, those three thousand fans, with their unabashed support, and significantly outnumbered in the crowd, would be as good as an extra man on the ice for Team Canada.

As well, it appeared that the Canadian public which had been ambivalent about its support for Team Canada after their disappointing effort in Canada also began to show their support. Thousands of telegrams and other correspondence started to arrive in Moscow. The dressing rooms and hallways were plastered with words of support and encouragement from every part of Canada. Canadians were behind the team as it began the final steps of its quest.

There was real tension and anxiety as the teams lined up for the ceremonial opening. And while certainly not planned, Phil Esposito fell unceremoniously on his rear end during the player introductions. His impromptu reaction to this embarrassment was a theatrical bow to the crowd, and while a small thing at the time, it helped relax Team Canada just before the game began.

And then began maybe the most exciting, hard-played, dramatic four-game hockey series of all time. From the last game in Vancouver, Sinden made several player changes, most notably putting Tony Esposito in goal. The only line still together since the Series began was Ron Ellis, Bobby Clarke and Paul Henderson.

From the opening faceoff it was good hockey. Team Canada took several minutes to get their skating legs, but their style of play was much less aggressive and more composed than in Canada. Both Tony Esposito and Vladislav Tretiak came up with some big saves in the first fifteen minutes to keep the game scoreless. On the larger ice surface—it was approximately twelve feet wider than the standard NHL rink—there was a premium on good skaters. It became evident immediately that the extra space was going to be a big advantage to players like Henderson, Yvan Cournoyer and Gilbert Perreault, who had explosive speed. However, the extra ice put more pressure on the defencemen. To cover the extra space, the forwards had to backcheck, and defencemen could not wander too far from the goal when they chased the puck into the corners. The forwards had to help out in the corners more than on an NHL-sized rink, and running around would be deadly. Team Canada had to play controlled, positional, composed and disciplined hockey. And they had to be mentally and physically tough.

The Soviets picked up right where they left off in Vancouver. They too were ready, and displayed a confidence in their game that was almost cockiness. In their home rink, with a friendly crowd, and up one game in the Series, they started Game Five confident that they could win the Series. From the outset, Team Canada had its hands full.

Team Canada drew first blood late in the opening period. The first goal in a game is always important, but this goal put to rest any doubts the players had about scoring in this strange arena. They were outplayed in the period, but left the ice with a 1–0 lead. I was sure it was a great relief to have the period behind them; the goal was a bonus.

Team Canada gained control of the game early in the second period, making it 2–0. When he played in Canada, everyone acknowledged Valery Kharlamov's speed. It was even more explosive and dangerous on the larger ice surface. The Ellis, Clarke, Henderson line was given the responsibility of neutralizing Kharlamov, who was definitely a handful. Both Ellis and Gary Bergman gave Kharlamov shots that earned them penalties. Team Canada knew how potent the Soviets power play could be, but allowed no one to score during the penalties.

Just past the midway point in the game, Henderson, ever the opportunist, drilled a shot by Tretiak to make it 3–0. No one on either team was skating around the rink quicker or more free-wheeling and confident than Paul. His game was custom-made for the big ice surface, and his focus was unparalleled. He was a man on a mission.

Then near disaster struck! On Henderson's next shift, he was tripped by Alexander Maltsev, who was racing him for the puck in the Soviet zone. Paul was pulled off his skates and unable to get turned around as he slid on the ice towards the end boards beside the Soviet goal. He hit the boards with a sickening thud, his shoulders, back and head taking the brunt of the collision. Foster and I were very concerned as was everyone in the arena. There was a hush in the rink. Henderson lay motionless, unconscious. The trainer raced onto the ice, and after a few minutes, Henderson came around and was assisted off the ice. The thought of the loss of Henderson to Team Canada was enough to make every Canadian sick. The game resumed, and Team Canada maintained the 3–0 lead through the second period.

In the dressing room between periods, Sinden faced two key issues. The first was the status of Henderson. He had definitely suffered a concussion, and the team doctor advised Paul to sit out the remainder of the game. He pleaded to be kept in. Sinden left the decision up to Paul. He chose to continue playing.

The second issue was the score. A 3-0 lead is the worst lead in hockey. As a player, it's hard not to think you had an insurmountable lead and that the game was won. But 3-1 puts the opposition back into the game and usually with some momentum. Sinden had to convince his troops not to let up, to keep taking the game to the Soviets. Team Canada players knew only too well that the Soviets weren't out of it, even at 3–0.

In the other dressing room, I could only imagine the tongue-lashing the Soviet team was getting from their coaching staff. It was no surprise when they came out for the third period ready to get back into the game. And into it they got. And quickly! Yuri Blinov broke in alone on Tony Esposito and, with lots of room, skated around the helpless goalie and slid the puck into the empty net. The score was 3–1, still a two-goal lead for Canada.

Just over a minute later, Henderson streaked in behind the Soviet defence to receive a perfect long cross-ice pass from Clarke. With the Soviet defence in hot pursuit, he moved in on the goal without being hauled down this time and beat Tretiak with a clean, quick wrist shot, restoring Team Canada's three-goal lead. With little more than fifteen minutes remaining, it looked like Team Canada was going to win the first game in Moscow.

Then, as had happened before in the Series, it all started to slip away from them. The Soviets had a habit of scoring in bunches, and they got it started when Viascheslav Anisin deflected a point shot to narrow the gap to 4–2. Eight seconds later, before Team Canada could collect themselves, Valdimir Shadrin, assisted by Anisin, made it 4–3. Anisin and his linemates continued to be a headache for Team Canada.

The dynamo was picking up momentum. With just over ten minutes remaining in the very important first game in Moscow, it was still Team Canada's game to win, or lose. But the Soviets just kept coming. A long slapshot from the point beat Esposito to tie the game. Team Canada was hanging on for dear life. But they lost their grip. As happens so often in hockey, a missed opportunity at one end of the rink ends up with the puck in the net at the other end. With a chance to give Team Canada the lead again, Jean Ratelle hit the post. Moments later, the ever-pesky Kharlamov made it 5–4 and sealed Team Canada's fate.

There were just over five minutes to play, and Team Canada still had a chance. But they were reeling after four unanswered goals in less than six minutes. With that remarkable comeback, the Soviets stole the game. Team Canada again saw a much needed win slip through their hands. The Soviets just didn't quit, no matter what the score.

My post-game comments summarized Team Canada's critical situation. Only three games remained, and they had dug themselves into a hugely deep hole and had no room to dig it any deeper, or they would be buried in it. They had to win all three remaining games to win the Series. It would require desperate, passionate and gutsy hockey. The comeback of the century—nothing less would do!

—ɯ—

Game Six was scheduled in two days. Team Canada had its back against the wall. There could be no more slippage, no more mistakes and no more giveaway games. Team Canada had to find a way to win three games in a row. Even though they hadn't lost their enthusiasm for Team Canada, some Canadian supporters in Moscow were skeptical that the team could make such a comeback against such a formidable opponent. Especially in the Soviets' own backyard.

On their days off, the players got a chance to visit some of the renowned sites and attractions in Moscow. We were doing some between-period features on the team and its players, so I had the opportunity to join them. Visits to Red Square, Lenin's tomb, the GUM department store and a private tour of the Kremlin were included.

We got to see the Moscow Circus, certainly one of the most unique in the world. It was presented in a venue designed like an ice-cream cone; the rows of seats were vertical and went all the way around, focusing on one show ring at the bottom. The circus was all around and over us, the trapeze acts almost close enough to touch and the famous bears near enough to pet. Like its hockey team, the famous Moscow Circus was a Soviet showpiece. And the ice cream they served there and in the arena was one of the real food treats in Moscow.

September 24. Twenty-three days into the Series. Five games played, and Team Canada had won only one. That win seemed like a light year ago. But with that win in the back of their minds, the players knew they could beat the Soviets. This team that had been continually forged under fire and tested with adversity after adversity, some self-inflicted, was ready for the battle of their lives. The most over-used sports cliché did apply: there really was no tomorrow. Lose again and return to Canada disgraced and in shame. The fear of losing was overwhelming and would become an inspiration and provide motivation.

From the broadcast booth as we set up the importance of Game Six, we were all terrified knowing that the Series would be over if Team Canada lost, making the last two games an unbearable nightmare for everyone. They must win!

In spite of the disappointing loss in Game Five, Sinden didn't make wholesale changes to his lineup for Game Six. The big change was putting Ken Dryden in goal. He hadn't played since Sweden, and his confidence level was low, but Sinden gambled that he would rebound and do the job between the pipes so desperately needed. All Canadians hoped he was right.

The Soviet coaches, smelling blood, sensing the kill and maybe a bit overconfident, made a lot of changes to their lineup. They replaced some experience with youth and speed, and they tried to use their most potent team. Tretiak continued to carry the goaltending load.

Right from the singing of "O Canada," in which every Canadian in the Moscow arena joined with patriotic fervor, the loyal fans let their team know they were behind them all the way. Team Canada needed all the help it could get.

It became obvious early in Game Six that the hockey was going to be trench warfare, a cold war fought by determined warriors on both sides. Team Canada couldn't afford to give up an inch of ice without a fight, and it was going to be Canadian-style hockey all the way, the only game Team Canada knew. They were determined to make it work, even against the impressive Soviets.

From the opening faceoff, both teams made it clear they had come to play all-out to the end. While the play was fairly wide open, with end-to-end rushes, the hitting and checking were fierce. Dryden was forced to make some big saves early, which gave him and his teammates much-needed confidence. Both teams had some good scoring chances but were unable to convert them into goals, as both goalies were solid in the nets. Even with a double minor penalty to Phil Esposito, the first period ended scoreless. So far so good.

The Soviets began the second period with a play started by Alexander Yakushev. Yuri Liapkin struck for the first goal of the game to give the Soviets a 1–0 lead. Yakushev had emerged as the Soviet counterpart to Phil Esposito; he was a big forward who could set up and score important goals. A few minutes after Liapkin scored, Dennis Hull picked up a rebound and fired it past a sprawled Tretiak to tie the game. The momentum slowly started to shift to Team Canada. Red Berenson, who had been used sparingly, centred a line with Cournoyer and Jean-Paul Parise. After a save by Dryden, Berenson led a rush. Team Canada got control in the Soviet zone and moved the puck around. A shot by Pat Stapleton from the point ended up behind the net. The inspired and tenacious Berenson retrieved the puck and fed a quick pass to Cournoyer in front; Cournoyer scored to give Team Canada a lead.

Between Game Five and Six, Sinden and Ferguson spotted a weakness in the Soviet team, and they didn't have many: they had difficulty getting the puck out of their end if the Canadians were aggressive in their forechecking and puck control. The Soviets had a system for every situation. Disrupt the system, and they didn't adjust well or quickly. In the Canadian way, Team Canada had been dumping the puck in and chasing it. The Soviets would take possession and move it out of their zone just as quickly. Sinden instructed the players to carry the puck into the Soviet zone, set up control, pass the puck around, disrupt and break down their defensive system, then wait for and create better scoring opportunities. Combined with disciplined positional play and hard checking, the strategy was working.

For the first time in the Series, Team Canada had the Soviets off balance and rattled. Henderson, ever the opportunist, intercepted a rare errant Soviet pass in the centre zone, took a few strides towards the Soviet defense pair and snapped a quick slapshot that beat Tretiak cleanly. In one minute and twenty-three seconds, Team Canada had erased the Soviet lead and replaced it with a 3–1 Team Canada lead. I commented that for the first time, the Soviets had opened the door a crack, and Team Canada had rushed through like a freight train. The team's confidence was growing, and I and the Canadian fans in the arena were delighted. But we knew the Soviets could also score in bunches and the game was less than half over. No time for celebration yet!

And as if the hockey challenge wasn't enough, Team Canada's worst fear about partial officiating started to be realized. The two officials in Game Six were the same Josef Kompalla and Franz Baader who had handed out numerous penalties to Team Canada in Sweden. As soon as Canada took the lead, the officials started to influence the game, looking for opportunities to give Team Canada penalties. While many were deserved, some of the penalties they called were questionable. I knew that Team Canada couldn't let the officials dictate the outcome of the game. It was easy for me to say; not so easy to achieve. Several players started to lose their control and composure on the ice, and the parade to the penalty box accelerated. All of a sudden, Team Canada's offence got parked on the bench.

The team focused its vicious and unrelenting attacks on Kharlamov, who was to the Soviet offense what Henderson was for Team Canada. They felt he must be stopped, so everyone ran at him at every opportunity. Some took the do-or-die mindset to its extreme, and no one more than Bobby Clarke, one of the most aggressive and intimidating Team Canada agitators. The officials missed it, but from the broadcast booth, I was shocked and disgusted when I saw Clarke viciously chop at Kharlamov's left ankle. Play continued, but it was immediately apparent that Clarke's two-handed slash had in fact hurt and hobbled Kharlamov. Had Team Canada's desperation come to this? Kharlamov was certainly one of the top Soviet players, but did Team Canada need to resort to these tactics to stop him?

No one wanted a win against the Soviets more than I did. I still had a vivid and painful memory from my 1964 Olympic Winter Games loss in the gold medal game. I knew what it was like to lose to the Soviets, and I didn't like it. I wanted Team Canada to win, but not this way. I hoped they would win by playing better hockey with more talented hockey players, not because they were tougher and dirtier, certainly not by intentionally injuring the other team's star players. Winning in sport shouldn't be everything. But emotionally these games had clearly gone past sport for Team Canada and had truly become unrestricted war on ice. And take no prisoners! I knew Team Canada, with its back firmly against the wall, would fight right to the end, and win or lose, they would show great courage. However, I couldn't condone Clarke's action or those who might have put him up to it, but I understood and appreciated that Team Canada was playing with intensity, desperate to keep their hopes alive in the Series.

Realizing they missed the Clarke penalty, the officials gave Hull a questionable slashing penalty. And just nine seconds into the Soviet power play, Yakushev scored in a goalmouth scramble to close the gap to 3–2. Team Canada was again on thin ice.

About half a minute later, all hell broke lose. Phil Esposito received a five-minute major penalty for cutting big Soviet defenseman Alexander Ragulin. Led by Sinden and Ferguson, the Team Canada bench went ballistic, screaming and shouting, throwing towels and generally losing it. The Soviet fans displayed their displeasure and disapproval of Team Canada's behaviour using their traditional ear-piercing whistle, in international hockey a signal of disapproval.

I realized that if Team Canada didn't get a grip quickly and restore their composure and discipline, their chances of winning the game and staying alive in the Series were going to go down the drain. As difficult as it was, Team Canada had to stop wasting so much of its precious energy on berating the officials, accept that they also would have to beat the officials as well as the Soviets, and get focused on the business at hand. This is the most difficult lesson to learn in international hockey, and they were learning it the hard way. It took more than just hockey ability to be a successful international hockey player, and it was a frustrating experience.

For his participation in the bench fracas, Ferguson was given a bench penalty, which put Team Canada two men short. Kharlamov, who had been used sparingly since his ankle injury, was on the power play. The Soviets set up in the Team Canada zone, an easy thing to do with the big ice surface and with a two-man advantage. They moved the puck around the outside of the defensive triangle with confidence and authority. The last pass was to Kharlamov, who was parked all alone to Dryden's left. He one-timed a shot to the top corner for what looked like a sure goal. However, somehow Dryden ended up with the puck in his glove. No goal!

Did Kharlamov score or not? To this day, no one is absolutely sure whether the puck crossed the goal line. From the broadcast booth, Foster and I had a clear look at the play. While it was politic to say it didn't go in, I wasn't sure then, and I'm still not sure. But when the official blew the whistle, Dryden had the puck in his glove on the safe side of the goal line. I'm inclined to think that if there had been today's sophisticated replay capabilities available, it might have shown that the puck actually hit the netting that hung down inside the goal before Dryden caught it. But at the time, I had never heard of a goal being counted if the goalie ended up with the puck outside the goal line, even if his glove crossed the plane of the goal line as he caught it. The cameras in Moscow couldn't answer that question, and it all happened so fast.

For the first time in the Series, fate may have shone favourably on Team Canada. In spite of some mild protests by Kharlamov and Vladimir Petrov, there was no goal. Had Kharlamov's shot counted, it would have tied the score at 3–3, and who knows what might have happened? A tie would have been no good to Team Canada. They needed a win. When the second period ended, Canada had a very fragile 3–2 lead.

Sinden knew that in the dressing room he had to control his frustration and anger and collect himself so he could calm the players, who still had to go out in the third period and win the game. Team Canada was fighting a two-front war: one against the Soviet players, the other against the officials. The second front they couldn't win, so they had to focus on the first.

There was a delay at the start of the third period. Foster and I wondered where Team Canada was. Sinden held back his warriors for almost five minutes. He said he was waiting for the ice to dry. But in reality Team Canada was in the dressing room getting its act together to face the challenge of a lifetime for every one of them.

When they got on the ice, they played like they were possessed. No third-period collapse, like in Games Three and Five. They started the period short-handed but weathered that storm, then shut down the Soviets the rest of the way. Even a late penalty, an attempt by the officials to give the Soviet power play one last chance to tie up the game, failed, and Canada earned a 3-2 victory. While still a long way to go with one hundred and twenty minutes of hockey remaining, Team Canada had created its own tomorrow. Team Canada had entered Game Six on mouth-to-mouth, but left it breathing on its own, alive and well. One battle won, two to go!

—⁓—

The next day, many of the players and their wives toured Moscow or just took a much-needed break from the hockey wars. In the evening, Foster and I and our wives were invited to join Team Canada at a reception hosted by Canadian ambassador Robert Ford. He had hosted a similar reception in 1969 when I played in the Izvestia Tournament. For the players, the Canadian embassy was a piece of home away from home, a temporary refuge. They could relax and enjoy a break from the close scrutiny in Moscow. It was a brief but important break from the unreal reality they were experiencing outside the embassy. They were recharged by Canadian hospitality and Canadian food. All too brief, it was back to the war.

The win in Game Six was their first since September 4, which seemed like a lifetime ago. But they were confident they could beat the Soviets and win the Series. It certainly wouldn't be easy, but in Game Six when the Soviets had Team Canada to the brink, they weren't able to push them over. Team Canada was no longer awestruck by their opponents. Formidable they were, but also beatable. The pendulum had started to swing back Team Canada's way.

The Soviets seemed less confident and cocky than they were before Game Six. They were entering uncharted territory. Virtually every opponent they played in recent years had collapsed under the relentless pressure of keeping up with them for sixty minutes. But the NHLers hadn't folded. The Soviets had at last met their match, and I suspect they knew it.

After six of the most exhausting games any Team Canada player had experienced, attrition was a factor Sinden had to consider.

However, he decided to make only two changes to his winning lineup. One was putting Tony Esposito back in goal. The Soviets dropped Kharlamov because of his ankle injury, and the coaches went back to their Game Five lineup in the hope of ending this nail-biting Series.

Game Seven was another do-or-die game for Canada. Foster and I had exhausted our normal repertoire of sports clichés. We couldn't overstate the importance of the game. And to think, they didn't have to win just once, but twice. It was emotionally exhausting just to watch; I could only imagine the stress and strain everyone involved with Team Canada was going through as they gyrated through the full spectrum of emotions.

Early in the first period, an impotent Team Canada power play was winding down, and the power-play unit was still on the ice. Phil Esposito, from his favourite spot in the slot, took a pass from Ellis with his back to the net, and as if he had eyes in the back of his head, then turned and fired a shot that beat Tretiak to make it 1–0 for Team Canada. Once again, Phil got Team Canada off to a good start. As Esposito had become the leader of Team Canada, Yakushev had emerged as his Soviet counterpart. Midway through the period, with a burst of power and speed, Yakushev raced up the ice and from the top of the face-off circle fired a blistering slapshot that Tony Esposito couldn't handle. The goal tied the game.

Both teams played brutally rough and tough hockey. No one was more pumped or aggressive than Phil Esposito. He cross-checked Boris Mikhailov and was so incensed he was still gesturing to him from the penalty box. I was worried by Esposito's lack of control. He couldn't lead his team from the penalty box and his presence on the ice was the key to any hope of a Team Canada victory.

The Soviets made it 2–1 on a power play, then tried to strike again, but Esposito was back on the ice and got a pass from Serge Savard in the high slot, which he converted quickly into a wrist shot that beat Tretiak just inside the post to tie it up again. The Soviets couldn't contain Esposito when he set up in the slot area. It was a tough period for Team Canada, but they escaped tied at 2s.

In the second period, the teams seemed to be trying to kill each other. The composure and discipline evident early in the game had evaporated, and I commented that Team Canada was slipping into very dangerous territory. The officials handed out seven penalties in the period, four of them to Team Canada. Fortunately, Tony Esposito came up huge in goal, and Phil, when he wasn't in the penalty box, controlled the ice surface when killing penalties. Contrary to their normal stoic passiveness to rough play, the Soviets became active participants. Not being their normal style, it reduced their effectiveness. While Team Canada was out-chanced and somewhat out-played in the period, the score remained tied.

Again, it was to come down to the last period to decide the outcome of this cliff-hanger. Team Canada started the third period strongly: Rod Gilbert gave them a 3–2 lead. It stood up for just over three minutes, then Yakushev was left uncovered at the edge of the goal crease and had an easy tap in on a goalmouth pass to tie it up again. So far it was the Espo and Yak show.

With less than fifteen minutes left in the game, it was still anyone's game to win or lose, as neither team could establish any advantage over the other. And just when we thought it couldn't get any rougher, it did. Stick work, slashing, cross-checking, butt-ending were now the norm, not just for Team Canada but for the Soviets as well. It was vicious, brutal and mean-spirited hockey, hardly a game any longer. Boris Mikhailov was one of the most willing Soviet players to mix it up with Team Canada. He almost seemed determined to prove he could play rugged hockey with the best, Canadian style or any style one chose to play. And Gary Bergman had been a ticking time bomb on a short fuse in every game he played. He struggled constantly to keep his composure on the ice. Mikhailov had Bergman pinned on the boards behind Team Canada's goal; Bergman took exception to it and exploded. All hell broke loose. Everyone jumped into the fray, pushing and punching. Then Mikhailov kicked Bergman hard enough to break his shin pad and draw blood. I commented that the game was teetering precariously, almost out of control. It was as close to playing Canadian style hockey as the Soviets would get in the Series.

The officials confined their censure to the two main combatants, Bergman and Mikhailov, assessing them five-minute majors for roughing. The Soviet crowd once again indicated displeasure with the ugly incident with ear-piercing whistles, which followed the players to the penalty box. Bergman was out of control even after he got in the penalty box. There was visible hate and anger between many players on each team and it threatened to destroy the game.

Foster and I were relieved when play finally resumed. The Soviets showed signs of running out of gas, but they only needed a tie to win the Series. To stay alive, Team Canada had to pull a rabbit out the hat: only a win would do.

With more room on the ice to move, Henderson approached the Soviet defence tandem with two players in hot pursuit, and with some slick moves got both the puck and himself past the pair. Then Valery Vasiliev got a piece of him and knocked him off his skates. As he fell towards the net and Tretiak, Paul snapped a wrist shot over Tretiak's right shoulder and just under the crossbar to score. The goal gave Team Canada a precarious 4–3 lead with just over two minutes to play.

As if the game needed any more problems. The goal light didn't go on when Henderson scored; the goal judge seemed to be waiting for an indication from the officials to allow or disallow the goal. Team Canada players rushed onto the ice and smothered Henderson with congratulations, and then almost as an afterthought the goal light finally glowed red. Score 4–3 for Team Canada. I noted that the game wasn't over yet. The Soviets tried to storm the Team Canada goal to tie the score. Team Canada hung on to win. From near death, with the grave dug and one foot in it after Game Five, Team Canada had scratched, clawed and fought its way out of its deathbed. It had been desperate and ugly hockey, but Team Canada had gotten the job done. Who would have thought when the Series began that it would come down to this: one game, winner take all? Team Canada had created another tomorrow.

Team Canada had a day to lick their wounds and get some much-needed rest and relaxation. Some of the players went to see the world-famous Bolshoi Ballet. The magnificent Bolshoi Theatre was splendid to behold. Seeing ballet was a unique experience for the players and for me. Stan Mikita thoroughly enjoyed the dance and appreciated the skill and athleticism of the artists, and he had a good sense of humour about the experience. At the end of the ballet he asked: "Why were the dancers always on their toes? Why don't they just get taller dancers?"

—⁓—

Before Game Eight, all sorts of games were played off the ice by the Soviet hosts who turned very inhospitable. I wasn't sure what expectations they had at the start of the Series, but in Moscow before a home crowd, they displayed an urgency to win similar to Team Canada's. The Cold War would get a lot colder before the Series concluded. On the ice it was one acrimonious and hard-fought battle after battle, and it was going to go right to the bitter end. The Soviets had never played against a team like Team Canada which had such a determined spirit to win and never-say-die attitude.

The most important question before Game Eight was who the officials would be. After the officiating in Game Six, Andrei Starovoitov, a leader in the Soviet Ice Hockey Federation, apparently agreed that Baader and Kompalla, the two West Germans, wouldn't work any more games. Then the Soviet team management, using every ploy and edge available changed their mind and insisted that Baader and Kompalla work the last game. Sinden and Eagleson were incensed at this about-face. Both sides stonewalled, and Team Canada said that if either West German officiated, they wouldn't play. The Soviets had met their match in Eagleson. He drew his line in the sand and wouldn't budge. An impasse. So the Soviets did an end run around him and went the political route: they appealed to Senator Arthur Laing, the senior Canadian government representative at the games, and to Hockey Canada officials, using Ambassador Ford as the diplomatic facilitator. The Soviets were assured that Team Canada would take to the ice for Game Eight. I would have loved to be present when Eagleson was told that the politicos had kicked out the footings of his negotiation position and compromised Team Canada's stance.

A few hours before the start of Game Eight, Team Canada still was not satisfied with the officiating. The backroom boys worked at it, trying to get an acceptable solution. After much screaming, threats and shaking of fists, an acceptable compromise was reluctantly reached:

each team would select one official. The Soviets picked Kompalla. Team Canada selected Uwe Dahlberg of Sweden. He was ill, so they selected Rudolph Bata of Czechoslovakia. With both sides certainly not happy, but having saved some face, the game was on.

For a week we had all been out of touch with what was happening in Canada, in fact in the rest of the world. We were very much behind the Iron Curtain and communication with the outside world was minimal. Foster and I were only vaguely aware of the interest the Moscow games had attracted in Canada. It wouldn't be until we returned to Canada that the impact the games had on all Canadians would become evident. You couldn't have dreamt up a more dramatic climax to any sports event than the one that lay ahead.

—◊◊◊—

Having made Game Eight the most important hockey game ever, Sinden had some tough decisions to make in setting his final lineup. In spite of injuries and aches, he stuck mostly with his Game Seven roster. The biggest decision was who would be in goal. Coaches have hunches. In spite of his outstanding performance in Game Seven and readiness to play, Tony Esposito was dropped. Both Sinden and Ferguson felt Dryden was due for a big game. The lineup decisions made, it was up to the players.

Across the rink, the Soviet coaches went with what they thought was their most experienced and best lineup and made only two changes: they dropped Ragulin on defence and reinserted Kharlamov at forward. Even though Kharlamov was reported to have a fractured ankle, the Soviets thought his presence would help lift the Soviet team. And for the eighth game in a row Tretiak was goaltending for the Soviets.

From our broadcast booth, we could see that the crowd was abuzz. Expectations were high on both sides; tension was evident everywhere. There were extra police and militia in the arena. The Soviets would not chance a crowd getting out of control. The Canadian fans made noise that exceeded their numbers tenfold. Team Canada wouldn't be out-supported in the stands.

It all came down to sixty minutes for all the glory. Did Team Canada have enough adrenalin in the tank to get successfully to the end? Phil Esposito, with Cournoyer and Parise started for Team Canada against Yakushev, Vladimir Shadrin and Anisin. Vsevolod Bobrov followed his starting line with Kharlamov, Alexander Maltsev and Vladimir Viku-lov. Although Kharlamov was clearly hobbled, he demanded watching. And in the opening moments, the Soviets moved the puck well and tested Dryden early. He looked steady, which was a good sign.

The game was only two and half minutes old when the reviled Kompalla called his first penalty on Team Canada. And then anoth-er penalty, putting Team Canada two men short. The Soviet power play quickly took control in the Team Canada zone. There was too much ice for Esposito, Park and Bergman to cover, and after a couple of attempts on goal, Yakushev parked in his favourite spot, to the side of the goal crease, took a rebound off the post and swept a backhand shot by the helpless Dryden to give the Soviets a quick lead.

The officials continued to call marginal penalties; Kompalla espe-cially seemed to smugly delight in penalizing Team Canada players. He knew his masters in the IIHF could get him the plum assignments, and he wasn't going to let Team Canada affect his opportunities. The officials seemed to be doing their best to ruin the game. The officiat-ing generally had been inferior, even incompetent, throughout the Moscow portion of the Series and Team Canada's worst fears were realized in the early stages of the game. I would be the first to admit Team Canada deserved many of the penalties they received, but in this deciding game of the Series, the officials should have let the players play. They didn't seem to know the difference between close checking and legitimate penalties. They tried to influence the outcome of the game. It was a tough environment to play in.

And then in a flash, the second Team Canada time bomb exploded: Parise snapped. Incensed at his penalty, he muttered something de-rogatory to Kompalla and banged his stick on the ice in anger. He was given a ten-minute misconduct. Then he really went berserk. Like a raging bull, Parise left the penalty box, cruised around the rink, went to the Team Canada bench for consolation, then headed towards Kompalla, who was on the other side of the rink by the penalty box.

By the time we got to Game Eight, Foster and I thought we had seen it all and there wasn't much left to say, but we were wrong; we hadn't seen anything yet. I was terrified to think what Parise was going to do next. He seemed barely able to keep himself from hitting Kompalla over the head with his stick. Kompalla gave him a game misconduct. The game, like so many of its predecessors, escalated into another full-scale battle, the last decisive battle of the war.

I'd played a lot of international hockey against the Soviets, and knew how frustrating it could be. But I'd never seen anything like this. Everyone involved with Team Canada was out of control: players berated the officials; Sinden and Ferguson threw chairs and towels onto the ice. The Soviet fans were whistling with disapproval—and the whistling felt like someone drilling a nail in my ear. The Canadian fans were chanting, "Let's go home!" Not only was the game getting ugly on the ice, the fans were also in a potentially dangerous mood. I sensed that the powder keg could blow at any moment.

The Soviet organizers had to accept a big part of the blame for the explosive situation. In their own desperation to win, they increasingly harassed and played mind games with Team Canada to distract and disrupt their focus: voiceless telephone calls in the middle of the night, changed practice schedules, tampering with the team's precious food supply, imposing incompetent officials into the games, and the constant surveillance and scrutiny of Team Canada's every move. Everyone was as tight as a piano wire and ready to snap. Any more tension and we would have a dangerous international incident on our hands.

As awful and disruptive as the Parise incident was, the message was clear: if the officials continued to tamper with the outcome of the game, it was at the risk of causing a riot. Team Canada wouldn't stand for it any longer. There was no enjoyment in the game for the players on either team; it was all serious business.

It took at least ten minutes to restore order on the ice, behind the team benches and in the stands so the game could continue. I commented to a man that Team Canada must collect themselves and go back to playing hockey in spite of the officials. They must keep cool heads if they were to have any chance to win the game. They were just going to have to beat both the Soviet team and the officials. Easy for me to say! When play resumed, Team Canada had to kill off the initial Parise penalty, which they did. And they got their first power-play opportunity. Sinden had Esposito, Ellis and Henderson on the ice, with Park and Guy Lapointe on defence. Working the puck around in the Soviet end, Park got a point shot on goal. Tretiak made the initial save, but Esposito was there to bang home the rebound to make it 1–1. As he had in Game Seven, Phil once again scored Team Canada's crucial first goal. Esposito repeatedly led Team Canada and was their tower of strength in every game.

The penalty calls continued: interference, holding or hooking penalties almost every time two players came in contact. The officials seemed not to accept that hockey was a contact sport. These types of penalties were symptoms of a tight close-checking game. There was no flow to the game. At least now both teams were being penalized. Cournoyer took Team Canada's third interference penalty and the fifth interference call of the period. The Soviets sensed an advantage. Broken ankle or not, Kharlamov was on the Soviet power-play unit. And before we knew it, a screened slapshot from just inside the blue line made its way through a maze of players, eluded Dryden and gave the Soviets the lead. The game's three goals had been scored on power plays. The penalty parade was going to kill Team Canada.

Late in the period, the game settled down, went from a very tight, close-checking style and the flow and tempo picked up for both teams. On a nifty two-man play, Park joined the rush with Ratelle and took a crisp return pass as he moved in on the Soviet goal. A perfect shot over Tretiak's blocker glove to the far upper corner tied the game at 2–2. Team Canada's play became surprisingly loose. Both teams were taking chances in the final minute. Dryden was forced to make several key saves to preserve the tie. One long, turbulent and volatile period finished; two to go. Nothing decided.

Between periods, Foster and I found out there were difficulties with the transmission feed to Canada for the television coverage. We assumed it was just one more Soviet effort to interfere with the Series. We couldn't do anything about the technical difficulties, so we kept covering the game, hoping the millions of fans trying to watch at home could see the finale of the truly incredible Series.

Almost off the opening faceoff of the second period, Yakushev fired a long shot that was high and wide; it hit the screening behind the goal. The puck rebounded off the screening and came almost straight out past Dryden. He took a futile swing, trying to stop it, and it went right onto Shadrin's waiting stick. Before Dryden could recover, Shadrin drilled the puck for a goal to give the Soviets a 3–2 lead. It was probably the only fluke goal of the Series, a tough one to give up, particularly at that time.

For the next ten minutes the game opened up offensively, both teams going from end to end, creating good scoring chances. Both goalies were called upon to make big saves. It was the longest stretch of penalty-free hockey in several games, and featured the Canadians' best team play.

Bill White snuck in from his defensive position to convert a perfect Rod Gilbert goalmouth pass into a tip-in for the tying goal. So far, Team Canada had come back three times in the game.

The Soviets just kept on coming. Dryden had his hands full as the Soviets got repeated clean scoring chances, but he was on his game. A save on Mikhailov was Dryden's most spectacular of the Series so far. And then, as he had done so often before, Yakushev found himself with the puck all alone in front of Dryden. With Ken at his mercy, Yakushev made a quick move and slid the puck in for a goal. Yakushev's team-leading seventh goal put the Soviets ahead for the fourth time in the game.

The Soviets continued to push, sensing they had the Canadians on the brink again, and it could be their last chance to push them over. As if he hadn't already done enough, "Mr. Everything" Phil Esposito took a turn at playing goal. After some sloppy play in the Team Canada end, Blinov faced an empty net. Dryden was completely beaten. And then, out of nowhere, Esposito skated through the goal crease and stopped Blinov's shot, as well as a rebound from Mikhailov. It looked to me as if Blinov couldn't believe he hadn't scored.

Then there was yet another dreaded Soviet power play. The Team Canada penalty killers held off the Soviets for the first minute and a half, but with only fourteen seconds left in the power play, Shadrin tipped in a goalmouth pass from Vasiliev. The goal was mistakenly credited to Vasiliev, but Team Canada didn't care who scored it, they only cared that it was now 5–3 for the Soviets. It was the third Soviet power play goal. Penalties were killing Team Canada.

Team Canada couldn't get back into the game during the remainder of the second period in spite of a power play opportunity late in the period. But at least they stopped the bleeding behind the stellar goaltending of Dryden. With two periods behind them and a two-goal deficit, winning might not be an insurmountable task, but certainly it was a Herculean one.

In the broadcast booth between periods, I could only imagine what was going through the minds of every player on the team as they got ready for the most important twenty minutes they had ever played. I wondered how many times Team Canada could come back.

The Soviets showed how desperate they were to win when they announced between periods that in the event of a tie, they would claim victory based on a two-goal advantage in total goals for and against. It jarred my memory of what had happened in the 1964 Olympics, when a similar arbitrary formula was hatched to break a possible tie for the medals.

When informed, Eagleson went ballistic and stormed into the Team Canada dressing room to tell the players and coaches of the latest Soviet attempt to hijack the Series. But the players didn't throw up their hands in frustration and despair. The news had a positive effect. The devious off-ice tactic provided the final motivation the team needed to go out there in the final period, win the game and ruin the Soviet plot. Every player went back to the well one more time to find a last supply of energy and adrenalin. Hopefully, they wouldn't come up empty.

When Team Canada took to the ice for the final confrontation they did so with quiet confidence and determined resolve. They had played twenty-three periods of the most intense and grueling hockey any of them had ever played. They had only twenty minutes to grasp the gold ring. They had confronted and overcome one obstacle and challenge after another, coming out of each more unified, strengthened and determined. Over the previous twenty-seven days, Team Canada had evolved into an incredible team before our eyes. They were convinced they were going to win. Team Canada was a group of true tempered and hardened veterans of the international hockey wars. They were ready for one last battle. Needing the comeback of the century, scoring the first goal was absolutely vital; it would put Team Canada within striking distance. Three goals down could be insurmountable.

They took the game to the Soviets right from the opening faceoff. They left nothing in the dressing room. The Soviets were also determined; if they could just hang on for another twenty more minutes victory was theirs.

Dryden made a tremendous save early in the period, then Peter Mahovlich, on an inspired rush, got the puck in the corner to the left of the Soviet goal. He fell but made a desperate pass across the goal-mouth. Phil Esposito kept his eye on the bouncing puck and after two swings connected to bat it between Tretiak's pads. Again, Phil had scored a clutch goal that kept Team Canada's chances alive, his most important so far. He and Yakushev had seven goals each in the Series. And, early in the period, it was 5–4. There was lots of time to work on the next two goals.

The game got increasingly tense. I could see that both teams were fighting off fatigue and near exhaustion from the heat in the arena; they played on sheer guts and determination. Gilbert took exception to a late hit by Yevgeny Mishakov and started swinging. His outburst was a reflex reaction to the pressure-cooker situation. Fighting was uncommon in international hockey, and players who fought usually were ejected from the game. However, the officials seemed to be making up the rules as they went along, and fortunately both players were only given five-minute major penalties.

When the first half of the third period ended, Team Canada was still trailing 5–4. As was the rule in international hockey, the teams changed ends at the ten-minute mark of the final period. (This practice originated when most games were played outdoors and the sun and wind were factors.) The short time out gave Team Canada a chance to collect themselves for one last push for glory. The three thousand Canadian fans sounded like thirty thousand as they urged-on their warriors.

For several minutes, the pace of the game was slowed down by the close checking and cautious play of both teams. Team Canada used short shifts, keeping players on the ice who were as fresh as possible under the circumstances, with the hope they could take advantage of any opportunity that presented itself. The Soviets checked relentlessly, but they were less aggressive offensively, handling the puck a lot more and making extra passes to kill time. Were they consciously or unconsciously sitting on their one-goal lead? Or were they also exhausted and hanging on for dear life?

With less than ten minutes remaining, Team Canada had to force the play for the next goal. Who better to lead the charge than Phil Esposito? And he did. He took a rink-wide pass from Brad Park at centre ice, then raced down the right wing. Phil was a man possessed.

Surrounded by four Soviet players, he got away a high shot, which Tretiak stopped but couldn't control. Esposito kept coming. The puck bounced behind the net to Tretiak's right. Esposito followed it and finally got his stick on it. He tried to get it out to the front of the goal, but Tretiak intercepted and directed it into the corner. Not to be denied, Phil like a bulldog after a bone saw his next attempted backhand slide over to an anxiously hovering Cournoyer, who fired instantly. Tretiak made the initial save, but before he could smother the puck it squirted loose, and both Cournoyer and Esposito pounced on it. Cournoyer got to his own rebound first and whacked a backhand under a stack of Soviet players and past Tretiak. They had done it! Against overwhelming odds, Team Canada had come from behind for the fourth time to tie the game at 5–5 with just over seven minutes left to play.

Now what? There was a ruckus going on in the stands. Eagleson, from his seat with the Canadian fans, noticed that the goal light again failed to come on. Would the Soviets' games never end? Eagleson was in a frenzy and was precipitating a dangerous incident at a critical time in the game. The goal was not being disputed, but Eagleson tried to make his way to the timekeeper's bench. An army of militia and police grabbed him and started to drag him out of the arena. All hell broke loose on the ice and in the stands, and the bombastic and often profane Eagleson was right in the middle of it. The Team

Canada players saw what was happening and raced over to assist him. Seeing Al disappear amongst the uniforms, Peter Mahovlich vaulted over the boards to the rescue, wielding his hockey stick like a sword. The police released Eagleson, who shuffled across the ice surrounded by his Team Canada bodyguards, defiantly waving his fist. Now we'd seen it all! Or had we? Hopefully the Eagleson fiasco hadn't disrupted Team Canada's momentum. The game didn't need any more distractions or sideshows.

The interruption gave Team Canada a bit of a rest, and then the final seven minutes began. They hadn't come back all that way to tie the game. Only winning would do; a tie was a loss, plain and simple. The Soviets had blinked and Team Canada had a chance to seize the moment. How would it be decided? So far, the goaltending was good but not decisive on either side. It was a goal scorer's game, not a goaltender's. Team Canada needed a "chosen one" to score and win the Series.

Both teams knew the next mistake could be decisive. The pace of the play slowed as fatigue took its toll; both squads were cautious defensively, waiting for an opportunity to make an offensive burst. As the clock ticked down, Dryden blocked a long, dangerous point shot to nullify a good Soviet scoring chance. The play became ragged, and there were a lot of whistles. On every stoppage, both teams took time between faceoffs to take one last breath before play continued.

Sinden paced back and forth like a crazed tiger behind the bench, knowing time was his biggest enemy. With just over a minute and half left in the game, there was a faceoff in the Team Canada end, to the left of Dryden. Sinden took his time getting the players he wanted on the ice for one last push. Esposito came back out to centre Cournoyer and Peter Mahovlich. Savard and Lapointe were on defence. Just before the faceoff, Phil called a huddle to confirm their strategy. The Soviet crowd whistled disapproval at this delay, but the cheering Canadian fans quickly drowned them out.

It was in the final minute, time was rapidly slipping away. Stapleton replaced Lapointe on defence, and Henderson jumped on to take over for Mahovlich. It was a long shift for Esposito and Cournoyer, but with no whistle they stayed on the ice for one last attack. The

Soviets couldn't get off either and were desperately hanging on. Cournoyer slapped a weak shot that ended up beside the Soviet goal, out of Tretiak's reach. Vasiliev took possession of the puck and instead of keeping it along the boards for a faceoff or putting it into the corner to kill time, he fired it weakly around the boards, hoping to clear it out of the Soviet zone. But it went right to Cournoyer, who was just inside the blue line. He spotted a streaking Henderson moving towards the net and fired a rink-wide pass. Paul tried to one-time the pass for a shot, missed, was hooked off his skates by Vasiliev and fell sliding into the end boards to the right of Tretiak. He was on his skates instantly and headed to the front of the goal. The bouncing puck caromed off the boards and slid towards the faceoff circle, where two Soviet players tried to get control of it but couldn't. Esposito chipped the puck towards the goal. Tretiak made the save but couldn't control the rebound. Henderson was in front of the goal and took a quick shot, but again Tretiak stopped it and went down to cover the crease. The puck squirted loose and came back to Paul, who, as he moved across the goalmouth, slid the puck past a sprawled-out Tretiak just inside the goalpost. Foster screamed: "Henderson has scored for Canada!" They'd done it! The goal, scored at 19.26 from Esposito and Cournoyer made it 6–5.

The Team Canada bench emptied, and everyone raced over to mob Henderson. But there were still thirty-four long seconds left to play. Not time to celebrate yet. Team Canada knew thirty-four seconds was an eternity and lots of time for the Soviets to score. Back to work. And they didn't give the Soviets any chances and ran out the clock with the Canadian fans counting down the last ten seconds. And then Foster exclaimed: "The game is over…and Canada has won the Series!"

The scene that followed was sheer bedlam. The Canadian fans erupted in delirious joy, while their counterparts were devastated. Everyone involved with Team Canada rushed onto the ice to join the celebration. The war was over. In spite of complete exhaustion both physically and emotionally, there was a combination of sheer ecstasy and incredible relief. The piano wire couldn't have tightened any more without snapping. By the thinnest of margins, Canada had won. Thank God it was over!

The teams proceeded to line up to shake hands for one last time. The Series had been bitter and hard fought, every game an all-out battle, but the players concluded the Series as sportsmen, shaking hands and expressing unintelligible words of respect and admiration for their opponents.

The Soviet players left the ice stunned, dejected and silent. For them it was incomprehensible that they'd lost. Against outrageous odds, Team Canada won three out of four games in Moscow to snatch the Series. The Soviets couldn't believe it.

For Team Canada and every Canadian in Moscow, the celebrations began. In post-game interviews, players and commentators tried to explain what the win meant. The common thread was that they were proud to be Canadians.

—⟶⟨⟨⟵—

After a night of celebration, Team Canada left early for Prague for an exhibition game with the Czechoslovakian national team, which would be televised to Canada. After what Team Canada had just been through, all they really wanted to do was go home. But the pressure was off, and the hockey in Prague would truly be an exhibition game.

I had played against the Czechoslovakian team when I was with the Nats. In my opinion, they were every bit as good as the Soviets. But like the Nats, they had failed to win the big games at the WHCs and Olympics.

I liked the Czechoslovakian style of play, which was a blend of Soviet precision and Canadian rugged individualism. Czechoslovakia was very proud of its identity. The Czechoslovakians were an oppressed people, under Soviet domination, and the hockey games between the two countries rivaled the intensity and emotion of what we had just seen in the Series. Hard to imagine, but true.

The game gave Stan Mikita the opportunity to visit his native land and play before family members who still resided there. Some of the players who had seen little or no action in the Series had a chance to play. The Czechoslovakian team also wanted to show Team Canada they too could play with the best. Team Canada scrambled in the late stages of the game, but Serge Savard scored his second goal with only four seconds remaining to salvage a 3–3 tie. By game's end, Team Canada realized that both the Czechoslovakian and Swedish teams were also pretty damn good.

At last, the hockey marathon was over. Had Team Canada lost the Series, it could have been very uncomfortable to go home. But now the players went home to a hero's welcome and the thanks of a grateful nation.

The Birth of the World Hockey Association

IN THE fall of 1972, the NHL planned to expand to sixteen teams by adding Atlanta and Long Island. The original NHL expansion of 1967–68 doubled the league to twelve teams. In 1970–71, Vancouver and Buffalo joined the league. Many fans who could remember the Original Six teams thought the expansions diluted the major-league level dramatically, because each team had only a few quality players. But most of the expansion was into cities in the US, where many of the fans didn't know the difference between the quality of major and minor-league hockey. And the NHL's primary concern was making money, not preserving the quality of the game.

On the surface, expansion seemed to be good for everyone involved. Veteran players could extend their careers, journeymen developed into stars, and many young aspiring players, and some older minor leaguers, were given the opportunity to play major-league hockey, something denied to most of them before expansion. Salaries definitely went up because there was more demand for players, but NHL teams could still control the escalation. The NHLPA was stronger, so players got better collective bargaining agreements, with improved minimum salaries, conditions of employment and benefits. But major-league professional hockey in North America was still operated by the NHL with monopolistic like control with all its implications.

Even after expansions, several potential major markets in North America didn't have major-league professional hockey franchises.

Enter two enterprising Californians: Gary Davidson, a lawyer, and
Dennis Murphy, a promoter. Neither had any real hockey experience,
but that didn't stop them from seeing and seizing what they thought
was an opportunity to create another major professional hockey league
in North America outside the domain of the NHL.

I first heard about the World Hockey Association (WHA) while
in Fort Worth. Rumours circulated about the prospects of another
league in competition with the NHL, and it was the buzz in all professional hockey leagues in the last half of the 1971–72 season. Another
major league would be like a dream come true for many players in
the minor professional leagues around North America. Davidson and
Murphy saw many good market areas that could and would support
major-league professional hockey, and they might as well be WHA
franchises instead of NHL ones. They thought even some NHL markets could sustain two major-league teams.

Initial franchises were twenty-five thousand dollars plus some
guarantees, compared to the six million the NHL demanded. There
were lots of takers. On February 12, 1972, the WHA conducted its
first player draft to stock twelve teams in two divisions: New England, Philadelphia, New York, Quebec City, Ottawa and Cleveland
in the Eastern Division; and Los Angeles, Houston, Minnesota (St.
Paul), Chicago, Edmonton and Winnipeg in the Western Division. All
professional players, including NHLers, were available for draft. Play
would start at the beginning of the 1972–73 season.

The NHL didn't see the WHA as a serious threat, and was scepti-
cal it would actually get started. Then a bombshell dropped on the
NHL: Bobby Hull, a major marquee superstar with the Chicago Black
Hawks, signed a ten-year multi-million-dollar contract with the new
WHA. He would coach and play for the Winnipeg Jets. When Hull
signed, the WHA went from rumour to reality. And while the NHL
recovered from the shell-shock, the ambitious and aggressive WHA
moved quickly, and recklessly raided the rosters of NHL teams and
minor professional hockey leagues where they saw potential players
who could help make the WHA an instant major league. Nothing or
no one was sacred.

During its expansions, the NHL had managed to keep the lid on salaries. All that changed when Hull jumped to the WHA. NHL owner's worst nightmare became a reality. For the first time, the NHL had to compete for the services of major-league hockey players, and overnight it became a player's market: the lid on professional hockey salaries was blown sky-high. Hull's salary, though modest by today's standard, was the breakthrough contract all pro hockey players dreamed of, and it became the standard by which all players valued their worth. While the summer of 1972 is best remembered for the historic Canada–Soviet Hockey Series, the formation of the WHA changed the dynamics and economy of major professional hockey in North America, and affected the game and business of hockey all over the world.

Once Hull made the jump, the floodgates smashed open and the exodus from the NHL began. Agents shopped their players around for the best deal they could get. Players went to the WHA and its promise of big bucks. As the supply of major-league calibre players diminished, demand and cost went higher. Professional hockey players looked upon the opportunity to choose between leagues as freedom to market their skills to the highest bidder. It was a first for all professional hockey players.

The talent pool of legitimate major-league players in North America had been significantly drained by the three NHL expansions and the initial raids by the WHA. The WHA recognized the deep, untapped pool of talented players in Europe, specifically Sweden and Finland. The Winnipeg Jets were the first to dive into the European player pool when they signed the Swedish tandem of Anders Hedburg and Ulf Nilsson as linemates for Bobby Hull. Access to the Soviets and Czechoslovakians was still restricted.

In the opening game of the new league, on October 11, 1972, the Ottawa Nationals (Nationals) played the Edmonton Oilers in the Ottawa Civic Centre. CBC television planned to broadcast the game. I had just been the colour commentator on the Canada–Soviet Hockey Series (Series), and CBC asked me to do the colour commentary. Don

Wittman was the play-by-play announcer. Ron Anderson of the Edmonton Oilers had the distinction of scoring the WHA's first regular-season goal. The Nationals went down to defeat in their first game 7–4. From a broadcast point of view, the game was interesting: the hockey was decent and entertaining, but each team had only one or two name players, surrounded by a supporting cast of journeymen.

The general manager of the Nationals was A.J. "Buck" Houle, and Billy Harris was coach. Buck had been the general manager of Canada's National Team (Nats) during its last season in 1969–70. I played on that team with Billy Harris as a linemate. Now Buck and Billy were running the Nationals. Buck had been associated for years with the Toronto Marlboros as part of the Toronto Maple Leafs organization and knew the minor leagues as well as anyone in hockey. By the fall of 1972, the pool of major-league players was getting shallow. And the Nationals didn't have a lot of money to dive into the deep end of the available hockey pool. With the limited dollars available to him, Buck assembled the best group of players he could at the time.

The Nationals weren't one of the elite teams in the WHA. The original franchise had the corporate name Ontario Nationals and had the WHA rights for the whole province. The original principles were Doug Michel and Nick Trbovich. They wanted to locate the team in Hamilton, where there was talk about building a new facility and tapping into southern Ontario's market in the Golden Horseshoe area. But in the short term, there was no major-league facility in Hamilton, although the mayor, Vic Copps, dreamed of building a facility there. That dream wouldn't be realized until 1985 when Copps Coliseum was eventually built. But that's another story for later. So the Ontario Nationals went to Ottawa.

During the summer of 1972, Buck contacted me and asked if I would play for the Nationals. I had great curiosity about the upstart WHA, but I didn't give playing serious thought because I was involved with the Series, and I had a broadcasting job with CKLW-TV in Windsor. My broadcasting career had progressed well after my detour with the Detroit Red Wings organization.

Buck asked me again after my return from the Series; I had a choice to make. I was ambivalent about whether to continue to play hockey or to use the Series experience as a springboard to a better broadcasting career. I hadn't decided before the Nationals took to the ice for their first WHA regular-season game. After the game, I bumped into Buck, who was still trying to fill out his roster with some experienced pros. The invitation was still there if I wanted to play.

I returned to Windsor to discuss and consider the options with Susan. I had been very fortunate to be involved as a colour commentator in a couple of high-profile events, but such events were few and far between in the broadcasting business at the time. Adding playing in the WHA to my resumé might help my broadcasting career. But the real truth was that I still preferred to be on the other side of the microphone or camera, if not as a player then as a coach or manager, instead of being a spectator or sports broadcaster. Susan would support whatever decision I made.

A few days later, I contacted Buck and we agreed on a one-year contract. The previous April, I thought my playing days were behind me, but here I was again, planning to play "one more season." By the time I got myself and my family organized to move to Ottawa, the season was well under way. I had missed the training camp and several games. However, I kept myself fairly fit, and it didn't take me long to get ready to play.

The Nationals were an interesting combination of players. Only a few had any significant NHL experience. The core group were minor pro players who had been elevated to major-league status overnight. Buck filled out the roster with some former top Canadian and US college players and some over-age major juniors who had not yet turned professional. Without the WHA, many of them would never have played major professional hockey. We were far from the strongest roster in the WHA, and Billy Harris had his hands full trying to make us into a playoff contender. We were major league in name only.

It took some time for the assortment of players to meld as a team. Inconsistency was our most consistent trait. On some nights, when it came together, we were a very competitive team and played good, entertaining hockey. However, on most nights we were a goal away from a win, and that goal too often was a bad one, scored because of our team's poor defensive play. But we all enjoyed the opportunity the WHA gave us, and we all tried to make the league as professional as we could.

The season was barely under way when we began to hear speculation in Ottawa about the future viability of the team and the league. Susan and I had just moved into our rented townhouse when the media started suggesting the Nationals wouldn't survive in Ottawa, and would move to Milwaukee before Christmas. The rumours were very unsettling for the players and their families. Most of the players kept their heads down and kept on playing: enjoy it while it lasted was the mindset of WHA players and owners alike.

The Nationals kept fighting to qualify for the playoffs. As the regular season wound down, Billy struggled to keep our playoff hopes alive. I remember a key game in Chicago against the Cougars. Both teams were at the bottom of their divisions. In a game we should probably have lost, we scored two short-handed goals and won by a goal. It was after this most unlikely win that the team started to play better and win its share of games, and we won enough to climb our way over the New York Raiders and the Quebec Nordiques to grab the last playoff position.

There was a scheduling conflict at the Ottawa Civic Centre, so the Nationals moved their home playoff games to Maple Leaf Gardens in Toronto. The move didn't really bother us. By the end of the regular season, we had generally accepted that the Nationals would not be in Ottawa for the next season, if there were to be a next season.

In the opening round of the inaugural WHA playoffs, the Nationals were up against the New England Whalers, who had finished in top place in the regular season with an impressive ninety-four points, twenty more than we had. The Whalers were very strong, with many former NHL players, such as Ted Green, Brit Selby, Tom Webster, Jim Dorey, Rick Ley and Al Smith. We played our best hockey of the season, but were overmatched and bowed out in five games. At least the Nationals were beaten by the WHA's first league champions.

The Ottawa Nationals franchise struggled on and off the ice every day of its existence. Team founder Doug Michel quickly realized the financial burden was too heavy and looked for additional investors. Nick Trbovich, a businessman from Buffalo, New York, seemed to have both interest and the financial depth to fund the team. He ended up with the majority controlling interest, probably reluctantly. No one in Ottawa was prepared to participate financially. It became obvious by mid-season that there wasn't any future for professional hockey in Ottawa at the time. If the franchise was to survive, the team had to move. Hard to imagine that Ottawa wouldn't or couldn't support a pro hockey team with a top ticket price of $6.50.

Because the Nationals held their home playoff games in Toronto's Maple Leaf Gardens, the media speculated that the team was moving to Toronto. Johnny F. Bassett, the entrepreneurial son of John Bassett, Sr., had dabbled in several professional sports franchises in the Toronto market. Why not another pro hockey team to compete with the Leafs? Bassett, a group of friends, and some of Toronto's most influential entrepreneurs—among them John C. Eaton, George Cohon, Steve Stavro, Peter Eby, Ron Barbaro and Allan Flood—began negotiations to buy the Ottawa franchise from Trbovich.

After only one season, the cost of a WHA franchise had skyrocketed to around $1.8 million. In spite of the speculative and inflated price, Bassett and his partners formed Can Sports Inc., bought the Ottawa franchise and transferred it to Toronto in the spring of 1973. They planned to play their home games in the Gardens, right under the nose of their NHL rivals. Apparently, Harold Ballard, who still controlled the Gardens while doing his time in jail, was prepared to take money from anyone who wanted to use his arena. The new WHA franchise would bear the name Toronto Toros.

I had enjoyed my season with the Nationals, but after the team's last game, I remember sitting in the dressing room realizing that this time my professional hockey-playing career was truly over. So at the conclusion of the 1972–73 season, I was again at a fork in the road. Where to next? Should I return to sports broadcasting or try my hand at coaching and management? For some time, I thought that with my broad experience and interest in teaching the game, that I might be good at it; I wanted to contribute something to a game I had loved and lived for most of my life. I was truly a student of the game.

Late in the previous season, with the Nationals slipping out of the playoff picture, Buck had approached me before a key road game. He said if the Nationals didn't win the game, he planned to relieve Billy Harris of his coaching duties and wanted me to take over for the remainder of the season. I felt strange during that game. I wished Billy no ill luck, but I realized this might be the start of my coaching career. For some time, Billy had struggled to motivate the team, and we wallowed around at the bottom of our division. I thought he probably sensed the precarious position he was in. Generally, players don't want to be coach killers, but sometimes it happens. As fate would have it, it was the fluke win in Chicago that brought Billy the reprieve he needed to survive the season. My coaching opportunity would have to wait.

I knew Johnny Bassett from our high school days at Upper Canada College (UCC) in Toronto, and I approached him in the off-season about a coaching opportunity with his new Toronto Toros. Johnny and I had a long talk about our aspirations in professional hockey, he as an owner and I as a coach or general manager. I still remember a comment he made that day: "You've a great sense of the way things should be, but not a great sense of the way they are." Johnny knew I thought professional hockey might be better played, coached and managed. I don't think he thought I was crazy, but I do think he thought I was too idealistic and practical to be successful in professional sports. In any event, he had no plans to change Houle and Harris for the first season of his new team. However, Buck knew of my coaching and management interests and was aware of an opportunity in the minors that might be a good place for me to get started on the off-ice side of the hockey business.

Coaching and Managing in the Minors

THE EASTERN Hockey League (EHL) was the bottom of the North American professional hockey totem pole in the 1960s and early 1970s. The league was notorious and legendary in the hockey world, had some great glory years, and to its fans, it was the best. Many aspiring young players started in the EHL, eking out a modest living and chasing the elusive dream of making it to the majors. For most, it was a dream they'd never realize.

During the league's glory years, the Clinton Comets were one of the most prominent and successful teams. Clinton had about two thousand residents and was known as "the biggest little hockey town in the USA," with a hockey tradition that went back to 1927. In Clinton, Saturday night was hockey night. The Clinton Arena, built in 1949, held about two thousand and two hundred people, and for years it was consistently packed to the rafters, the fans dedicated and noisy. The Clinton Arena was a typical old small-town arena, not unlike many in Canada—as much a community centre as an arena. It was not a fancy place by any stretch of the imagination, but it had seen and experienced a lot of barn-burning hockey over the years, and it was the hometown arena, the centre of entertainment and excitement, and the pride of the community. The Comets played rugged and competitive hockey, and made the community proud. The Clinton Comets were Clinton's team.

By the end of the 1972–73 season, the WHA and the NHL had dug deep into the minor pro ranks for talent to stock their newly formed teams. In the EHL, attendance fell, and teams had to pay more to travel (the bus was the transportation mode of affordability for the league). The EHL covered a lot of territory—from New York to Florida—and became impractical to operate. At the end of the season, the league dissolved, leaving a vacuum in many places where professional hockey was well supported and financially viable. The Comets ended their EHL participation with a whimper, and finished the season in last place. Despite the sad finish, the team's franchise was purchased by eight local businessmen, led by Victor Ehre, chairman and CEO of Utica Mutual Insurance Company. The Comets would become almost a department of the company, using its resources as well as those of Ehre and his partners. The partners' bonds were their love of hockey and their sense of community. All they needed was a good coach/general manager—and a league to play in.

Shortly after the EHL dissolved, a group made up primarily of former team owners started the North American Hockey League (NAHL). Their goal was to preserve the EHL teams in the northeastern US, as well as set up some new franchises. They wanted to keep the league compact geographically to reduce travel. They also planned to keep the focus on development and keep costs down, so they added a requirement: each team would include several players younger than twenty-two, as well as several who were American born.

The NAHL began with seven teams: Syracuse, Mohawk Valley, Binghampton and Long Island in New York, Lewistown in Maine, Cape Cod in Massachusetts and Johnstown in Pennsylvania. The Comets had found a league.

While the EHL was still going, Buck Houle, manager of the Ottawa Nationals, placed a few fringe Nationals players with the Comets. Buck knew about the new league, and he knew the new owners of the Clinton–Utica franchise. He suggested me as a potential coach and general manager.

On a warm, sunny, late June day in 1973, Susan, Sean and I drove from Ottawa to Exit 31 on the New York Thruway, bound for Utica. It was our first visit to the Mohawk Valley, in central New York. We immediately fell in love with the area, particularly Clinton. And I was offered the job of coach/general manager. The mandate was simple: make and keep hockey financially viable in the Mohawk Valley. The owners would give me all the non-financial support I needed, but I had to pay the bills from gate receipts. How I achieved it was my challenge. The job was an opportunity to create my own success with an ownership group that wanted nothing more than to have a hockey game to go to on Saturday night. I accepted, made plans to move and prepared to begin my new career.

Clinton is about eight miles southwest of Utica, a sleepy, picturesque college town nestled in the historic Mohawk Valley. The Conacher family moved early in July, 1973. Our house was within walking distance of the Clinton Arena, but then so was everything else in town. It was small town USA; it was wonderful! Full of optimism and enthusiasm, I plunged into the next phase of my hockey career.

The obstacles to overcome to reinvent and revitalize the Comets as a hockey franchise were many and varied and began the moment I arrived. The new Comets ownership group needed a fan base that would support the new team economically, and that fan base would have to include the whole Mohawk Valley. And the Clinton Arena was not large enough to sustain a franchise in the NAHL. The first two things the new owners did were to change the team name to the Mohawk Valley Comets, and to move at least half of the team's home games to the Utica Memorial Auditorium (UMA), in downtown Utica, a city of some ninety thousand residents, but with no history of interest in professional hockey. So right at the start, I faced two challenges: first, to enlist fans in Utica, and second, to get the diehard hockey fans in Clinton to share their team. The Comets were a team stuck between two communities.

The first thing I did after arriving in town was meet the manager of the Clinton Arena. Ed Stanley was a crusty old-timer in his late sixties. He was the founder of the EHL Clinton Comets and had sold the Comets franchise to Vic Ehre and his group. As part of the deal, he would be a governor and treasurer of the NAHL and a consultant for the team. I needed a relationship of respect and hopefully friendship with Ed, particularly since the new Comets were going to be in his arena almost every day.

It was a beautiful day outside, but I got a frosty reception from Ed when I entered his small office in the Clinton Arena, an arena Ed had been instrumental in building in 1949. He was known as "Mr. Hockey" in Clinton and was a revered pillar of the community. It was immediately obvious that he had been a reluctant seller of the Clinton Comets. I knew right from that first meeting that I was going to have my hands full trying to garner support for the new Mohawk Valley Comets from the old Clinton fans. From meeting Ed, I learned that Clinton residents did not like the prospects of sharing "their team." Nor did they like the idea of travelling to Utica to watch the Comets play. The UMA seated four thousand and was an attractive, circular-style building, a style common in New York State at the time. But it was used primarily for concerts and community events and activities, not for hockey. Converting the Clinton fans was not going to be easy!

I had no second thoughts about the decision to take the job, but I quickly realized it was going to be a huge task to make the new Comets a fan and financial success. As general manager and coach, I had many duties: by October 12, I had to set up a new organization and put together a whole new team to be ready for the first game in the new NAHL. It was a clean slate and my opportunity to put all my pent-up ideas about hockey into practice. And it would be a chance to gain the hands-on experience I would need for an eventual major-league opportunity. And in the professional hockey world, there was no place to go but up.

I knew I needed help. I started by hiring a competent trainer to handle all the equipment and manage the dressing room. When I was with the Nationals the previous season, I met a young trainer with the Ottawa 67s (a major junior team) named Rick Dods. I approached him, and he became my first hire. He was nineteen and hoped one day to be a major-league trainer. He saw the Comets job as a step in that direction.

One of the first things Rick and I had to resolve was our travel arrangements. The NAHL would be a "bus league," like the EHL had been. The bus company was immediately across the street from the Clinton Arena, and we went over and introduced ourselves to the owner. George Marsh had been a solid supporter of the Comets over the years and wanted to continue. He led us to the very back of the parking lot, past his fleet of buses, most fairly new. In the back corner was this old bus, a 1960 Flexble, that looked like it had been retired from service. It was, except for when the Comets used it. In its day, the Flexble was top of the line, with all stainless-steel exterior side panelling and trim. But after a dozen years or so and a lot of hard miles, our bus was definitely tired looking. The inside was even more depressing. It was early vinyl; there was no toilet; many of the windows didn't open; and I could barely stand up in it. Simply, it was an old bus. George assured us it was still functional, if not fancy. And it was going to have to do for now, as it was all we could afford, and George's newer buses were all busy on other routes.

George introduced us to our designated driver, Jim Beebe, a huge, good-natured chap who had driven the Comets for years and looked forward to continuing that tradition with the new Comets. I didn't realize it at the time, but I would spend many long late hours keeping Jim company, as we would head straight home after most away games. The team bus would become our second home. Its ID number was 101, and my son affectionately named it "the 101 Beauty."

Vic Ehre was a very busy man, but his new hockey interest was a labour of love. I noticed immediately that he was also a very proud man, with a strong military background and bearing, disciplined and authoritarian. That was how he ran Utica Mutual Insurance, and he was determined to make sure the Comets didn't fail under his watch. Vic generously made company resources available to help the Comets as required. In fact, the whole ownership group was very generous with their time and support.

Vic assigned a young and enthusiastic employee named Bill Randall to act as the team's public-relations director and promotional advisor. Bill had no hockey experience, but his energy and enthusiasm more than offset this shortcoming. The first thing we needed was a season-ticket campaign. Modest as the ticket prices were—from $2 to $3.50—selling the residents of the Mohawk Valley on the new

Comets was going to take some doing. Generally, Clintonites chose to reserve judgment: they were non-committal and wanted to wait until they knew if the new version of the team could replace their beloved Clinton Comets. Other residents of the Mohawk Valley needed to be sold on hockey. Until the new Comets took to the ice, it was difficult to get commitments, though there were a few hundred or so loyal and dedicated fans, most of them members of the Comets Fan Club. The season-ticket campaign was much more difficult than expected, but a very important component for the financial viability of the franchise.

With Bill in charge of the tickets, I shifted my focus to putting together a competitive team, hopefully one that was better than the previous season's Comets. As a novice coach, I modelled my coaching methods and style after my mentor, Father Bauer, the best coach I ever had. Were it not for his tutelage, I would never have made it to the NHL. He taught me how to play better hockey, both offensively and more importantly defensively. And through his leadership qualities (teaching, communication-motivation skills, example and charisma), he could take a group of individual players and mould them into a team unit that collectively was greater than the sum of its parts. A rare gift! He left an indelible mark on every player who ever played for him. It was this ideal coach I wanted to emulate. I also had my own definite opinions about how the game of hockey should be taught, coached and played. The Comets seemed the ideal place to start.

In recent years, the emphasis on the "Canadian" style of play had been based more on physical strength, intimidation and violence; the fundamental skills of the game—skating, puck-handling, passing, playmaking and shooting—seemed less important. As was evidenced in the 1972 Canada–Soviet Hockey Series, Canada had fallen behind in skill-based hockey development.

Hockey is a contact game—it always has been and always should be—and players need to be physically rugged and tough to play it. However, a player shouldn't have to be a fighter to be a good hockey player. By 1973, some coaches employed marginally talented goons to instill fear in their opponents; the goons terrorized the skilled players

Rare times with my Dad and my older brothers, in 1953 at Baron Renfrew Public School. From left, Brian, father Lionel, Lionel Jr., David. My father, Lionel "The Big Train" Conacher was Canada's Athlete of the Half-Century (1900-50). He died suddenly in 1954 when I was twelve, after he was hit in the head playing softball on Parliament Hill.

The Conacher family, 1952. Deanne, mother Dorothy, Lionel Jr., father Lionel, Connie, David, Brian.

With my brothers at the ceremony for my father's posthumous induction into Canada's Sports Hall of Fame in 1955. With photo of Dad Lionel Conacher, from left, Lionel Jr., David, Brian.

My father, Lionel Conacher (left) and one of his brothers, Charlie, in the 1930s. My Uncle Charlie was the first Leaf ever to score in Maple Leaf Gardens, on opening night, November 12, 1931. Lionel and Charlie were two of the three Conacher brothers, along with brother Roy, who ended up in the Hockey Hall of Fame—the only three brothers to be inducted.

BRIAN CONACHER
Centre.
Born-Toronto. Aug 31,1941

Toronto Marlboros

As a member of the Toronto Marlboros, 1960.

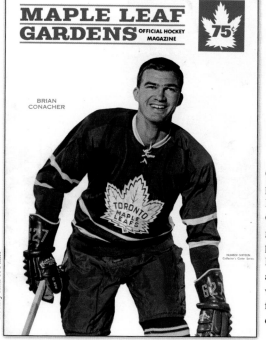

On the cover of the Maple Leaf Gardens program and a member of the 1966-67 Maple Leafs team. I've had a strong connection to the Gardens for much of my life. I went to Leaf games there regularly as a child, where my parents had seasons tickets, played in Maple Leaf Gardens when I was a Marlboro and then as a Leaf during that memorable Stanley Cup winning year, and returned there some thirty-five years later to manage the entire building's operations.

The Canadian Olympic hockey team that represented the country at the 1964 Games in Innsbruck, Austria. I'm in the middle of the second row, right behind the goalie in centre, and Father David Bauer, our coach and a big influence on me, is in the front row to the right of the goalie.

ROCHESTER AMERICANS
1965-66

The 1965-66 Rochester Americans. I played one season for the AHL team during my first year of pro hockey alongside such notables as Don Cherry (back row, third from left behind goalie), Al Arbour (to the right of Don Cherry), Dick Gamble (back row, third from right), Jim Pappin (front row, third from left), and Mike Walton (front row, second from right). I am to Al Arbour's right, (back row, fifth from left).

Facing off for the Leafs against the great Gordie Howe, #9 for the Detroit Red Wings, with referee John Ashley in the middle of the action, during the 1966-67 season.

The 1967 Stanley Cup Champions, Maple Leaf Gardens, May 2, 1967. I'm congratulating goalie Terry Sawchuk.

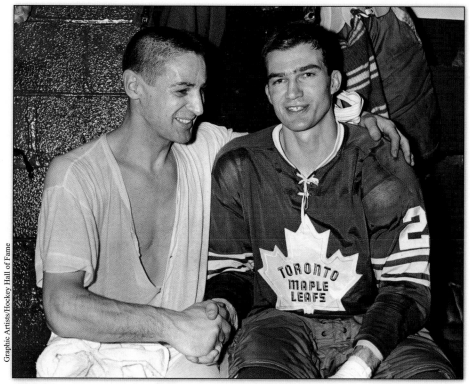

In the dressing room with legendary goalie Terry Sawchuk (left) after the '67 Stanley Cup win.

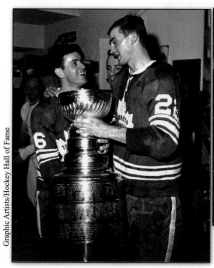

With teammate Mike Walton and the coveted Stanley Cup.

With my wife Susan and the Stanley Cup, 1967. We were married on May 15, 1967, and she has been by my side for every twist and turn in my career, no matter which way the puck bounced.

The 1969 Canadian National Team at the Izvestia Tournament in Moscow. I am in the front row, centre, with the fur hat. Billy Harris is in the front row at right and Ken Dryden is in the middle of the back row in the red sweater.

BRIAN CONACHER

DETROIT RED WINGS

1971-72

The last stop in my NHL career, I played for the Detroit Red Wings for one season in 1971-72.

with their fists, neutralizing their opportunity to play a skill-based style of game. I never liked the goon style of play and didn't condone it. Simply, a lot of pro hockey teams and leagues were being hijacked by brutes and bullies with limited ability.

On the ideal team, all the players can take care of themselves, and all stick together against anyone who tries to intimidate or challenge them; they become "team tough," not needing designated goons to act as team protectors and enforcers. The ideal player is tough, rugged but also skilled, a real asset to any team.

I wanted to emphasize basic skills combined with speed, grace, rhythm and flow, and creativity—offensive and defensive skills that make hockey such a beautiful game to watch and play when played within the rules. I believed in a well-disciplined style of play, particularly defensively where every player had defined responsibilities when our team did not have the puck. Talented offensive players were becoming scarce; I thought a team that was strong defensively from the goal out could win close games. However, I knew from experience that the challenge would be to teach the players a strong defensive awareness, which was predicated on discipline and hard work. And hopefully the players were team tough. With these lofty ideals in tow, I began my coaching career.

I had no real idea how good a player needed to be to compete in the new NAHL. I just wanted to recruit and sign up the best players I could get access to. The salary range in the league was generally between $200 and $350 per week; a few star players might make as much as $500 per week. With my owners' clear directive to live within my meagre budget, I was able to sign mostly players in the $200 to $250 range. There was no shortage of willing candidates—this surprised me—but I wasn't sure what kind of talent those modest dollars would get me. The owners expected a competitive team, but they were only prepared to pay so much for it. The rest would have to be done by my coaching and teaching skills.

I wanted the Comets, like other minor-league pro teams, to establish a working relationship with a major-league team. I went to Buck Houle and the Toronto Toros, and Buck agreed to continue the agreement he'd had with the EHL Comets. When the WHA

started up, players and teams were signing two- or three-year contracts. Some of the players were now not talented enough for the
improving league; if a manager fired them, he still had to pay out
their contracts. Buck assigned these extras to the Comets, and I
paid a small portion of their salaries: in effect, I was renting them.
I expected these players to be my most skilled and talented, much
better than the players I could afford. Buck also agreed to play a
pre-season exhibition game against the Comets. It would be the
team's first game.

I thought it made sense to try to recruit a few of the former Clinton Comets players still in the area. One such player was Jack Kane,
who had a long and very successful EHL career and had been captain
of the Comets. While his career was mostly behind him, he was an
exceptional skater, and I knew he could still keep up in a younger
league. I hoped his involvement would warm up the Clinton fans. Also
I hoped that Jack, because of his experience and age, would be almost
like an assistant playing coach. He could guide the younger players
and set a good example.

The Mohawk Valley Comets training camp came all too quickly.
I already had half a dozen Toros players, and had committed to Jack
Kane and a few other veterans, so I invited only a small group of
prospects to fill out my seventeen-player roster. Training camp went
well. There was lots of energy and enthusiasm, and enough skill to
fill me with hope.

In the end, the roster I was able to assemble with all the unknowns,
inexperience, financial and time restrictions included a few local veterans, some WHA castoffs and prospects, a local American goaltender
and a few young hopefuls. I thought we had the necessary roles filled:
we could skate; we had size; we had a blend of experience and youth;
and we seemed to have team toughness. In practice the team looked
pretty good, but I wouldn't see its real character until we were in a
game against a NAHL team. Would the new Comets have enough
talent and heart to be competitive in the NAHL? That was the big
question. Everyone was optimistic.

Before I knew it, our first game was upon us. We were scheduled
to play the Toronto Toros on October 2 in a pre-season exhibition

game in the UMA. The game would launch a whole new era of hockey in the Mohawk Valley. With the marketing help of Tom Garber, a member of the ownership group, we had a new logo based on the original red, white and blue colours, and an all-new uniform. The new Mohawk Valley Comets of the new NAHL were ready to make their debut. Advance ticket sales were brisk, and we expected a capacity crowd as we unveiled the new team and started the season. Certainly a big part of the attraction was a chance to see a major-league professional team play.

It was a beautiful early fall evening; the crowd was making its way to the arena; the Comets were in the dressing room getting ready; the ice was newly painted and flooded. After almost three months of round-the-clock work, everything was ready for a new beginning for minor professional hockey in the Mohawk Valley. But where were the Toros?

It was very close to the scheduled starting time, and the Toros should have arrived hours ago. I anxiously phoned Buck Houle. The Toros were having transportation trouble, and they weren't going to make it to the game. What was I going to do?

In a state of shock, I informed the Comets in the dressing room; I met with the owners; I advised the staff that the game was cancelled. I then went to the front lobby of the UMA and apologized to the sellout crowd as they left the arena. It was a disaster. What a way to start my career in the hockey business! An ominous beginning.

In spite of the disappointment and negative impact of the Toros no-show and false start, I didn't have time to stew about it. I took a deep breath and plowed ahead. We were scheduled to play a few pre-season exhibition games with other NAHL teams. These games were my first real chance to test the team I'd assembled.

The Comets started with home-and-home exhibition games with the Syracuse Blazers. Their coach, Ron Ingram, was a veteran minor-league general manager and coach, and the Blazers, an established team, had been last year's EHL champions. The first period of our first game wasn't over before I had an awful feeling in the pit of my stomach: the team I had so naively assembled probably wasn't going to be good enough.

The Blazers were bigger, stronger, more experienced and most definitely tougher and more aggressive than we were. In a word: they were better. And they had a player named Bill Goldthorpe who was a terror on the ice, a classic hockey goon. He represented all the things I despised about the way a lot of pro hockey was played: uncontrolled intimidation and thugery on the ice. To compound the Comets problems, the Blazers had several good players who enjoyed great success in the comfort of Goldthorpe's protection. If the Blazers were to be the team to beat in the NAHL, the early indications were that the Comets didn't have the personnel to do it. My hands were going to be full trying to develop the Comets into a competitive and respectable team.

—⋙—

After on-ice opening ceremonies, the Comets played their first regular-season game in the inaugural NAHL season. They played solid, smart hockey and won their first real game 3–2 against the Binghampton Dusters. A promising start. The early optimism was short-lived; things on the ice quickly went sour, then steadily deteriorated. A pattern was established: win one, lose three, win another one and lose six, and so on. The losses added up at an alarming rate, and it wasn't long before the Comets were looking at the league from the bottom up.

I found that many of my ideas about a better way to play the game were predicated on having a certain level of talent available, and the time to develop it; and also on having players with the interest and capacity to accept new ideas and learn to be better players. Simply, some of my players were threatened by the learning process. Most developed as hockey players based primarily on natural ability. They weren't flexible, secure or confident enough to abandon their old habits and grow their abilities. Some were trapped by limited ability and were clearly on a dead-end road on (and sometimes off) the ice.

A successful team needs two elementary components: a head and a heart. My Comets had neither. And there were two things the fans insisted on: goals and fights. There too, we could provide neither. Apparently we lacked the talent and the character to compete successfully. We were in most games and often kept them close, but game after game, when the opposition pushed, we didn't have the grit to push back. We just lost too many of the decisive battles for the puck and our place on the ice. And the veterans (Toros and EHL alumni) failed to provide leadership and set an example, which I expected and desperately needed. As for the younger players, I soon realized that you can't teach experience. I needed time to teach and develop many of my players and wondered if I could afford the time to do so.

The arrangement with the Toros turned out to be a mixed blessing. While the price was right, some of the players wouldn't get their head around the fact they had had their chance to play major-league hockey and they weren't good enough, and there was little or no hope of another shot. The Comets became the dumping ground for these castoffs. Some were difficult to motivate and handle. The dream of making the WHA was a magnet that lured many aspiring players to think they could make a living in hockey. For but a rare few this dream would never come true.

Goonism seemed to be a necessary criterion for a minor professional hockey franchise. I wanted to sell hockey based on skill and finesse, not brute strength, aggression, intimidation and fear. But the talent level available to most NAHL teams dictated the rough-and-tumble style of hockey. I quickly learned that you can't teach aggression; either you have it by your basic nature or you don't. Fear and intimidation are great neutralizers of ability and too often reduce talent to the lowest level, creating the bully syndrome on ice. When the goons were on the ice, the pace of play slowed with players wary of the goons, whose primary purpose was to instill fear through intimidation. Against the Comets it worked. My skill players were scared into paralysis by tough teams like the Blazers. Skill was not enough.

I was conflicted as a novice coach; I desperately wanted the Comets to be a skill-based team, not a bunch of hockey thugs, but I also had to win to survive. The classic coach's conundrum. As the season rolled out, my success as a rookie coach was minimal at best. I had some very capable players with real skill, but unless they were prepared to fight for their space on the ice every shift, they would never get a chance to show their skills. I had empathy for my players, as the NAHL basic style of play was not what I wanted to preach, teach or see played.

The Comets were not tough enough—as a team or individually—to compete against most teams in the league. The Comets played scared, and it showed on the scoreboard.

The NAHL struggled to establish its identity as a developmental league. Some coaches, general managers and players wanted to emphasize the base elements of fear and violence as the building blocks and image of the game and new league; and key components of success on the ice and at the box office. The role of the goon became inordinately important to the success of an NAHL franchise.

It didn't take long before some of the owners started to show their frustration at the team's performance. They wanted more than just hockey on Saturday night, they wanted winning hockey on Saturday night. It was something I'd noticed over the years. Many owners in hockey lived and breathed for the success of their teams, and they took losing personally. Whether ego, vanity, greed or a combination, they just wanted to win. It was first time I truly felt the intense pressure and necessity to win to survive.

The relationship with the Toros also started to show some strain. My owners were still stinging from the pre-season no-show, and when the assigned Toros players failed to perform to expected levels, I too was unhappy. Was it my coaching inexperience or their lack of interest in playing in the minors?

I had to improve the talent level of the Comets. The panic button was pressed! I started to replace some players I had under direct contract in an effort to improve the team. A few months earlier, I never imagined or anticipated that I would be trying to rebuild the Comets a third of the way through my rookie season as coach. I became a disillusioned and disappointed coach.

The Toros recognized my problems with some of their assignees and attempted to help. The revolving door began to spin. It was with real regret that I let some of the young, inexperienced and promising players go so early in the season, before they gained the experience to adjust to minor pro hockey. I met every player individually for an exit interview. For those I thought were wasting their time pursuing the dream of professional hockey, I counselled them to get on with the rest of their lives outside the world of hockey and into another career with more long–term stability and potential. For players without much formal education, these meetings were often traumatic. While not a pleasant experience for either party, I tried never to cut off a player in an abrupt and impersonal way; these meetings were often very demanding on both of us. For these young men, the dream of being a professional hockey player often ended after the meeting.

Another issue that compounded the Comets' on-ice futility was the officiating in the NAHL. It was a new league, and many of the more experienced officials had been promoted to the WHA, leaving the NAHL with too many referees and linemen who didn't have the experience, authority or respect to control the likes of a Bill Goldthorpe. Like all coaches, I wanted to blame the officials for my team's on-ice inadequacies. During too many games, it seemed like the inmates were running the asylum. There were inconsistent calls; the refs had little control over the goons. Many games slipped quickly out of control. And then there were coaches like Ron Ingram and John Brophy (the "Silver Fox," who coached the Long Island Cougars) whose teams thrived on the rugged, aggressive and intimidating style of play. And their presence behind the bench was often enough to influence penalty calls. Many of the NAHL officials became major-league referees and linesmen, but at the beginning of the NAHL's first season they were as ineffective as I was as a rookie coach. It was a challenging hockey environment in which to work.

I remember one game in the Clinton Arena against the Cougars when Brophy went berserk after a call against one of his players. Brophy was a former EHL legend, known for his rugged play; the Clinton fans loved to get him wound up, and he loved to accommodate them. At this particular game he started behind the bench, then he was standing on the bench, and then he was walking along the edge of the rink boards in front of the bench. John's face was bright red, in sharp contrast to his shocking white hair, and he spat a tirade at the official who dared make a call he took exception to. Then a chair flew across the ice in the direction of the penalty box, and eventually Brophy was kicked out of the game. His display of temper was entertaining for the fans, but it created chaos on the ice. And in my mind it didn't do much to develop good hockey players.

With less than half the season remaining, the Comets were mired in last place. We had dug ourselves into a deep hole, and if we wanted a playoff spot we'd have to start climbing out very soon. I had to change my idealistic coaching strategies for more realistic and practical ones. A coach has to play with the team he has been dealt, not the team he would prefer to have. I would have to maximize the abilities and strengths of the players I had. I felt I could get all of my players to work better defensively, so we could keep games close. Then maybe we could generate enough offence to win our share. Even this simple coaching strategy was based on having a reasonable level of team toughness and commitment—qualities the Comets lacked. My coaching inexperience and shortcomings as the bench boss showed, as I made changes based on desperation rather than skills or talent, in the random hope that I would somehow end up with a winning combination. But most nights we were out-hustled, out-muscled, out-skated and of course out-scored. It wasn't in the cards.

When a team is losing, frustration and despair can set in. Eventually the team starts to play as if it expects to lose and doesn't mind. I hated losing, and I hated the way we lost. Our mounting losses gnawed at me. I kept hoping the Comets would be one of the five teams to make the playoffs. It wasn't always gloom and doom on the ice. In some games rays of hope would shine through the window of opportunity and the Comets really gave me confidence that we could make the playoffs. There were some satisfying wins that made both the players and me feel good. Unfortunately, these wins surfaced too infrequently. With about fifteen games remaining in the regular season, with the team realistically out of the playoff race as the window of opportunity steadily closed, many of the players rolled over and died on me. The Comets were in free fall; it was something I'd never experienced in my sports life, and I was at a loss how to stop the descent. I hoped the players would have enough pride not to totally embarrass themselves or the franchise in the remaining games. Possibly, they could act as spoilers for teams above them still fighting for a playoff spot or playoff positioning. Surprisingly, the Comets managed to win six of the last twelve games and made the inevitable at least bearable. With a final record of 20 wins, 52 losses and 2 ties for a total of 42 points, the Comets who spent most of the season looking up from the bottom of the standings missed the playoffs by 26 points. The long season from hell finally ended.

I had the illusion that I was going to be a super-coach when I began only a few months earlier. I naively thought I could take average players and, in a matter of weeks with good coaching and discipline, grow them into skilled and talented players, then mould them into a cohesive unit. I either couldn't motivate them or I didn't have enough talent; it was probably a combination of both. The stark reality of it was—and is—that a great coach can make average players better by imposing disciplines and developing skills, but star players have natural and instinctive gifts and creativity—things a coach cannot teach. Great coaches generally are fortunate enough to coach great players. There's no substitute for talent!

In that one very, very long season, I realized that I was no Father Bauer. My gamble with Jack Kane failed. Several WHA castoffs made it known that if they weren't WHA calibre material they had no interest in wasting their time on the road to hockey nowhere with the Comets or any other minor pro team. Other players left because they realized that being a pro hockey player was a tough way of life and they weren't physically or mentally suited to it. I understood that if your heart and your head are not committed to playing pro hockey, you're visiting purgatory every time you step on the ice. It's not a safe workplace for doubters.

Life in the Minors

BEING THE general manager and coach of a struggling minor pro franchise was more than a full-time job. In fact, it was several jobs rolled into one. I worked from dawn to well past dusk every day, and my duties were many: I conducted team practices, travelled to and coached away games, coached home games, helped lay out the souvenir game program, sold program advertising, dealt with the media, promoted and kept track of ticket sales, paid the bills and generally managed and did anything else that needed to be done.

On occasion, I even drove the Zamboni ice-conditioning machine. The UMA was a poorly operated facility, and its management knew little about maintaining ice for hockey. I realized this one Saturday morning when the local minor hockey organization had the use of the UMA. Group after group went onto the ice, but there was no rink attendant to scrape and flood between sessions. It occurred to me that if this continued all morning, there would be no ice surface for my game that night. I mentioned this to the organizers, who felt if I was worried about the condition of the ice I could flood it for them between sessions.

So there I was, never having driven a Zamboni before, trying to figure out exactly how it operated and getting ready for my first experience of flooding ice. Although I had seen it done thousands of times, I had no real experience. As I started up the machine, I was nervous about bashing into the boards or stalling and having the hot water spill out and melt a hole in the ice. However, I managed to get around and resurface the ice several times throughout the morning. It became a Saturday morning ritual whenever the Comets had a Saturday night game in the UMA. Whenever Rick and I were around the UMA, we took care of the ice and painted the markings, particularly in the goal crease area, which received excessive wear. Fortunately, the Clinton Arena was well maintained and operated under the steely eye of Ed Stanley.

A big part of the season was spent in the 101 Beauty. Except for the short runs to Syracuse and Binghampton, road trips began early on game day. The team and the radio broadcast announcers would meet in front of the Clinton Arena and we'd head out for anywhere from a six to a ten-hour bus ride, with a stop somewhere on the road for a midday team meal. Each player received a very modest meal allowance. I generally sat in the front right seat, either by myself or with our radio play-by-play announcer, Lee Hamilton.

Lee was a young, hard-working, aspiring broadcaster with WIBX in Utica. In addition to doing the Comets broadcasts, he hosted a daily sports talk show and was totally committed to hockey. His personal goal was to one day get a major-league job. We were at the same stage of our respective careers and established a very good professional relationship, and later a personal one that exists to this day. No one followed or supported the Comets more than Lee. He was always positive about the team, win or lose. He went on to a very successful sports broadcasting career in California.

If I wanted to talk to an individual player, I'd invite him to join me up front. Conditions on the bus were tight and less than ideal for comfort, but there were usually enough seats for each player to have a double seat to stretch out and rest as best they could. A few of the seats turned around, to make room for card tables. Team members took turns playing, generally euchre or poker to pass the monotony of the long bus rides. Others relaxed, read or slept. And it didn't take long for every player, like school kids, to establish his seat.

Rick, the trainer, generally sat in the front left seat behind our driver, Jim Beebe. Rick was the same age as many of the players, but mature enough not to mix too closely with them, as he knew he was management. He was very loyal to me and was a good pipeline, giving me feedback on the mood of the dressing room.

The long road trips were always exhausting. Without toilet facilities on the bus, we often had to make pit stops, which really slowed us down until someone came up with a creative solution for at least the liquid part of the problem. The bottom step of the front door was right over the road. We rigged up a funnel with a hose, drilled a hole in the bottom step and pushed the hose through, and that was our simple if not sanitary solution.

In the fall of 1973, the first major energy crisis gripped the US. The OPEC oil embargo tightened the supply of gas and diesel fuel, which led to rationing. At the gas station I used in Clinton, the dealer pumped his monthly quota until it was gone and then closed his station, leaving drivers stranded. The shortages caused great anxiety for the American public, and certainly didn't help attendance at the Comets games, as people were very selective as to where they drove. When we drove the bus to away games in Johnstown, Pennsylvania, we worried about whether we would have enough fuel for the return trip. I remember seeing the long, long lines of cars and trucks, with drivers anxiously waiting to get their share.

We usually arrived for away games an hour or so before game time. The players unwrinkled themselves, then went for a short walk and had a cup of coffee to get their bodies going again. We often felt as if we were losing 1–0 before we even went into the visitors' dressing room. Road games were killers for all the NAHL teams, but some handled them better than others. We didn't have the talent or depth on our bench, and we were often intimidated by other teams' arenas, so we enjoyed little success on the road—most games, we might just as well have saved the time and bus fuel and mailed in the two points.

The trip to Johnstown, in the heart of Pennsylvania coal and steel country, was the longest and by far the toughest, as it included a lot of mountainous roads. We usually approached the city after an all-day journey, so it seemed always to be grey, dull and smoggy. The road went down a long hill, and it felt as if we were driving into an open pit mine. The best years of the steel industry were behind, but the mills still spewed their caustic clouds of pollutants. The whole area was generally depressing and depressed.

Before every game against the Johnstown Jets, I'd talk to Johnny Mitchell, the team's crusty, wily and veteran general manager. His office was in one corner of the arena high above the seating. Johnny had been around minor pro hockey for years, and when I first introduced myself, he gave me his usual greeting: "Come on in son!" He had known my uncles Charlie and Roy, and told stories about the Conacher boys and the "old days" of hockey. Johnny projected a fatherly image, but he was a very shrewd and astute hockey horse trader. My visits with him were generally the only memorable part of otherwise forgettable trips.

And getting there was only half the trip. As soon as the game was over, the players showered, loaded the bus, picked up some food and a few beers, then the bus would turn around and head straight back to Clinton. We often arrived home after the sun came up.

I seldom slept on the bus on the way home. Win or lose, I was always wired after coaching and generally chatted with Lee or with Jim, the driver, until the players drifted into fitful sleep. Jim stretched out in the bus and slept while the game was on. He sometimes drove as many as eighteen hours in a day. (Regulations about the number of hours a driver could drive in a day were not closely monitored, and the Comets could not afford a second driver.) So I rode shotgun in my front right seat and talked to Jim most of the way home, as much to keep him awake as to resolve the world's problems with our wide-ranging discussions.

In the middle of one long night on a return trip in the dead of winter, we were in the final miles on the New York Thruway. It was a snowy, messy night, and that highway could be treacherous in the winter. Fortunately there was not a lot of traffic to worry about. But the snow was heavy, and it was difficult to make out the roadway. The snow constantly coming at the headlights must have been hypnotic, and Jim momentarily dozed off. There I was talking away when I realized he had fallen asleep at the wheel and we were headed off the left shoulder of the highway into the median. I shouted at Jim, and he jerked awake, then regained control of the bus, saving us from God knows what. I kidded him that it must have been my stimulating conversation that put him to sleep. After that near disaster, I never slept a wink on a return trip.

We usually arrived in Clinton in the middle of the night or early morning. The players carried their equipment bags into the dressing room, unpacked and helped Rick hang up the wet equipment. Then the players headed home to complete their disrupted sleep. I too would stagger home for a few hours sleep. After an away game, practice was usually around 11:00 in the morning. Then I had to attend to my managerial responsibilities. Often, one day melded into another with but a few hours of sleep in between. It was a brutal and exhausting existence, but it was the norm in minor pro hockey.

—〰—

By the end of that first long and stressful season with the Comets I was as emotionally and physically spent as a whipped dog. The season had been a never-ending series of challenges and disasters on and off the ice, and the team struggled at the gate. When we didn't make the playoffs, our future seemed uncertain.

The ownership group was more upset with the players than with me. I think they realized I did a reasonable job with the talent I had. The owners and I were disappointed with most of the Toronto Toros castoffs; they hadn't performed to our expectation. In my performance review, we discussed whether I should step down as coach and focus on being general manager. Each was a full-time position, and then some, especially without the assistance that most had; maybe I'd spread myself too thin. However, when we combined the experience I acquired in my first season with the economics of hiring a new coach, plus the uncertain future of pro hockey in the Mohawk Valley, we decided I would continue to shoulder both responsibilities for at least another season.

To go forward into year two, we all agreed that we needed a better team. And we would need more financial commitment from the hockey fans. We also agreed unanimously that the UMA needed to be upgraded to better accommodate the needs of a professional hockey team. It was a nice-looking facility from the outside, but the inside had suffered from real neglect, lack of funding and staffing short-ages. There were missing light bulbs, rink dasher boards were broken, doors didn't work, seats were ripped, the roof leaked and the place was generally filthy. It was an operational mess.

The ownership group was very supportive and generous with time, but none of them wanted to commit any significant money to keep-ing the franchise afloat. I constantly struggled to keep my head and the team's above water. We needed a bigger season-ticket base, so we decided to initiate a "Save the Comets" campaign in the summer.

The Clinton fans hadn't really warmed up to the new Comets, preferring to live with the memories of past glory. Some of the Utica crowds were quite good, and there was an occasional sellout, but gen-erally, people in the Mohawk Valley seemed ambivalent about hockey; it was hard to tell how much they cared about having a professional team in the community. We still had the loyal and supportive Comets Fan Club, but there was no broad base of support. Even in the NHL, a very rabid, vocal and dedicated core group of supporters can give the impression that there's broad interest in and support for a team, when in fact there isn't. Some teams have learned that their financial base is built on quicksand.

Another obstacle reared its head. The mayor of Utica, Ed Hanna, decided he would play political games with us. The city and state had provided some much-needed funding to upgrade the UMA: new lighting, new rink boards, better seating, some painting and a general clean-up and fix-up. It finally looked like a proper professional hockey arena. The mayor felt that an upgraded UMA was worth more rent.

Ed Hanna was a real character. He had an open-door policy: any-one was welcome to meet with the mayor, and his office at City Hall was always open to the citizens. His waiting room was like a giant liv-ing room and occupied by a broad spectrum of citizens: street people, lobbyists, political hacks, media.

Vic Ehre didn't want the Comets' rent to become a general public debate; he preferred a more conventional meeting. However, the may-or insisted on an open public forum. Our meeting was scheduled for an early summer evening. The mayor's waiting room was filled with the usual cast of assorted characters, and his office door was open so all could hear. Our presentation was fairly simple: the Comets games in the UMA were economically positive for Utica, attracting people downtown in the evenings when otherwise the area was deserted; and the Comets were fighting for their financial existence, and an increase in the rent would be prohibitive. Playing all our games in the Clinton Arena would not bring in enough money. An acceptable resolution of the rent issue was a prerequisite to the Save the Comets campaign. No use of the UMA, no Comets. Always a man to be perceived as the people's mayor, Ed Hanna wanted to win something in the negotiations. The dealmaker was my offer to give the City of Utica a small percentage of the net gate receipts.

Another one of my many responsibilities was selling advertising for the Comets Hockey Magazine, published for every home game, and collecting payment for that advertising. In the summer of 1974, there were still several delinquent accounts, and we needed every penny to make ends meet. Ads sold for $100 to $500 for the season, and most of them cost about $250. Most advertisers apologized for late payments, but one took exception to my persistent attempts to collect.

A pizza place ran an ad in the magazine for the whole season; the ad generated some significant post-game business, because it was close to the UMA. After several unanswered letters and phone calls, I decided to drive over to the pizza place at lunchtime. I waited in line, then finally stood face to face with the owner, a big burly Italian gentleman, though "gentleman" is not really the right word to describe this character. To put it mildly, he was incensed that I had the nerve to ask him to honour his commitment to pay for an ad he benefited from all season. No explanation of how important payment of every ad mattered; he didn't care about the Comets, and if I persisted in trying to collect the measly $250 he'd have "his boys" take care of me. And he meant it. I returned to my car. If someone wasn't prepared to pay $250 to support the Comets, I wondered whether professional hockey had a real chance of making it in the Mohawk Valley.

Response to the Save the Comets campaign was not overwhelming, but there was an acceptable expression of interest from hockey fans, and the owners agreed to proceed for another season. And with what I had experienced and learned in season one of what it took to survive in a minor pro hockey league, I planned to be better prepared on and off the ice for season two.

Although a few other franchises were also struggling economically, the NAHL made plans to expand for the 1974–75 season. All seven original teams committed to return, and a new team was added: the Philadelphia Firebirds. With eight teams, six would be eligible for the playoffs. The Firebirds were well funded and considered viable.

I was full of enthusiasm and optimism as I prepared to assemble a better Comets team. I still had tight financial restraints on my player budget, so I would have to get a better bang for my buck—and from Buck and the Toros. And because of concerns about our ongoing working relationship with the Toros, I also set up a second working agreement with the Indianapolis Racers, a new WHA expansion franchise.

That's how I met Chuck Catto, director of player personnel for the Racers and a bundle of nervous energy. Chuck received his major league opportunity because of the WHA, as did many of the players he scouted and recruited. The WHA was heading into its third season, and the calibre of player and play had improved noticeably. Like the Toros, the Racers had to scramble to recruit and sign players, though many of them would also prove incapable of playing at the WHA level. One or two of the Racers' assignees turned out to be legitimate prospects.

I knew the 1974–75 Comets had to be better than the previous edition to attract fans, so my plan was to improve the talent level from the previous season. Practically, I couldn't afford to discard all last year's players and start over again. A lot of work had gone into developing those players, and I hoped that in their second season they would perform better. The 1974–75 team included a few Toros returnees, a few new Racers prospects and a few returning and established minor-leaguers. Also, because each team had to have a minimum number of American-born players, I had three highly touted young prospects out of Minnesota.

The other big project over the summer was our team bus, the 101 Beauty, the most spartan bus in the league. One of our problems the previous season on our road games was how we got there. The seats were cramped; the heat was either on full blast or not at all, it was uneven—roasting in the front and freezing in the back; there was still no proper washroom; you could often smell exhaust fumes in the bus; the radio didn't work at times. Simply, it was an old, tired, worn-out bus. After ten hours in the 101 Beauty, players needed time to get their circulation and skating legs going. And too often, they never did get the kinks out.

We still couldn't afford to rent one of George Marsh's newer, more spacious and comfortable buses, so I convinced the owners we should buy the 101 Beauty and spend some money making it more suitable for the Comets' needs. This we did. The biggest improvement was a convertible bunk-bed system that could be raised and lowered above the seats, so players could stretch out and catch a few winks. Members of our faithful and supportive Comets Fan Club made new red, white and blue curtains to dress up the interior. It wasn't a new bus, but it definitely was more functional and comfortable.

As the season got underway, it was evident that the Comets were an improved team. We were not as tough as was generally necessary in the NAHL, but we had several strong offensive players, who would end up in the NAHL's top twenty-five regular-season scorers.

The expansion Philadelphia Firebirds quickly established themselves as a very competitive team. Greg Pilling, an experienced former minor-league player, was their general manager and coach, and he was a great addition to the NAHL. The Firebirds had working agreements with the Philadelphia Flyers and the Washington Capitals of the NHL, as well as a very generous player budget. They immediately became one of the top teams. I envied Greg's instant ability to ice a top-level team, and was pea green when they showed up in Utica for their first game in a spanking brand-new bus with all the latest bells and whistles, first-class travel in the bus leagues.

Greg liked to stretch the rules and was always looking for whatever edge he could get. He was a very creative bench coach. He had a favourite trick, which he caught me on once; I saw it coming but couldn't get the officials ready for it, no matter how I warned them. The Comets were desperately hanging on late in the game to a one-goal lead. With the clock running down, Greg pulled his goalie and sent two players onto the ice, instead of one. I screamed at the referee that there were too many players on the ice. The referee started counting: one...two...three...four... Then the Firebirds scored and the whole team poured onto the ice, and the referee lost count. While against the rules, it was a clever move. If Greg got caught, the goal would be disallowed and he'd get a penalty for too many players on the ice. But it was worth a try. I was infuriated—not that he tried it, but that he got away with it. And I'm sure he used the same tactic against other teams.

The Syracuse Blazers quickly established themselves as the team to beat. The Comets were generally an easy two points for the Blazers, particularly in games in the Syracuse War Memorial Auditorium.

The fans in Syracuse loved to harass the Comets. There was not much of a barrier behind the away-team bench, and the fans continually ridiculed the players. I wasn't spared, either. There was one woman who heckled me about every move I made. She used to call me Clark Kent (Superman's alter ego of comic book fame) because I wore black horn-rimmed glasses and a trench coat. (The building was cold, and getting sprayed with beer was not an uncommon occurrence.) She would get the whole section behind the bench into the act, calling, "What are you going to do now, Clark?" Many times I had to bite my tongue not to react, knowing the worst thing I could do was acknowledge her jibes. I was always trying to think of a way to shut her up. Finally, I came up with what I thought might be the perfect comeback. During one of the Comets' last regular-season games in Syracuse, she started with the usual relentless Clark Kent taunts, trying to get a reaction. At an appropriate time, I turned and looked her directly in the eyes, but said nothing. Then I took off my glasses; unbuttoned my trench coat; loosened my tie; and then I started to unbutton my shirt. Everyone in the area was wondering what the hell I was doing. Underneath my shirt I had on a Superman T-shirt. She was speechless, and everyone around her broke up. It was probably the only cheer I ever got in Syracuse. After the game she approached me and we both had a good laugh. I never had any problems with her again.

The 1974–75 season was certainly better than the previous one, and the Comets were much more competitive, though we were still a long way from being a championship team. Personnel problems with some Toros assignees continued; the Toros management continued to change their loaned skaters at the most inappropriate times, which annoyed me and the owners. This was one of the prices all minor pro teams paid for working agreements with major-league teams.

One of the real strengths the Comets had in their second year was in goal. Good goaltending in hockey is like good pitching in baseball: you can never have too much of it. Jim Park and Michel Dion both had major-league potential. And two more different personalities you could not find, nor two more different styles of tending goal. Jim was a big goalie who played the angles well and was very good at poke-checking the puck away from any shooter who got too close to him. He loved to handle the puck, particularly if the opponents pulled their goalie late in a game. His goal as a goalie was to score a goal. He could shoot the puck the length of the ice as well as any skater.

My favourite memory of Jim Park is from after a home game in Utica. He had played exceptionally well and faced about fifty shots, but in a losing effort. After the game, a member of the local media asked him the usual mundane question: whether it bothered him to have so many goals scored against him, did the red light give him a sunburn, and how did he feel about the crowd booing every time the other team scored. Jim's response was priceless: "How would you feel if you were a business man in your office at your desk, and every time you made a business mistake, a red light would flash in your office and a booing noise would be piped in through the public address system?" Jim had a good perspective on his job as a professional goalie.

Michel Dion, from Granby, Quebec, had been a baseball catcher, a prospect of the Montreal Expos. But being a major-league goalie was his real passion. Michel's style was quite different from Jim's. Michel had a very good and quick glove hand and was much more a reflex goalie. He was a legitimate Racers prospect, and the extra work he got tending goal for the Comets only made him a better goalie. In mid-season, he got called up to the Racers to play one game against the Quebec Nordiques in Quebec City; it gave the whole team a lift when one of the Comets players got a chance to play in the majors. That was the first game of many for Michel with the Racers.

Not all the Racers assignees had Michel's positive attitude and approach. One in particular, Conley Forey, played only six games for the Comets before he quit the team and went home to Montreal. At the time, I thought I would never see Conley Forey again.

The Comets made the playoffs, beating Long Island for the final spot with a record of 31 wins, 38 losses and 5 ties for a total of 67 points, a 25-point improvement over their first-season results. The Comets faced the Binghampton Dusters in the best-of-five quarter-finals. The Comets used up all their gas getting to the playoffs, and the Dusters eliminated us. The 1974–75 season, while not all smooth sailing, had been a considerably more successful and rewarding than 1973–74.

By the summer of 1975, I had spent two very demanding and stressful seasons juggling the dual roles of coach and general manager. And with minimal success as coach. I realized I was probably too idealistic to be an effective professional coach. However, I had become a very competent administrator and was financially accountable, which gave my owners comfort. We all agreed that I should focus on being the general manager. The Comets would have a new coach for the 1975–76 season.

Late that summer, the NAHL held its annual meeting at a resort hotel on Cape Cod. The general managers met with league officials to discuss and plan changes, schedules and the like for the upcoming season. Over the previous season, I had become involved in several league issues. Scheduling was always a contentious issue, as all the teams wanted their home games on Friday and Saturday nights, to take advantage of generally better ticket sales on the weekends. I spent hours with my pencil and eraser trying to develop a balanced schedule that was reasonably fair to all the teams. My idea made no one really happy, but I worked closely with the NAHL office to develop a better one, as well as on other issues. I wanted to contribute to making the NAHL a better league, both on and off the ice.

The Comets had been a more competitive team in the 1974–75 season; we made the playoffs, and we made a bit of money. At the annual meeting, I was voted NAHL General Manager of the Year, a recognition I really appreciated. The couple of years of hell had started to pay off. My role as a general manager was developing well. It was a great way to end the summer.

In the off-season, there were more changes in the NAHL structure. The Long Island Cougars withdrew from the league, then the league expanded again, this time bringing in three new franchises: the Erie Blades, the Buffalo Norsemen and the Beauce Jaros (in Beauce, Quebec). The league was divided into two five-team divisions; four teams in each division would qualify for the playoffs. My only concern with the expansion was that there would be more overnight road trips, particularly to Maine and Beauce.

Beauce got into the NAHL because their owner, André Veilleux, was a very affluent businessman who bought his way in. When it admitted Beauce, the NAHL became truly North American. I remember the first time I met André. He drove down to Clinton to discuss operating an NAHL franchise. He showed up in a new Rolls-Royce or Bentley, I can't remember which. He was a big, good-looking, flamboyant Frenchman with the confidence of the wealthy. André made it clear that he would spend whatever it took to ice a very competitive team from the opening whistle. He even offered me a job as his general manager. But in spite of the challenges and financial limitations with the Comets, my family and I were well settled in the Mohawk Valley. Susan and I both loved the area, and Sean was in school and had made lots of friends. We were hoping our next move would be to a major-league city, not another minor-league one.

I was spending more time on NAHL administrative and planning matters. As long as I was in the NAHL, I wanted to see the quality of play and officiating improve; I wanted all the teams to be competitive. There were several teams in the league with wealthy owners who did not hesitate to splash money around to get better players. The Comets were a community-owned team and clearly the poor partner in the NAHL. If player salary levels escalated too high, the Comets would not be able to afford competitive players. The Comets already struggled to be competitive, and a real part of the challenge was our financial limitations.

Jim Matthews of the Binghampton Dusters was the first president of the NAHL. I had great respect for Jim. He had lots of money and wasn't afraid to spend it to make his Dusters a first-class, competitive franchise. But I was able to make him understand that it wasn't healthy for the NAHL, or any league, if one or two owners bought themselves the best teams and ran away with the regular-season races. The key to success is reasonable parity from top to bottom. To survive, the lower teams had to be competitive enough to give their fans hope that they could make the post-season. Otherwise the fans would abandon their team, which would threaten its financial viability. This could jeopardize the whole league and potentially cause it to collapse. A healthy league is one where every team is competitive enough to be a playoff contender. Jim Matthews occasionally made sure that the Comets remained a competitive and viable member of the NAHL. For example, Ted McCaskill.

Ted had spent most of his playing career in the minor leagues. He flirted with the NHL for four games in the 1967–68 season, then got a second major-league chance when the WHA came along. Ted played with the Los Angeles Sharks for their first two seasons. I hadn't met Ted, but I saw him play with the Binghamton Dusters in 1973–74. He was a big, strong, hard-nosed player, a tough guy but not a goon. Ted was in his late thirties, and his playing career was nearing its end; he wanted to get into coaching. Jim Mathews referred him to me as a good candidate to coach in the NAHL. I signed Ted to be the Comets' new coach. We hit it off well right from the start, despite our very different personalities. I looked forward to the 1975–76 season.

Ted had two children, a daughter and a son. His son, Kirk, was a good hockey player and had been drafted by the WHA Winnipeg Jets. But he was also a very promising baseball prospect. Kirk had a chance to go to a good US prep school on a baseball scholarship, but that would mean abandoning his hockey dreams. Ted agonized over the decision his son had to make. But he made the right decision. Kirk gave up his hockey aspirations, continued on in school and became a very successful major-league pitcher with the California Angels.

After two disappointing seasons, the Comets' relationship with the Toros was significantly reduced. Over the summer, the Comets developed and expanded the working agreement with the Indianapolis Racers. Chuck Catto and Racers president/general manager Jim Browitt had a few young players they wanted to assign to the Comets, hoping one or two of them might be called up to the Racers during the season. Ted and I made a trip to the Racers' training camp to look at players. While I was there, I found out the Racers planned to get all new equipment. I managed to beg, borrow and conscript about twenty full sets of used equipment. (The Racers' and the Comets' colours were the same: red, white and blue.)

And Vic Ehre was able to impose on personal friendships with Seymour and Northrup Knox, principals with the NHL's Buffalo Sabres. Ted and I also spent a few days at the Sabres training camp hoping to get a couple of their players assigned to the Comets. George "Punch" Imlach, my former general manager and coach when I was with the Leafs, was general manager of the Buffalo Sabres. And Joe Crozier, who had been my first pro coach, when I played with the AHL's Rochester Americans, was the Sabres' coach. My last contact with Punch had been when he unceremoniously dumped me from the Leafs in 1968. I didn't know what to expect when I showed up at his training camp. Some seven years older with real hockey management experience under my belt, I better appreciated some of the decisions Punch made over the years now that I too was trying to build a team and remain competitive and financially viable both on and off the ice. To my surprise, we got along very well, and he made a real effort to help the Comets. It was an interesting evolution of our relationship. The world of professional hockey was truly a small one.

It became apparent early that the 1975–76 season was going to be yet another interesting season. We were solid in goal with the returning tandem of Jim Park and Michel Dion, always a good place to build from. Jim had a chronic shoulder problem that continued to plague him and limited his availability and dependability. We had some good skaters, but again we were not team tough.

The biggest challenge Ted and I had was keeping a healthy roster. Injuries were killing us. Almost literally: one player, Billy Horton, was hit in a random drive-by shooting as he left a bar in downtown Utica after a game. Fortunately the bullet only grazed his neck, but he was out of the lineup for a few games.

There's nothing like always scrambling for players to ruin your player budget. I can remember many times Ted and I sitting at my kitchen table trying to figure out our roster for an upcoming game. It got so bad we were below the league minimum of players to be dressed for a game. Against my better judgment, Ted conscripted me to play a few games until our roster was restored. I played in three games in the NAHL, scoring two goals and getting one assist. One of those games was a home game against the Johnstown Jets. They had the three Carlson brothers, who played together as a line. As a trio on the ice they were scary; they gave a new meaning to the word "goon."

And then there were the Beauce Jaros. Trips to Beauce ranked right up there with trips to Johnstown. Only a lot colder! I often joined Ted and travelled with the team on the road. I remember one trip to Beauce in the dead of winter. It was so cold that we left our bus running all night because we were afraid it wouldn't start the next morning. But the Beauce arena was overheated by a very rabid French-Canadian crowd, who incited their hometown Jaros into a frenzy.

The Jaros had a player named Gilles Bilodeau. He was a bigger version of Bill Goldthorpe and just as scary on the ice. He liked to intimidate and beat up opponents so his skilled teammates could have free range on the ice. The Comets were no physical match for his on-ice insanity. It was a throwback to a Goldthorpe game. In spite of the efforts by the NAHL to improve the quality of play, it took only a few Carlsons or a Bilodeau to wreck it all. He was the catalyst to the chaos on the ice: bench-clearing brawls and stick-swing melees. It was potentially very dangerous stuff. The officials lost control. Ted was a tough, hard-nosed player in his day, with an explosive temper, but even he was fed up with the situation. We agreed to pull the Comets off the ice to put a stop to the mayhem; both of us were disgusted with how the game had been permitted to degenerate to nothing more than a gang war on ice. It was no longer hockey. And their fans encouraged it. It was the most ridiculous game of so-called hockey I'd ever been involved in.

It took several policemen to get the arena under control. Then Ted and I permitted the Comets to return to the ice and resume the game. I knew I stood to be reprimanded by the NAHL for my actions, but enough was enough. Either the NAHL was a bona fide professional hockey league or it was a hockey joke. As far as I was concerned, all the positives of having Beauce in the NAHL were eradicated that night.

Hollywood Comes to the Mohawk Valley

LATE IN 1975, while checking my telephone messages, I found one from Roone Arledge of ABC Sports Wide World of Sports in New York City. He was the guru of sports television at the time, certainly in North America and quite possibly the world. As the Comets were struggling on and off the ice and were the brunt of some local ridicule, I assumed the call was a practical joke from a local sportscaster. I was swamped trying to keep the Comets competitive and financially viable, and I didn't respond to the message. Over the next week or so, I received several more messages from Arledge's office, requesting me to please call back as soon as possible.

From my home office a few days later, I finally returned the call. When the person who answered said, "Mr. Arledge's office," I just about croaked. I had absolutely no idea why Roone Arledge would be calling me.

Apparently, Johnny Esaw, of CTV's Wide World of Sports, Canada's affiliated counterpart of the ABC Sports show, had recommended me to Roone. ABC Sports had acquired the television rights to the XII Olympic Winter Games in Innsbruck, Austria, in early February 1976. One of the sports they would have to cover was hockey. ABC Sports had never covered hockey and asked Esaw to help them put together a broadcast team. Johnny recommended me as the colour commentator.

As soon as I hung up, I called Johnny to see if this was serious and to seek his counsel. Sure enough, it was for real. He had suggested two people to help with ABC's maiden hockey coverage: me and Ralph Mellanby, director/producer of Hockey Night in Canada. Johnny said I should definitely pursue the opportunity, and fast.

I immediately set up a meeting with Vic Ehre to discuss the opportunity. Vic and the rest of the ownership group thought it was a great personal opportunity for me; they also thought the publicity might benefit Utica and the Comets. And a couple of weeks away from the continual pressure cooker might be a good break for all concerned.

My initial tardy response was fortuitous. When I next called ABC Sports, I was surprised by their approach. Time was very much of the essence, and they said, "If you're available, the job is yours." I accepted so quickly I didn't even ask what I would get paid. They wanted me to fly to New York to meet with all the people who would be working for ABC Sports on the Olympic Winter Games.

I arrived in New York City in a daze, grabbed a cab and said, somewhat in disbelief, "Take me to ABC Sports on Avenue of the Americas." When I entered the ABC Television Network building, I was nervous as hell. I was ushered into a meeting room set up like a theatre. As I took my seat I looked around and recognized many faces I had seen regularly on television: Jim McKay, Chris Schenkel, Frank Gifford, Bob Beattie, Jim Lampley, Dick Button, Curt Gowdy. The only one missing seemed to be Howard Cosell; maybe winter wasn't his season, or perhaps when they said he had to wear ski pants he declined their invitation.

When we were all seated, Roone Arledge took the stage. His message to the approximately three hundred people assembled was clear, direct and concise. ABC's overall ratings were suffering, and the network was behind both NBC and CBS. ABC planned to use its coverage of the Olympic Winter Games to regain first place among the top three networks. He felt he had put together the broadcast and technical teams to get the job done. ABC Sports was going to pull out all the stops to achieve the network's objective.

Following Arledge's presentation, everyone was directed into another room to receive details of their particular involvement. I felt like

I was a rookie with the Leafs again, afraid to say anything. I spoke only when spoken to. I spied Ralph Mellanby, whom I knew casually from *Hockey Night in Canada*, and went over to chat with him. Ralph and I were the only Canadians on this exciting project.

I was introduced to Curt Gowdy; Arledge had chosen him to do the hockey play-by-play. Curt was an icon in US sports broadcasting with his unique voice and style, well known for his award-winning series, *The American Sportsman*, and his play-by-play coverage of baseball, football, basketball and a wide range of other special sports events. Despite his impressive résumé, Curt had limited experience in hockey. Arledge chose him because of his sports broadcasting status and because he had done at least some hockey play-by-play. I looked forward to working with this veteran of the sports broadcasting world.

I hadn't really followed the international hockey scene since 1972, and Canada was still boycotting international hockey competitions, so they wouldn't have a team at the Olympic Winter Games. We would focus on the US Olympic Hockey Team (Team USA), and I had lots of research to do to get up to speed before the Games began on February 4.

A large group of us flew to Innsbruck together from New York. On the plane, I sat beside Curt. It was an overnight flight, so I had time to develop a rapport and brief him on my hockey and broadcasting experience. When I told him I had been to Innsbruck as part of Canada's 1964 Olympic Hockey Team and that I had been the colour commentator for the 1972 Canada–Soviet Hockey Series, he seemed to feel more comfortable with me. It was the beginning of a great professional relationship, which developed over the next few weeks.

Arriving in Innsbruck was like a flashback. Little had changed since 1964. The Olympics were in the same facilities, which had a few upgrades. It was very familiar, and I felt quite comfortable with the surroundings.

A production and broadcast team was assigned to each of the competing sports. Jim McKay was the anchor host, and Arledge was the puppet master. Each broadcast team would follow their designated sport throughout the Games, focusing primarily on medal contenders, particularly Americans.

The show produced by ABC Sports was a compilation of high-lights from all the sports. Each day, Roone reviewed the highlights and built the show for taped delayed transmission to the North American market in prime-time evening programming on the weeknights. On the weekends, some events were covered live.

Hockey wasn't considered a high-profile sport, because Team USA wasn't expected to be a serious medal contender against the elite teams of the Soviet Union, Czechoslovakia, Sweden and Finland. But in games against France, West Germany, Poland and other second-tier teams, Team USA was expected to make a decent showing. Each game Team USA played was taped in its entirety by Curt and me as if it were a live broadcast. Only small portions of a few games were covered live; the rest were taped post-game highlight packages.

It was a strange emotional experience for me to be at an international hockey event cheering for Team USA. But Canada wasn't participating, and I was employed by ABC Sports, so Team USA became my team for two weeks. And it was a much more relaxed feeling to broadcast for a team that wasn't really mine. As well, Team USA was a real long shot as a medal contender. So the whole experience was low pressure and most enjoyable. Curt and I had a good time doing our broadcasts.

Bob Johnson was the coach of Team USA. "Badger Bob" was one of the top college hockey coaches in the US and had brought the University of Wisconsin Badgers to national prominence. (He would go on to leave his mark at the NHL level as the coach of the Calgary Flames.) Bob had an infectious personality. He was a very positive guy, always with a smile and a congenial attitude. And he lived and breathed hockey! He coined a phrase that became his trademark: "It's a great day for hockey!" And he lived his life as if every day was a great day, right up to his untimely death in 1991. He reminded me in some ways of Father Bauer, one of those rare individuals who have a gift to motivate and inspire people with their unique personalities.

Bob was always co-operative and accommodated our requests for interviews throughout the Games. The hope was that Team USA could give some of the top teams a good game and a possible scare, and be the best of the teams that wouldn't win a medal. They were a gutsy team with a lot of enthusiasm and an inspiring coach. All their games were interesting and competitive. Unfortunately, their early 4–1 loss to West Germany dashed any hopes of a medal.

As the medal contenders came into focus, ABC Sports planned to cover at least parts of key or final games even though Team USA was not involved. Because I hadn't followed international hockey for several years and wanted to be as informed and prepared as possible for any game Curt and I might have to broadcast, I went to as many games as I could. Some of the games ABC Sports did not cover were among the best of the tournament. The game between the Soviets and the Czechoslovakians was very intense and reminded me of the emotion and intensity of the Canada–Soviet Hockey Series. The Sweden–Finland game was also keenly contested, as the two countries were archrivals for hockey supremacy in Scandinavia.

In the Olympic Icehalle, hockey and figure skating alternated. On the off hockey days, I could attend other events. (My media pass got me into every Olympic activity.) Curt and I sat in our hockey-broadcasting seats to watch the women's figure-skating finals. A young skater named Dorothy Hamill was the USA's hope for a gold medal. She was the darling of ABC's coverage, and figure skating was one of the top TV audience attractions of the Olympic Winter Games. Curt and I were in our prime seats at centre ice, about fifteen rows up from the ice. (The Icehalle had no proper broadcast booths for hockey; temporary booths had been built in the general seating area. It reminded me of the Luzhniki Sports Place in Moscow in 1972; we worked with someone looking over our shoulder.) We had just settled into our seats when a young lady came down the aisle towards us. As she approached, Curt uttered a very friendly, "Hello Caroline." We made room for her to join us, and then it dawned on me that this young lady was Caroline Kennedy. She was somewhat shy and reserved, trying not to attract attention. She settled in beside us for an evening of electrifying figure skating, and Dorothy Hamill won the gold medal. (In 1994, when I was working at Maple Leaf Gardens, I introduced myself to Dorothy, who had come out of retirement to skate with the Ice Capades, and related that memorable evening.)

It wasn't all fun and games. There was a six-hour time difference between Innsbruck and the US east coast. After we had taped a game, we waited for Roone to decide how much hockey coverage to include in that day's show. On a few occasions, it was the whole game, but generally he picked a period or a highlight package. Curt and I would go over to the Broadcast & Media Center and with our director and producer would edit and prepare the hockey package for that evening's show. On one occasion, Roone called when I was asleep; he decided he wanted more hockey coverage and wanted Curt and me back immediately. In spite of the late hour, I was happy to accommodate because I knew Roone thought it would make a better show. It was a privilege to work for him.

I found the process of editing and packaging a most fascinating part of my involvement. Our challenge was to make our coverage seem live to the audience at home, when in fact the game usually had been completed several hours before. When the highlight package was determined, Curt and I would do our voice-over commentary. In the game with Finland, their goalie was particularly strong along the ice. One of my comments suggested that if Team USA was going to score on this goalie, they would have to start shooting for the top of the net. Of course, I knew the game's final outcome and that the Team USA players had gotten to the Finnish goalie by doing exactly what I said to do. It made me look more astute and knowledgeable than I really was. But it was sports entertainment, and Roone wanted his colour commentators to communicate some perceptive insight into the games—something the ordinary viewers generally did not know.

Because of his limited knowledge and involvement with hockey, Curt was desperate to pick up any information about Team USA and their opponents. When the US played the Soviets, I mentioned that their coach, Boris Kulagin, was nicknamed "Boris the Bear" because he was like a big grumpy Russian bear behind the bench. Curt liked the image. The first time the camera isolated a shot of Kulagin behind the bench, Curt not only grabbed my line but also made it sound like Kulagin was his new best friend. I quickly learned to keep my thoughts to myself until I could drop them in during the coverage.

It was a real thrill to work for ABC Sports on its coverage of the 1976 Olympic Winter Games, and ABC realized its objective of catapulting itself to the top of the ratings with its coverage. And later, Ralph Mellanby, our director, won an Emmy Award for the hockey coverage. I was very grateful for having been a small part of its success.

—⁘—

When I returned from Innsbruck, I was delighted and proud to find that my wife, Susan, as my designated interim general manager for the Comets, managed a winning record in my absence. Of course Ted helped, but maybe all they needed was a little motherly encouragement! Things were never dull around the Comets. With about a month to go in the regular 1975–76 season, my promotions director, Gary Clark, said he'd heard a rumour that plans were afoot to make a major Hollywood movie based on a team in a minor league like the NAHL or the old EHL. I thought it was just one more of the many fanciful rumours that floated around the minor leagues and made good conversation on a long bus trip.

However, over the next few weeks Gary and I got several phone calls from advance people with Universal Pictures. They were requesting information about the UMA and seeking the opportunity to meet the Comets to tell us their plans. I agreed. I was as curious as everyone else to find out what it was all about.

The rumours had been true: Universal Pictures was indeed going to make a hockey movie based on a minor-league professional team. Further, Paul Newman was going to star, and Academy Award winning George Roy Hill (*The Sting*, 1973) would direct. It certainly sounded like it was going to be a big-league movie.

Universal wanted to start on-location production during the NAHL playoffs. They were prepared to pay about $250 per day for extras, more if there was a speaking part. That was as much as I was paying most of my players for a week! I knew where they would prefer to be, if given a chance to be a part of a real Hollywood movie starring Paul Newman.

Over the last month or so of the regular season, Universal Pictures sent people to scout locations and look for hockey talent to fill some of the player parts, and also acting talent to fill some of the speaking roles. They wanted any NAHL players interested in being in the movie to sign up. As you can imagine, this was a major distraction, and many of my players became more interested in being in a Hollywood movie than in playing hockey for the Comets.

Universal had approached me about renting the Comets bus for six weeks, starting immediately after the Comets' last game, which the way they were playing was rapidly approaching. I threw out the amount of $6,000 ($1,000 per week). Done! It was probably the best deal I made the whole time I was with the Comets, particularly since the 101 Beauty wasn't even worth that much.

Universal also suggested I might be suitable for a referee role in a segment they planned to shoot in the Syracuse War Memorial Auditorium. It would be no conflict, as the Comets' season would be long over by then. I thought it would be an interesting experience to be around a real movie set on location, and I willingly accepted the opportunity.

The Comets ended the regular season in a distant third place in the NAHL Eastern Division with 30 wins, 40 losses and 4 ties for 64 points. That was three less than the previous season, but it was good enough to get us into the playoffs for the second year in a row. Beauce ended up in first place overall, with 110 points. As expected, the Comets bowed out of the playoffs early.

I wondered where the idea came from to make a Hollywood movie about a minor-league pro hockey team. As it turned out, Ned Dowd, who played for the NAHL Johnstown Jets during the 1974–75 season, had kept a diary of life as a member of the team. Ned's sister, Nancy Dowd, was a screenwriter who lived in the Los Angeles area and around the Hollywood scene. The Johnstown Jets were a classic example of a minor-league professional team. With Ned's background material about life in the minors and his entrée to the Jets and the NAHL, Nancy originally planned to write a documentary based on the seasonal trials and tribulations on a minor pro team under the working title *Hat Trick*. Then she decided to expand the manuscript into a feature-length movie script and renamed it *Slap Shot*. With ribald humour, foul language and a fair bit of exaggerated violence, she developed an entertaining and colourful script. She called her fictional team the Charleston Chiefs (based on the Johnstown Jets), and some of the infamous NAHL and former EHL players became fictional characters. She caught the attention and imagination of Universal Pictures, and convinced them to make the film.

The real-life Johnstown Jets' three Carlson brothers became the movie's Hanson brothers, but Jack Carlson was playing with the WHA Minnesota Fighting Saints and unable to participate. Universal substituted Dave Hanson who also played with the Jets and became Jack Hanson in the movie. Strother Martin portrayed Joe McGrath, the crusty and irascible general manager of the Chiefs. Martin was a perfect clone of Johnny Mitchell, the veteran general manager of the Johnstown Jets—a great casting job. The movie's pugilistic Ogie Ogilthorpe was based on Bill Goldthorpe, the resident goon of the Syracuse Blazers, played by Ned Dowd. In fact, most of the players in the cast were based on real-life players in minor pro hockey leagues.

Working beside real actors like Paul Newman, Strother Martin, Michael Ontkean and Jerry Houser were players, coaches and general managers from NAHL and former EHL teams. Comets players Ross Smith and John Cook got parts, as did coach Ted McCaskill. Other NAHL people who had parts in the movie included Galen Head, Louis Levasseur, Ron Docken, Guido Tenesi, John Gofton, Reg Bechtold, Reggie Krezanski, Blake Ball, Connie Madigan, Dick Roberge, and Danny Belisle. These were but a few of the NAHL personnel who were part of the many game scenes in the movie. And even Nancy Dowd, the movie's screenwriter, made a cameo appearance.

Paul Newman grew up in New England, could skate fairly well and was more than capable of doing many of his playing scenes. Roddy Bloomfield, from the Binghampton Dusters, was enough like Newman in size and looks to fill in as Paul's double where required. Newman apparently commented that Roddy was the closest double he ever had.

The three Carlson brothers, Jeff, Jack and Steve, were from Virginia, Minnesota. Glen Sonmor, the general manager of the WHA Minnesota Fighting Saints, discovered the three boys playing together as a line and thought they might have some major-league potential. Glen's father-in-law was Johnny Mitchell, Johnstown's veteran general manager. Glen sent the Carlson brothers to play for the Johnstown Jets for the 1974–75 season. It was their first professional hockey experience.

The Carlson brothers were to the Johnstown Jets what Bill Goldthorpe had been to the Syracuse Blazers and what Gilles Bilodeau was to the Beauce Jaros— except there were three of them on the ice at the same time. They were a bespectacled and bizarre-looking trio. All over six feet tall and each weighing more than two hundred pounds, they were big, raw-boned and gangly, scary to watch and worse to play against. Look at one of them the wrong way, and you stood a good chance of being jumped by all three of them. Their role was to create chaos and terror on the ice, to disrupt their opponents' ability to play the game properly, and they were good at it. And yes, they did wrap their knuckles with tin foil so they could inflict some serious damage on their opponents but wouldn't damage their hands in a fight. Their American audience not only related to this style of play, they loved it. Playing the Jets was like demolition derby or wrestling on ice: a real circus. When they weren't on the ice wreaking havoc and terrorizing their opposition, they weren't bad hockey players.

When the Comets' season concluded, Universal Pictures took possession of the 101 Beauty, but I didn't report to Syracuse for several more weeks. As it turned out, the scene Universal Pictures planned to shoot in the Syracuse War Memorial Auditorium was based on an incident that took place in the UMA in a game against the Johnstown Jets when I was behind the Comets bench as coach.

In every game the Carlson brothers played in the UMA, fans jeered and baited them with the usual spectrum of ignorant remarks. In this one particular game, the Carlsons were out on the ice intimidating the Comets with their customary gusto. It was a normal high-tension game, and everyone waited expectantly for the inevitable lid to blow off. As one of the Carlson brothers skated near the Comets bench, an irate fan stupidly threw something, which hit the Carlson brother in the face. In a reflex rage, he hurled his hockey stick like a spear in the direction of the culprit. Then all hell broke loose on the ice and in the stands. Jets players scrambled over the glass barrier behind the benches and into the stands. Sparks flew as skate blades hit concrete and the seats. Patrons scrambled to get away from the enraged players. It quickly turned into an ugly and dangerous situation. There was chaos both on the ice and in the stands, and it took several minutes to restore order. It was all I could do to restrain my players from getting involved, but I managed to keep them under control.

As order was being restored, several Utica policemen appeared on the ice. The Carlson brother's hockey stick had hit a young boy whose father was a detective with the Utica Police Department—which happened to be right across the street from the UMA. When the boy got hit, the detective promptly ran across the street for help.

The lead officer approached me, and I pointed to the Johnstown bench. He proceeded to arrest a couple of Jets players, removed them from the game immediately and took them across the street to charge them. (Fans and players should never mix during a game and this scenario was as ugly as I'd ever seen.) Fortunately there were no serious injuries.

The final act of the incident took place during the off-season, when the Jets players had to come to Utica to appear in court. They were found guilty of assault, fined and put on probation in New York State.

A re-creation of this incident was being shot in the Syracuse War Memorial Arena, subject to some artistic licence. I reported to the arena, and checked in at the Pass Gate and moved from a warm sunny summer day into the world of Hollywood.

Over the next two days, they set up and staged the scene over and over and over again. It seemed to me they didn't know exactly how they wanted to shoot the scene, and were creating it as they went along. The cast had to wait around for frustratingly long periods. Between takes, while the director was figuring out if he had what he wanted, most of us would go onto the ice and play shinny. Paul Newman joined in on a few occasions.

My older sister Connie had driven down from Toronto with hopes of meeting Paul Newman. I asked him if he would mind having his picture taken with me and my sister, me in my referee's shirt and Paul in his Charleston Chiefs jersey. He was very personable and accommodating. I am fairly tall, six foot six on skates, and Paul is quite short. I never realized how short until I towered over him in the photo. (Unfortunately, in one of my many hockey-related moves over the years, I lost this much treasured photo.)

It was interesting to watch Newman. While he was on the set and around the cast, he was affable and one of the gang. He even enjoyed the occasional beer with the guys. But as soon as work was over, he made a beeline for the privacy of his trailer, and had no apparent interest in autograph seekers, picture takers or interaction with his fans. Away from work, he was a very private person.

I played a referee and patrolled the ice on the side away from where the cameras were shooting the incident in the stands. Consequently, I ended up on the cutting room floor (somewhat like my hockey career). However, it was a great experience and a lot of fun for all of us who participated. Some of the people probably made more money working on the movie for a few weeks than they did in a whole season with the NAHL.

Later that summer, I got a call from our bus company saying that the 101 Beauty had been returned and that I might want to come over and look at it. One of the luggage doors had been badly damaged. It looked like someone had taken a large can opener and punched holes in it. I made several futile efforts to contact Universal Pictures, to ask them to pay for the repairs. I realized that the $6,000 I had received was all-inclusive. (When *Slap Shot* came into the theatres in 1977, I finally found out the luggage door had been damaged by one of the players in yet another absurd hockey scene.)

Minor pro hockey leagues throughout North America were full of characters similar to those portrayed in *Slap Shot*. And while some of the goofy stuff was exaggerated for effect and humour, and didn't happen in the two and a half hours of a movie, over the three and a half years I was with the Comets, many of the far-fetched incidents were a lot closer to reality than one would imagine. *Slap Shot* became a classic sports movie, and has a cult following, websites and all sorts of memorabilia.

As a footnote to my very brief movie career, on October 22, 2005, Toronto hosted the First Annual *Slap Shot* Golf Tournament, a fundraising event for Paul Newman's Hole in the Wall Camps. It was an enjoyable day, and I saw many former NAHL players like Guido Tenesi and Ross Smith, who had small roles in the movie. I met cast member Paul D'Amato, the actor from New England who played the frightening Dr. Hook (based on Tim McCracken of the EHL Syracuse Bulldogs). And I met screenwriter Nancy Dowd. After *Slap Shot*, she won an Oscar for the screenplay of *Coming Home* in 1978. Finally, I met Bill Goldthorpe, Nancy's model for the infamous Ogie Ogilthorpe. We had a good chuckle when I told him how he had terrorized my Comets into paralysis thirty years earlier. Bill has had a tough life since his hockey days, but he is still a charismatic and likeable member of the diverse hockey fraternity.

—⚎—

As the Comets headed into the 1976–77 season, things were more settled than they had been since I began the job in the summer of 1973. Ted returned for his second year as coach, and I continued to concentrate on being general manager. Relationships with the NHL Buffalo Sabres and the WHA Indianapolis Racers continued, and we managed to pick up some free-agent players. There was real optimism as the season began.

About a month into the season, some of the Indianapolis Racers owners spoke to Vic Ehre. They were thinking of replacing their general manager, and my name was mentioned. Vic gave permission for them to approach me. My heart was beating a million miles a minute when I called the Racers. Making it to the major leagues as a coach or manager was my ultimate goal. In the previous three and a half years, I had at times lost hope that it would ever happen. There were several coaches and managers in the minor leagues with better knowledge and experience than their major-league counterparts. But similar to the players, opportunities were very limited. Luckily, after a grueling apprenticeship learning my trade, finally a major-league chance presented itself. A deal was done and plans put into action immediately.

The Comets held a farewell for me on the ice at my last home game. As I stood there with Susan and Sean, receiving very generous acknowledgement for my contributions to keeping pro hockey in the community, my whole time in the Mohawk Valley flashed before me. I remembered my first meeting with Ed Stanley, which seemed like an eon ago, and how we had become very good friends. I respected and often sought his counsel. (I kept in touch with Ed until he passed away in 1991. He was truly a fine gentleman.) I remembered Rick Dods and his invaluable assistance; the 101 Beauty, an experience I wouldn't miss; Vic Ehre and all the Comets ownership group, who were always so generous with their time and support, and who always encouraged any opportunity that came my way to get ahead, including the one before me; Mayor Ed Hanna, a truly original politician; the more than a hundred hockey players I'd coached or managed, some of whom drove me crazy but most of whom were fine young men trying to make an honest living in the tough business of hockey. (I've crossed paths with many of them over the years and I'm always glad to see them and hear what they're up to.) I remembered the Comets Fan Club members who supported the team with devout loyalty through thick and thin; the Comets staff I worked with—Bill Randall, Gary Clark, Marilyn Crandall, Bruce Manning and Elaine Kane, to name a few; I remembered key members of the local media, who in spite of the oft futile efforts of the Comets on the ice were always fair with me and the players—Lee Hamilton, Bill Higdon and John Pitarresi.

And I thought of the three and half years of life-long memories I acquired while I lived in Clinton and the many friends my family and I made in the Mohawk Valley, most of whom we still keep in touch with. Mostly I remembered our babysitters, Colleen and Rene, and the Christmas eve the Clinton police chief toured as Santa Claus and paid an early-evening visit to all the five-year-old kids. We heard his "Ho, ho, ho!" over his loudspeaker as he approached our house. I remember Sean's eyes when he opened our door to see Santa before him, Santa saying that his reindeer and sleigh were up on the hill waiting for all the children to go to sleep before he would return to deliver presents, Sean saying he wanted to go to bed one second after Santa left.

It was an emotional evening. As much as I had worked for and hoped for a major-league hockey job, and in spite of the myriad challenges I had faced with the Comets, Clinton was a great place to live and raise a family. Clinton, small-town USA at its best! I was truly sad to be leaving the Mohawk Valley, which held many life-shaping experiences and emotions. However, I headed out to confront my next hockey challenge in Indianapolis.

Managing the WHA Indianapolis Racers

WHEN I arrived in Indianapolis to take over as general manager of the Indianapolis Racers, I was excited about the opportunity, but also nervous about the unknown challenges ahead. There had been no time to do anything about moving my family, so once again Susan had to mind the home front, as she so often had to do over the years. The Racers put me up in a furnished apartment until I could find a proper place for us to live. While not the ideal family arrangement, it was the price to pay for the opportunity.

The WHA was in its fifth season, and the Racers had come into the league as an expansion franchise in the 1974–75 season, so they were in the midst of their third full season. The WHA was like a chameleon: every season since its inception, the configuration of the league had changed. It seemed as if the league had to see which teams showed up for the next season before they set up the divisions. Teams moved and changed their names: the Ottawa Nationals became the Toronto Toros became the Birmingham Bulls; some teams merely folded. Each season was a new adventure in the WHA!

The whole league struggled financially from its inception, and every team had to perform financial gymnastics to stay on its feet. The Racers were no exception. I asked myself why I wanted to get into another financial struggle, only with a couple of more zeroes added on. But the WHA was the major leagues and where the opportunity was. So the options had been pretty clear: either take the job and be a part of major-league hockey, or pass and stay buried in the minor leagues, possibly forever.

Indianapolis was centrally located in the WHA, which was ideal for travel, and Market Square Arena was an impressive new facility located right in the heart of the city, with a seating capacity of more than sixteen thousand. The Racers shared the arena with the Indiana Pacers of the National Basketball Association (NBA). It was real basketball country, and the Pacers were *the* team in town. But the WHA felt there was room in the market for a second major-league team.

For the 1976–77 season, the WHA was a twelve-team league with two divisions. The East included the Quebec Nordiques, New England Whalers, Birmingham Bulls, Cincinnati Stingers, Minnesota Fighting Saints and the Racers; the West was made up of the Houston Aeros, Winnipeg Jets, San Diego Mariners, Edmonton Oilers, Calgary Cowboys and the Phoenix Roadrunners.

The Racers were a reasonably competitive team. Pat Stapleton was probably the biggest name player; he was a top defenceman with the Chicago Black Hawks when he jumped from the NHL. I knew a few of the players from my WHA season in Ottawa in 1972–73. Because the Racers were an expansion franchise, many of their players had come from other WHA teams or out of the minor leagues. These included former NAHL players Michel Dion, Jim Park, Randy Burchell, Brian Coates and Mike Zuke. Jacques Demers was the coach. He had been driving a beverage truck in Quebec when his major-league hockey break came with the original (now defunct) Chicago Cougars. His story was not unfamiliar; the WHA created opportunities for many people buried in the minor leagues of hockey, players and management alike.

My contact with the team would be very limited. I introduced myself to them at a team meeting and gave the normal assurances that all was well and good in the front office. I secretly had my fingers crossed, hoping what I said was true. Jacques immediately staked his turf, establishing that the players were his exclusive domain and that I was not welcome to intrude into his dressing room world. Jacques probably would have preferred to be both coach and general manager. In his mind, my job was to get him the players he wanted and pay the bills; his job was to win hockey games, attract fans and court the media. It was a classic hockey management scenario: the coach feels threatened by the general manager. I was surprised at his reaction, and the only reason I could come up with was that he felt insecure because I had once played hockey and because I had coached. I assured him I had no interest in coaching. My sole focus as general manager was to make the Racers a financially viable WHA franchise. Jacques and I had to work with each other, but I basically left him to his job and I proceeded to tackle mine. (Some thirty years later, in November 2005, Jacques revealed publicly that he was illiterate, which helped explain his attitude and conduct. His accomplishments over the years are nothing short of astounding and commendable in light of his startling revelation.)

Some members of the ownership group had given me a cursory financial overview, but otherwise I knew nothing about the Racers' business operation. I felt as if I had jumped onto a fast-moving train. What I wasn't sure of was which direction the train was headed: to the light at the end of the tunnel or a wreck?

I inherited a fairly small front-office staff, including a few leftovers and floaters from the old management team. As the new boy in town, I made no snap judgments about the administrative and business operations, though my first impression was that it had been a very loosely managed operation.

The Racers were set up as a limited partnership of about ten local businessmen. Harold Ducote, an accountant, was the common denominator of the group, as many of the other investors were his clients. They were involved for varied reasons: some for tax purposes; some just to be involved in a major-league sports franchise; some for ego and vanity; and some to support the community. Harold was the managing general partner. The key members with whom I would have considerable contact were Harold, corporate legal counsel Tom Jones, and Tom Berry, Jr., who had made a lot of his money during the CB radio craze that swept the US. Berry, Jr., was one of the major investors. Based on an assessment undertaken by Harold and others, the ownership group had committed another $600,000 to get the team through the season.

With no family obligations in Indianapolis, I buried myself in my work. My first order of business was to get a grip on the financial status of the franchise. I started by reviewing all the player contracts. Signing players in the WHA was a real crapshoot as teams scrambled to get the right combination of talented, skilled and tough players. A lot of the available players were only marginally talented. But it had been a player's market when the league started, and still was for expansion teams like the Racers.

Under great pressure and anxious to make the Racers competitive from their opening faceoff, the original management group signed players with reckless abandon. I couldn't believe some of the absurd promises (financial and otherwise) they had made to some players, particularly those who had jumped from NHL teams. Contracts included ridiculous salaries and bonuses, advances for houses, free cars, deferred payments, multi-year deals, anything to get a wanted player. Promise them anything and defer as much as you can—it seemed to be the WHA negotiating strategy. And worry about how to honour your promises later. If there were a later.

I didn't condone the promise-them-anything approach. As a player, I had never liked management that made promises my gut told me would probably never be honoured, and I didn't want to be that type of general manager myself. I was a financial conservative and very cautious, particularly with other people's money. But that, evidently, wasn't the WHA way. Contractual promises to players had helped create the financial mess the team was in. I reviewed each player contract and charted the team's financial commitments; I was shocked and alarmed at the financial exposure, some totally boggled my mind.

There were still players on the payroll from the first two seasons, some of whom were no longer with the team. This financial millstone around the neck of the franchise could seriously jeopardize the financial buoyancy of the Racers. Player signing mistakes could be franchise killers. I was pretty sure the ownership group had no real knowledge of this area of the operation. My strategy for dealing with these contracts would be to try to negotiate buy-outs with the players, their agents and/or their lawyers.

The next pressing situation was a cash-flow challenge. It appeared that the modus operandi of some WHA teams was to use the current year's season-ticket money to pay off the previous season's outstanding bills. Season-ticket funds were money in trust, and should only flow into the operation as the games were played; using them this way was a very questionable practice, one that gave me great discomfort. The serious financial challenges of the Racers made those of the Comets seem minuscule. I felt as if I had jumped out of the frying pan into the fire, and a very hot one at that.

By the end of the first month, my business plan had two parts: short term, to get the Racers through the current season; long term, to make the Racers a financially viable WHA franchise. The short-term objective was top priority. And parts of it were urgent. From what I could determine, the ownership group had made their collective decision to sink another $600,000 into the franchise based on misleading information or mistaken assumptions. By the time the controller and I identified all the outstanding financial exposures, we agreed that $600,000 would not cover them, and it wouldn't get the Racers to the end of the season. It was not a pretty financial picture, and I had to be very careful how I delivered the message to the owners.

Harold Ducote, the general managing partner, was the owner I had to talk to first; he was the one who encouraged his partners to commit more money to the team. How could he have been so wrong in his financial assessment? He was shocked by my news. We reviewed my information carefully, both hoping I was wrong. Unfortunately, I was not. The previous management had not given him all the information, particularly information about some of the player contracts. The Racers probably should have folded before the owners hired me. And an accurate financial picture might be even worse than my research had so far revealed. My numbers were a reasonable calculated guess, but still a guess.

I developed a plan that required some real creative financial gymnastics. Only outstanding debts that absolutely had to be paid were paid, and not before I tried to negotiate them down or unless they were C.O.D., which started to happen as our suppliers sensed our financial distress. Indianapolis was still a relatively small community, and rumours travel fast.

I contacted all former players still on the Racers gravy train, and/or their agents and lawyers, and tried to negotiate minimum settlements to help stop this huge area of financial hemorrhaging. I approached Market Square Arena to get some relief on the rent. The owners and I agreed the Racers shouldn't take on any more financial commitments, which meant Jacques would have to make do with the players on his roster, whether he liked it or not.

Where would the money come from to continue to operate? By the end of the calendar year, most of the season-ticket money would be gone. There were about six thousand empty seats per game to sell, which was an opportunity. Ancillary revenue streams like merchandising and program advertising and sales were modest at best. There were really only two potential sources of funds: go back to the ownership group for more, and go to our bank.

I decided to start with the Indiana National Bank. It was the biggest bank in the city and well hooked. Whether because of overoptimistic projections for attendance and revenue, or because they wanted to support another professional sports franchise in the community, or just because they were hockey fans, the bank was between a rock and a hard place with the Racers.

After the account managers got over the initial shock, they were relieved that at least I could present them with some more accurate numbers and projections, as well as a business plan. I was soon spending more time with the bankers than in the front office. I had to make the bank see its dilemma; they had gone too far to go back and they stood to lose everything if they pulled the plug on our line of credit, the critical financial life-line to help see us at least through the season. Optimistically, it was still possible that I could salvage the situation for the bank, the Racers and the community. Working together as partners, we formulated a financial strategy that kept the bank onside.

However, the bank insisted on one key condition. The ownership group would also have to contribute more cash up front. It was my job to sell this part of the plan. The controller and I had some work to do before I was ready to make that presentation. And players think playing the game is tough!

Before talking to the owners, I had to make sure Jacques was onside. He was cruising along with the team as if everything was rosy, but I felt he needed to be aware of the real situation. Jacques didn't take it well. He shot the messenger. As far as he was concerned, I was the problem; there had never been any apparent problems before I arrived. Jacques thought the owners' sole obligation was to put money into the Racers, and his job was to spend it on assembling the best hockey team possible. He looked at me as his enemy, the enemy of "his" team. His lack of understanding of the situation, and the emerging alienation between us, did not bode well for the future.

People started to take sides: with me as the owners' representative or with Jacques as the team's. He was very much a player's coach. A very emotional personality, he became a pal to many of his players. A high-risk strategy for a coach in professional sport. However, in dealing with a lot of marginal talent, his encouragement, mentoring and close involvement with the players often maximized their performance. He was totally committed to the interests of the players, which ultimately were also his interests. One of the carrots he used to maintain his support was to get the players anything they wanted from management. The scenario I found myself in had Jacques siding solely with "his" team, casting me as the opposition trying to spoil his party. He failed to understand that he was an important part of the management team, and that his first obligation should not have been to the players. I started to feel alienated from the team.

Shortly before Christmas, the Racers were on the brink of insolvency, on mouth-to-mouth support, hanging on for dear life. The time had arrived for me to meet with the full ownership group. I presented a business plan to get us through the season. After that there would be some time to figure out the future.

A few members of the ownership group were not happy, to say the least. Unlike Jacques, they did not shoot the messenger. But some were very upset with Harold Ducote. After all, he had talked them into investing additional money, which they might not have done if they had accurate information.

I had to sell the owners on staying in the game at least until the end of the season. Fortunately, they seemed confident in my efforts so far. I took the positive approach: the glass was half full, not half empty. The season was almost half over; the Racers were a competitive team and should make the playoffs, which would help financially; the attendance was averaging about ten thousand, which would be a break-even figure were it not for all the dead weight the franchise was carrying; and the bank appeared to be onside and prepared to help. And no one wanted the personal embarrassment of the Racers folding in mid-season.

Some of the owners wanted out, but there were enough who still wanted to try to make the Racers successful and who were prepared to commit a little more. But before any money was put in, the remaining owners wanted me to meet with the team to see where they stood and what they might be prepared to do to help save the Racers. I immediately set up a closed-door confidential meeting with Jacques and the team. The team's reaction to my state of the union address dumbfounded me. They didn't get it, or chose not to get it. And it was implied that I was fabricating a crisis so the organization could save some money.

Led by some of the veteran players, who I felt should have understood the reality of the situation and known I was not trying to screw the players, the team would not budge. Even if it meant their jobs, their collective attitude was that the Racers had made financial promises to them, no matter how unrealistic, and management had to honour them. They didn't seem to understand that if the Racers folded, most of them would get nothing, and many would not be able to find jobs with other WHA teams. It was a tough sell and it didn't fly. The players' counter proposal to me was to get rid of a few of the marginal players and to hell with players who were no longer with the team. When I reported the team's attitude to the owners, the future of the franchise was hanging by the thinnest of threads. I wasn't sure what would happen next.

Around Christmas a payroll was due, and there wasn't enough money to cover it. The owners had a critical decision to make: pull the plug now or plow ahead. I felt that unless they were going to commit to the end of the season, why put more money in? Although the players were not prepared to help financially, if they continued to do their jobs on the ice they would contribute significantly to helping the team and keeping their jobs. I had not yet worked out the ownership reorganization and financing package, and I needed to deliver payroll cheques to the players. Only one owner stepped forward, Tom Berry, Jr. He wrote a personal cheque for $50,000 to help cover the payroll, and by the stroke of his pen that day saved the Racers' season. Tom was a real driving force for hockey development in the Indianapolis area, and exemplified all the good qualities that hockey ownership should try to emulate. Beyond our business relationship, we began a friendship that lasts to this day. He is the most honourable person I have come in contact with in the business of professional hockey.

As the second half of the season began, financial challenges continued. However, the revamped ownership group contributed some funding, and the bank helped out with the rest. As the bank became the principal investor and main creditor, I reported more to the two account managers than to the owners.

We needed to attract new fans with new money to buy as many of the approximately six thousand unsold seats per game for the remainder of the regular season, and hoped for long playoff run. Selling more tickets was a tricky proposition: most of the supporters in Indianapolis had paid full price for their tickets. If we sold dramatically discounted tickets (or some free ones appeared) to attract new and casual supporters, we might alienate our hard-core fans. No full paying ticket holder wants to hear someone bragging about the good deal they got on their tickets. If we weren't careful, we could very easily kill the golden goose.

While at loose ends in Indianapolis, not knowing anyone outside the office which was a constant pressure-cooker, I spent most of my free time trying to solve the housing problem for me and my family. Finally, early in March, the Conacher family was reunited when Susan and Sean joined me in our new house.

On the ice, in spite of the personal concerns of the players, who knew the precarious position the franchise was in; the Racers were a solid playoff team. To his credit, Jacques kept them focused on playing. Somehow, we got through the rest of the regular season. The Racers ended up in third place in the WHA East Division with 36 wins, 37 losses and 8 ties for a total of 80 points.

In the playoffs, the Racers met the Cincinnati Stingers in the first round and defeated them handily in four games, but in the second round, the powerhouse Quebec Nordiques eliminated the Racers in five games. The Nordiques went on to defeat the Winnipeg Jets in a seven-game final and win the WHA championship Avco Cup.

The Racers played their last game on May 2, and the focus shifted to the future of the franchise, a period of real uncertainty. Everyone involved still wanted it to survive and move forward. The community knew the Racers were on thin ice. I started a Save the Racers season-ticket campaign; set a target that would give the organization a proper financial platform from which to operate. As the main creditor, the bank took over operating control, almost like a receiver. I worked to reorganize the Racers financially. Harold Ducote's role was dramatically reduced; Tom Jones acted on behalf of the limited partnership, and the two of us represented the franchise at the league level.

Shortly after the season ended, the Racers were served legal notice that Conley Forey was suing them for $50,000. He felt he was owed this amount on his Racers contract when he was assigned to and made a brief appearance with the Mohawk Valley Comets. Of course, the Racers didn't have that much money, and Tom Jones decided we'd fight the claim in court. Forey had been signed by Chuck Catto and Jim Browitt. The contract wasn't clear, the records were a mess, and I wasn't optimistic about our chances in court.

I appeared in court on behalf of the Racers as the defendant, and it was a unique experience for me. There was a trial before a twelve-person jury. As I was the current general manager of the Racers, my appearance was a command performance, though I had had nothing to do with the contract. Chuck Catto was also called. Forey, who came from a well-to-do Quebec family, breezed into the court in a dapper suit looking cool and confident.

The first day was spent selecting the jury. Most of the candidates knew little or nothing about the hockey business or the Racers. Some men, some women, some white, some black. They were impartial people, a cross-section of the community, passing judgment on the goings-on in the world of the WHA and major-league sport, a world they generally only knew about through the media. It made me realize how insular and myopic the hockey business was.

My gut told me the Racers were hung before the trial began. It wasn't a pretty story as the evidence came out. A young guy from Canada was promised big money by so-called major-league hockey types, then he was arbitrarily cut adrift when the Racers reneged on some promises. His dream of playing major-league hockey was shattered. Most of the promises to Forey apparently had been verbal, but Forey told a compelling story, and denial by the Racers organization did not sit well with the jury. Talk about washing your dirty laundry in public. It was an example of an apparently wealthy sport magnate taking advantage of a poor young aspiring hockey player. The assumption seemed to be that the Racers owners had lots of money and had made some promises, and whether verbal or not, big business types should not cheat the little guy. Even I could not condone the Racers' conduct.

The trial took two days. The jury found the Racers guilty. Forey had put on quite a convincing performance. If he'd been that convincing on the ice he'd have been worth the $50,000. While a cocky victory for Forey, he was going to have to stand in line with the other creditors to get paid. I was embarrassed as I watched the charade unfold; it made the management of the Racers, and in fact the major-league hockey business, look inept, irresponsible and foolish in a public court. Not exactly the type of publicity the Racers needed at the time, or ever.

With the Save the Racers campaign in full swing, I felt like I was back in the Mohawk Valley. It was definitely déja vu. Here I was going to our hockey fans implying that if they didn't buy season-tickets early the team might fold and the community might lose its major-league hockey. This had to be handled very carefully. Hockey fans don't like being blackmailed into supporting a team. We had an enthusiastic and supportive base group, who loved hockey and committed quickly. To get a comfortable financial base, we needed to push the season-ticket sales to at least ten thousand; this objective was a much harder sell. However, sales were coming along nicely, and we were optimistic that the Racers would survive for at least another season.

And then the dynamics within the WHA started to change. Near the end of its first season, some team owners discreetly floated trial balloons with the NHL about a merger of the two leagues. Some owners planned from the beginning to crash the NHL party (not unlike what the American Football League had done with the National Football League). During the 1976–77 WHA playoffs, Howard Baldwin of the New England Whalers and Bill De Witt, Jr., of the Cincinnati Stingers renewed the attempt at a merger. The Racers and a few other teams—and the league as a whole—were struggling, but there were some very successful franchises.

At the end of the season, the WHA had eleven teams (the Minnesota Fighting Saints had folded in January). All the team owners were invited to attend a secret meeting. Tom Jones and I would attend on behalf of the Racers (the bank insisted I be there to monitor their interests). The meeting was held in a hotel suite in Chicago's O'Hare Airport. Tom explained why a general manager was attending, and after introductions things got under way.

Benny Hatskin, chairman of the WHA, chaired the meeting, which included a truly diverse and strange cast of characters. Johnny Bassett of the Birmingham Bulls (the former Toronto Toros) and "Wild Bill" Hunter from the Edmonton Oilers were the only owners I knew. Joining Hunter from the Oilers was one of their new owners, Nelson Skalbania. And there were owners from the Quebec Nordiques, Calgary Cowboys, Winnipeg Jets, Houston Aeros, Phoenix Roadrunners and San Diego Mariners.

The plan, concocted by Baldwin and De Witt, Jr., was simple. Instead of everyone losing everything with the eventual and inevitable collapse of the WHA, why not try to salvage a few franchises and see if the NHL would take them in. Not a bad plan. Except that the

Racers weren't invited to the merger party. Only six teams would go to the merger party: New England and Cincinnati, Houston, and three Canadian franchises (Quebec, Winnipeg and Edmonton). On the outside looking in were Indianapolis, Phoenix, San Diego, Birmingham and Calgary.

I was surprised the Racers weren't included. In spite of our operating difficulties, all of which I felt could be overcome with better management, I was confident Indianapolis, with an ideal Midwest location and a solid base of hockey interest, was as good an NHL location as New England or Cincinnati. But owners were looking out for their own interests first.

The "out" group's only question was: "What's in it for us if we bow out gracefully?" All the owners had spent a lot of money, and promised more. They didn't want to fold their tents without some financial indemnification from the group. Tom and I were there to listen; we would report the proposal to our principals. Several other franchises were wrestling with the same financial obstacles that plagued the Racers with respect to going forward for a 1977–78 season. For some of those teams, gracefully stepping aside might not be a bad resolution; some of the owners might be quite happy to get out of major-league professional hockey. A second meeting was planned for a few weeks later in New York City.

The Racers scenario was getting complicated. The Save the Racers campaign had to continue as if the team would participate in a 1977–78 WHA season. However, a merger with the NHL would preempt another WHA season; negotiating a reasonable financial indemnification might be an acceptable escape from the onerous financial position we were in.

The bank and the Racers decided to consider financial indemnification, if the amount were right, probably in the $2 million range. Tom and I headed to New York City for the next meeting.

Nothing was ever simple in the WHA. The league had some real urgency to get its ducks in a row if there was any real chance to get the NHL to take in the proposed teams for the upcoming season. Financial indemnification for the franchises who weren't considered in the merger was an acceptable concept, but no one knew where the money would come from. To put it in perspective: during the discussions, room service was called for coffee and doughnuts. The bill came to about $70. Not one person in that room was prepared to pay the bill, and here they were talking about a multi-million-dollar merger with the NHL. Talking about millions, and not having pennies to spend!

Meanwhile, the WHA had to be ready to start the 1977–78 season. If the league didn't operate, the NHL would win the war without the need of a merger. Several franchises—one of them the Racers— might have real difficulty committing to another season. Teams that folded early might not get any financial indemnification. It was a tricky poker game. With the vague direction of the owners, Baldwin and De Witt, Jr., continued to pursue the merger possibility with the NHL. Owners needed to know if there was a merger deal before the WHA annual meeting, scheduled for Toronto at the end of June. If there was no merger, the WHA would firm up plans for another season.

If financial indemnification were a real possibility, it would be difficult to turn down. The Racers' bank would probably grab whatever money it could get its hands on to get out of the hole it had been drawn into. The two Toms knew that would put me out of a job. They agreed to help me get another WHA job if the Racers folded. I appreciated their concern and support for my future, in light of their own financial plight.

As May moved into June, I had no real idea of how the scenario would turn out in Indianapolis. The bank seemed satisfied with my efforts on their behalf, and my relationship with the ownership group, particularly the two Toms, was good. But what did the future hold? Would the Racers survive for another season? What if the WHA merged with the NHL? What if the bank pulled the plug?

The owners decided to send me to the WHA's annual meeting on behalf of the Racers. The media constantly sniffed around and fed the rumour mill. The big questions were: Is there going to be a merger? Does the WHA have enough solvent franchises to operate for a sixth season if there were no merger? During the meeting, the attempted NHL merger was derailed. The WHA had to scramble to keep the league together for at least another season. Eight teams committed: Birmingham, Houston, New England, Cincinnati, Quebec City,

Winnipeg, Edmonton and Indianapolis. Calgary, Phoenix and San Diego folded their tents.

Before I went to the annual meeting, I met with Tom Berry. He encouraged me to use the opportunity to look for a position with another team. He suggested I contact Nelson Skalbania, one of the new owners of the Edmonton Oilers. At the meeting, Nelson and I spoke. He and Peter Pocklington had taken over control of the Oilers from the original owners. (I can't say they bought the franchise, because I'm not sure what the deal was.) Nelson and Peter would operate the franchise into the uncertain future.

There were several reasons I wanted to talk to Nelson. He and Peter had just let the Oilers' general manager go, and I assumed they were in the market for a replacement. I thought that, no matter what happened, Edmonton would end up with a hockey team. Finally, Edmonton was a Canadian franchise, and I felt it was time to go home. With or without hockey, I would feel more comfortable in Canada if I had to start over again.

Nelson and I continued to talk, and I'm sure he checked me out. Apparently the two Toms gave me positive references as a responsible money manager and administrator. Peter Pocklington had already gone ahead and hired Glen Sather as coach. Nelson wanted someone in the front office to keep track of the spending, and said I had been recommended. We worked out a deal before the meeting ended, and I headed back to Indianapolis to break the news.

The Racers were committed to the 1977–78 WHA season, but there were many financial hurdles to overcome before the team could play. I was torn: I liked Indianapolis a lot, and believed it could be a top major-league hockey city. But I couldn't risk getting stuck in the US with no team and no job.

My brief time in Indianapolis aged me ten years. There was never a moment without a crisis. We had enjoyed living in the US as a family, but even Susan was excited about going home to Canada. And by a stroke of luck we were able to sell our house with no real estate agent, and we got all our money out of a house we'd lived in for less than half a year. It's ironic: the only thing that went smoothly for me in Indianapolis was my leaving.

Managing the WHA
Edmonton Oilers

I HEADED for Edmonton in mid-July. I was emotional as I returned to Canada to take up residency again. While I had enjoyed my stay in the US and had made many good friends, I realized that I had maple syrup in my veins and was proud and happy to be returning to Canada. Alberta was the most vibrant province in the country, alive with unlimited optimism. It seemed to be the ideal place to land.

Nelson Skalbania was part of a small group of real estate speculators and developers in Edmonton. He, Peter Pocklington and a few others personified the phrase "wheeler dealers." They played Monopoly with real properties. Nelson and Peter were partners in the Oilers venture and some other deals in Edmonton and throughout North America, but they also often competed for properties. It was the Wild West, the ultimate high-stakes poker game. And Nelson and Peter were two of its most active players.

How did Nelson come to take control of the Oilers? Wild Bill Hunter and Dr. Charles Allard were the original owners, at the start of the WHA in 1972–73. Wild Bill had a long and well-established hockey background and had been president of the major junior Western Canada Hockey League and general manager of the Edmonton Oil Kings. He was confident Edmonton could become a top major-league professional hockey city and wanted to be part of the WHA. Wild Bill was a real maverick in Canadian hockey circles and a great promoter, just what the WHA needed. He was the league's first president and was instrumental in attracting many of the Canadian franchises. But he didn't have the kind of money to be an owner—that is, until Dr. Allard got hooked and funded the serious money behind the Oilers. Hunter provided his hockey business knowledge, management and considerable promotional skills. After several seasons of losing money with little prospect of improvement, Dr. Allard lost interest and wanted to sell all or part of the team. And along came Nelson, one of his real estate players, always looking for a deal.

Once Nelson got hooked by Dr. Allard, he quickly looked to lay off some of his exposure, for he immediately learned that professional hockey was a cash business. And some serious money! Enter Peter Pocklington, whose bread-and-butter business enterprise was a very successful car dealership in Edmonton. But like Nelson, Peter was always looking for opportunities. And what better place in Canada to find them in the 1970s than Alberta?

As the story goes, over dinner one evening with Peter and his wife, Eva, Nelson indicated he was looking for some partners to co-own the Oilers. Before the next mouthful, Peter removed a huge diamond ring from his wife's finger and slid it across the table to Nelson as a down payment for his involvement. Paintings and exotic cars followed. And before long, Nelson and Peter were co-owners of the Oilers. Little cash, a lot of kind.

Neither Nelson nor Peter had a hockey background. They saw owning the Oilers as a good opportunity to be part of the rumoured WHA–NHL merger: they hoped to make a financial killing with the Oilers as an NHL franchise. They both loved the art of the deal, and some of their deals were very creative indeed. Their games would be played off the ice, not on it. But they both found out very quickly that major-league professional hockey was a beast with an insatiable appetite, constantly needing to be fed with lots of cash.

When I took over as general manager of the Oilers, my initial impression was that their operation was in considerably better shape than the Racers' had been when I showed up there. Of course, "better" was a relative thing; the whole WHA was skating on thin ice that summer, as teams scrambled to get ready for the upcoming 1977–78 season. In my brief experience in the WHA, the standard modus operandi seemed to be crisis management, and success and survival were determined by how well you managed each crisis. And a crisis occurred almost daily.

I'd never met Glen Sather before I showed up in Edmonton, though I had run into him (literally) a few times on the ice over the years. As a major-league player, "Slats" was a hard-working, gritty, grinding, in-your-face journeyman. He had made a solid career out of his style of play. The previous season with the Oilers was one of his best. Towards the end of the season, Bep Guidolin, general manager and coach, had not been getting the response he needed from the players, so he appointed Glen as player-coach. Under Glen's direction, the struggling Oilers won their last two regular-season games and grabbed the last playoff spot in the Western Division from the Calgary Cowboys. In the first round of the playoffs, the Oilers were beaten out by the Houston Aeros in five games.

Prior to my involvement, Pocklington made Glen the full-time coach of the Oilers. He had the good fortune of stepping right off the ice into a major-league coaching job. I envied him that opportunity, one I missed several years before with the Ottawa Nationals. The way the hockey business was in those days, you might as well jump into the deep end of the pool right away, and not waste time learning your trade in the minors, probably getting buried forever as a minor leaguer. By the time Glen and I met, the seeds of my demise were already sewn. He was hired by Peter; I was hired by Nelson. I was not aware what Peter may have promised Glen, but Nelson made it clear that I was general manager. Having your two key management staff hired by two different people was certainly not ideal. Sather was full of self-confidence, cocky and ambitious. He had a personal agenda, and I wasn't part of it. Bruce MacGregor, one of Glen's hockey-playing buddies and a hometown Edmonton boy, became Glen's right hand and confidant. They handled all hockey matters; they saw my job as tidying up the financial and contractual mess from previous seasons, running the front office, marketing the team off the ice, figuring out how to pay the bills, and getting them the money they needed to hire some new and better players. In Glen's mind, I was merely the business manager, and he was, in fact if not in name yet, the general manager. I was an obstacle he had to endure until he could get rid of me and surround himself with "his" people. The obvious split between front office and team management wasn't ideal. The stars were aligned: Glen with Pocklington, me with Skalbania.

Glen envisioned a top WHA team. To achieve the goal, he wanted to build a different type of team from the current Oilers. It would require some new players—and a different type of player. The Winnipeg Jets had introduced a modified European style of play, with free-wheeling movement, speed and skill. That was the type of team Glen wanted, and with a touch of muscle added, just to keep everyone from taking advantage of the skill players.

Glen's hockey mentor and role model was Sam Pollock, the legendary brains behind the great Montreal Canadiens teams. Pollock had been a general manager. To fulfill his vision, Glen not only wanted, but felt it imperative, that he have full control over all aspects of the team: who to hire, who to fire, who played, how they played: everything. He immediately isolated me from the team and team issues, even more completely than Jacques Demers had with the Racers. I hadn't thought it was possible.

And so began another season of uncertainty. My job was to keep the Oilers on the ice, which would require more financial gymnastics. I was in a far from ideal working relationship, but I was determined to make the best of the situation.

Susan was still in Indianapolis, closing the sale of our house, which would happen at the end of August. She wanted Sean settled into our new house in Edmonton and ready to start school right after Labour Day. She also wanted the same moving company and mover she'd had when she went from Clinton to Indianapolis, and she wanted him to pack as well as move. When George showed up at Susan's door on packing day, she finally broke down and cried at the prospect of yet another move. George said, "I told the missus I didn't want to go to the Conacher house again." Susan and George had coffee and doughnuts, she collected herself, and they rolled up their sleeves and got to work on another move as a result of my being in the nomadic hockey business.

About noon on the Friday of the Labour Day weekend, George pulled his truck up in front our new house in Edmonton. This guy was a real pro. He opened his doors to start unloading, and the first thing off the truck was Sean's bike, followed by all the furnishings for his bedroom. Before it got dark, George had our whole house unloaded, unpacked and set up. And as quickly as he had arrived, he was in his truck and on his way back to Indianapolis.

We settled into the neighbourhood over the long weekend and began friendships that last to this day. Sean started school right after Labour Day, and came home to tell us he was in Grade 2 again. To this day, Sean thinks he was in Grade 2 twice. It made us very aware that moving affects the whole family.

Before the season started, I joined Nelson on a quick trip to Vancouver, his hometown. I met Nelson's wife, Audrey, and their two daughters and stayed at their beautiful home in the exclusive Point Grey area. By profession Nelson was an engineer, and his company was based in Vancouver. He took me downtown in his Rolls-Royce, which seemed to be the car of aspiring hockey team owners. Nelson pulled up in front of an office tower in a no-stopping, no-parking zone. He jumped out and told me to wait. When I suggested that I move the car, he replied, "When you're going in to borrow millions, don't worry about a parking ticket!" It was a world I'd never been exposed to.

Later I borrowed Nelson's car and drove over to see Father Bauer at St. Mark's College on the campus of the University of British Columbia. It was the first time I'd been there since the 1964 Olympic hockey team was stationed there. We drove around the campus in the Rolls-Royce, reminiscing. Father Bauer probably thought I was a long way removed from the idealistic youth who had played for him. But I hadn't changed all that much.

I'd been in Edmonton barely a month, trying to put the Oilers' financial house in order, when Nelson asked a question that almost knocked me over: how would I like to go back to Indianapolis and run the Racers again? I couldn't believe it. The Racers were still trying to ice a team and were still cash poor. The WHA wanted the Racers as the eighth team in the league for the 1977–78 season. They wanted Nelson to sell his interest in the Oilers to Pocklington and take on the Racers franchise. I knew my situation with the Oilers was tenuous, and that Nelson was my main connection, and that if he departed I would be on fragile ground. But I decided there was no going back to Indianapolis. If my hockey involvement came to an end, I would rather it happen in Edmonton than Indianapolis. No matter what kind of deal they gave Nelson to take over the Racers, I knew the team's future was problematic. Nelson wasn't thrilled with my response, but I hoped he understood.

Before the season started, Nelson became principal owner of the Racers. I heard he assumed their liabilities for $1. I don't know how my former ownership group fared in the deal or what promises Nelson had to make to the Indiana National Bank, but he hustled down to Indianapolis to take over the team. Ever the opportunist, Nelson appeared at the eleventh and a half hour to literally save the Racers.

With Nelson gone, it seemed pretty clear that Glen would eventually take over as general manager; it was only a question of when. I knew my days were numbered as soon as Nelson left. I liked Nelson. I admired his energy, enthusiasm and his mental quickness; I knew I was nothing like him, but thoroughly enjoyed being exposed to his deal-making creativity. Peter was quite different than Nelson; I never felt comfortable working for him. I just wasn't his type. Glen would successfully cultivate a close business and personal relationship working for Pocklington.

As the new owner of the Indianapolis Racers, Nelson planned a trip to Indianapolis on American Thanksgiving, when the Oilers were scheduled to play there. He wanted to fly down in his private jet, attend the game, stay overnight and return to Edmonton on Friday. Susan and I were invited to join him and his wife, Audrey, as well as another Vancouver couple and David Ingram, a business associate of Nelson's. I knew David from public school days in Toronto. I think Susan and I were invited because of my familiarity with the Racers. We were happy to be included and looked forward to the trip. And what a trip it was!

The business jet held eight people comfortably, but in close quarters. Susan chatted with Audrey most of the way there, and I spent some time getting caught up with David. I had never been in a social setting with Nelson and enjoyed his company. He was a very bright guy with an incredibly active mind, a financial wizard and juggler.

After the Racers–Oilers game, we went out for dinner. Friday morning we were all up first thing and ready for the return trip. Before we boarded, Nelson said he needed to make a side trip to New York City on a real estate matter. Susan and I tried to book a commercial flight to Edmonton, but it was Thanksgiving weekend, and nothing was available. No problem, first New York and then back home to Edmonton. Susan called our new neighbours, Gail and Fred McDougall, who were babysitting Sean, and they had no concern about keeping an eye on him for a few more hours. Sean and their son Ian were in the same class at school, so Sean wasn't with complete strangers.

We landed at LaGuardia Airport and piled into a limousine for the trip downtown, expecting to spend a few hours there while Nelson tended to his business. The limo pulled up in front of one of New York's most exclusive boutique hotels, the Pierre, on Fifth Avenue in midtown Manhattan. Initially, Susan and I thought nothing of it, but when Nelson told everyone to check in, Susan and I just about croaked. We had expected to be back in Edmonton before the day was out. Nelson and Audrey, sensing our discomfort, took us aside and said we were their guests and to relax and enjoy the experience. The plan for the rest of the day was to look around New York while Nelson dealt with his business issues. In the evening he was hosting a dinner at the Pierre for about a dozen or so business associates and friends. Susan and I had been on a lot of trips in our time, but this was our first experience with the jet set. Trapped in the situation, we decided we might as well enjoy it. It was quite a day, quite a dinner and quite a night.

Saturday morning we all had breakfast and again headed for the airport and the long anticipated flight back to Edmonton. On the plane the conversation turned to country music and the Grand Ole Opry. David had friends in Nashville, Tennessee. And in the blink of an eye, Nelson instructed the pilot to set a course for Nashville. Susan and I sat there in stunned silence. After all, what could we say or do at thirty thousand feet? Except laugh! This trip was definitely turning into an unforgettable North American odyssey. Everyone was having a lot of fun and getting along famously. And we thought this was just another short side trip on our way back to Edmonton later in the day. It certainly made me realize how easy and flexible it is to travel when you have your own plane.

Another limo picked us up at the airport and we headed for downtown Nashville. And again we were instructed to check in to a hotel. What did this mean? The first thing Susan did was call the McDougalls to give them an update on our remarkable trip home. No problem with them or Sean, who was having a good time. Keep in touch and have a good time, was their message. They probably thought we were real wacko parents and had abandoned our seven-year-old son.

It was mid-afternoon, and I wondered what was on the agenda for the rest of the day. Well, David, Nelson and Audrey had it all planned. I'm not sure whether they were improvising as they went along or whether it was planned all along, but by then we just went where we were told, and with a smile on our faces. David's friends invited us to an afternoon cocktail party, so off we went to meet a whole bunch of new people and enjoy some real Southern hospitality. Around seven, Nelson produced tickets and said we were off to the Grand Ole Opry. We saw Little Jimmy Dickens, Minnie Pearl and several other acts. It was a night to remember.

Sunday morning, we got up, packed our overnight bags, which had had an extended workout, and headed for breakfast and to get the day's agenda. At last the whirlwind trip was coming to an end: we were flying straight home. When the plane lifted off that afternoon, I had a window seat on the left side. An hour or so into the flight, as the sun started to set on the westerly horizon; it dawned on me that we were flying almost due west, not northwesterly towards Edmonton. I didn't know the flight plan from Nashville to Edmonton, so I gave it no further thought. Until I looked down and saw the snowy peaks of the Rocky Mountains. We were headed to Vancouver not Edmonton! Everyone but Susan and I lived in Vancouver. I reminded Nelson that we lived in Edmonton, and he shrugged and said he'd get us home.

So there we were in the Vancouver Airport about nine on Sunday evening, still a long way from home. Nelson got us two tickets on the next commercial flight to Edmonton, which turned out to be the Vancouver–Edmonton–Toronto "red eye." So after bidding our adieus and giving many thanks, Susan and I had about three hours to kill before we made the final leg of this truly unique travel excursion. Once again, almost in disbelief, Susan called the McDougalls. They graciously agreed to keep Sean for another night. I expected them to ask for rent. By the time we arrived at Edmonton International Airport and caught a taxi home it was about two in the morning. As we finally walked through our door and dropped our bags, we were like two giddy teenagers. We'd been on a lot of trips before, but never any like that one.

—⋙—

Average attendance for the Oilers was near the top in the WHA and the season-ticket base was decent, but keeping the Oilers afloat financially was a daily struggle. Against my advice, I was instructed to pre-spend some season-ticket money, leaving our net game receipts depleted as the Oilers headed into the home stretch of the season.

Trips to our friendly banker were a regular occurrence. Peter used the bank that handled some of his other business ventures, so the Oilers became one part of a much bigger financial picture, a financial juggling act. And Peter was learning he could leverage a hockey team only so far. Most players didn't want paintings, cars, jewellery or pieces of speculative real estate development deals; they wanted certifiable paycheques every two weeks. Cash, not promises, kept hockey teams afloat.

A brief diversion from the day-to-day grind was a trip to the WHA All-Star Game in Quebec City. Half a dozen of us flew down in Peter's plane. The big feature of the game was Gordie Howe playing with his two sons. Gordie was an amazing athlete, and still a force to be reckoned with on the ice at age fifty. The game was in the Quebec Colisée, and I ended up sitting beside Peter. A few minutes into the game, he asked me why they kept blowing the whistle so much. It made me realize how little he really knew about hockey as most of the whistles were for routine off-sides. I wondered if he thought a face-off was an obscene sex act.

Glen and Bruce ran the team, and I worked flat out, the way I had in Indianapolis, to generate revenue to get the Oilers through the season. And then one day I got a call from Peter. He wanted me to write eight cheques for approximately $11,000 each. "To whom and for what?" I asked. Well, Peter had bought a share in a race car with, of all people, Paul Newman, an avid race car fan and driver. I balked. I said the Oilers were struggling from payroll to payroll and were in the hockey business, not the car racing business. I said that each month we owed Revenue Canada payroll taxes and that I was personally responsible and liable, as the general manager and signing officer for the Oilers, if those taxes weren't paid. Peter was furious and said he wanted to see me the next day in his office.

I spent some anxious hours between that phone call and the meeting. Peter again instructed me to write the cheques. Again I balked. I said as he was the owner of the Oilers, he could sign the cheques if he wanted to, but in light of the current financial situation it would be irresponsible and wrong of me to sign them. I didn't know what to expect. Was he going to fire me? All he said was, "You're either with me or you're not."

I wasn't fired. But when I left Peter's office I knew that between the cheques incident and Glen's management aspirations, I was finished with the Oilers. I didn't fit with the way Peter operated. I expected my one-year contract, which expired at the end of the season, would not be renewed. In the interim, I continued to fulfill my obligations and not give Peter any cause for my early termination. I was proud of the job I was doing as the general manager of the Oilers. The front office was running more efficiently, effectively and responsibly than ever before, even though I knew I would be a footnote or the answer to a trivia question in the Oilers' history.

On the ice, the Oilers were a decent team, but nothing exceptional. Glen Sather would have to wait to build his dream team, as the Oilers had too many short-term contractual obligations and financial limitations to pay for the wholesale changes he wanted. They finished the regular season in fifth place and made the playoffs with 79 points on 38 wins, 39 losses and 3 ties. They met the New England Whalers in the first round and bowed out in five games. The Winnipeg Jets, who finished first overall in the regular season, went on to sweep the Whalers in four games to win the Avco Cup.

By the end of the 1977–78 WHA season, it was obvious I didn't fit the mould of a major-league general manager, at least not in the WHA. The wheeling-and-dealing styles of Nelson, Peter and eventually Glen were way over my head. What made these people so different from me was their ability to endure risk, and with a smile on their faces, never showing that their stomachs may be internally hemorrhaging. That just wasn't my style. I was a conservative, methodical, organized and responsible administrator and a practical money manager, all qualities and skills that should have been welcomed in any successful business. But they were not the qualities and skills most WHA hockey owners were looking for and they were qualities that were not to be found in any great abundance in the WHA. The whole league defied financial gravity, and it was an ongoing giant crapshoot as to who would survive.

My contract with the Oilers expired at the end of June. While I knew what Glen wanted, I wasn't sure what Peter might have in mind. So I set up a meeting with him. It was uncomfortable for both of us. Based on performance, Peter had no cause not to extend my contract. In spite of all the financial challenges off the ice, the Oilers were one of the most successful teams in the WHA, which I realized was only a relative thing. Glen couldn't take all the credit for the success, because the team's performance, while decent and competitive, had been nothing special. But I'd learned another of the harsh realities of business: that doing a good job doesn't mean you necessarily keep your job. I was dumbfounded when Peter offered me a new multi-year deal to continue with the organization. In what capacity, I asked. Well, Glen is going to be general manager and coach and doesn't want you around the team, so you could do scouting or something. It was a vague, awkward offer, and to my amazement for more money than I made as general manager. It was an offer I could refuse, and I did.

My family was settled in Edmonton, and it was going to take a pretty attractive opportunity to get me to move to another hockey job. I knew I didn't really fit in the WHA. After some soul-searching, I came to grips with the reality that my dream of being a long-term major-league hockey manager was at an end. I decided to stop chasing the twists and turns of the puck world and move on with life after hockey. I was thirty-seven and had been involved with the game and the business of hockey in one form or another on and off the ice for some twenty years. The time had come to build a life outside of the hockey world.

Edmonton after Hockey

MY EXIT from the Edmonton Oilers was unceremonious. In spite of the financial chaos that prevailed in the WHA and Oilers, Peter Pocklington honoured all the team's obligations to me. The bad news was that I was out of the hockey business, where I had invested so much time and energy seeking success. The good news was that I was fortunate to be in a dynamic and friendly community instead of in the US with an expired work visa. And my integrity and reputation were intact.

My years of chasing the puck had come at a cost to my family. They had supported every decision I made with optimism, courage and enthusiasm, but I think my decision to leave hockey was a great relief to the whole Conacher family.

Suddenly I was in the real-world job market. Like most players before and after me, I was scared as I faced the world outside hockey. I knew that this time there was no going back. However, I felt confident that my hockey experiences on and off the ice, as unorthodox as they were, would provide many transferable skills for life after hockey. And Edmonton was full of opportunity and in the midst of a real estate boom. I accepted a job with a major commercial real estate company. In 1968, I had worked in commercial office leasing in Toronto, so it seemed like a possible good fit that could get me into a more conventional work environment.

Real estate had one similarity to hockey: doing a deal was like scoring a goal, in that after each goal, I always wondered if I would ever score again. And it was a straight commission business, so it was difficult to project my income. It could be feast or famine. I'd been in the famine business too long and began to think I should try something more dependable and suitable to my personality and needs.

In early 1979, I received a call from George Hughes, the general manager of the Edmonton Exhibition Association, also known as Edmonton Northlands. Northlands owned and operated Northlands Coliseum, where the Edmonton Oilers played their games. George wanted me to meet with him and a few of the Northlands directors. I had no idea about what, but agreed to meet.

I had dealt with Northlands when I was the Oilers' general manager and had established a good working relationship with them. Now some members of the Northlands board of directors were concerned about the future financial viability of the Oilers, who were a very important licenced user and tenant of the Coliseum. The board wanted to know what I thought, so I told them there was no question the WHA was on financial mouth-to-mouth. The season had begun with only seven teams, and by December it was down to six when the Indianapolis Racers took their last breath. But whatever happened to the WHA or Peter Pocklington, Edmonton had a major-league hockey future. Several of the directors agreed with me.

After another meeting, Hughes offered me a job. The Northlands marketing manager was leaving, and if I was interested, the position was mine. Northlands was concerned that with all his wheeling and dealing in real estate and the money committed to Gretzky and the Oilers, that Pocklington wouldn't be able to do the financial gymnastics to meet the heavy cash flow required to operate a major league hockey team. Some people thought cash-flow pressures might be his financial Achilles heal that could cause his whole business empire to collapse. And if Pocklington lost control of the Oilers, Northlands wanted to be ready to take over ownership. No one on the Northlands staff had any experience in operating a major-league hockey team, which is where I fit in.

Even though out of the hockey business, Nelson Skalbania and I kept in touch; he would use me as a sounding board for his hockey ideas. Still the owner of the ever-struggling Indianapolis Racers, he called to ask me what, if anything, I knew about the young hockey "phenom" Wayne Gretzky. I said he was a scoring machine, was about seventeen years old, played for the Sault Ste. Marie Greyhounds, that he was the sensation of the OHL and all of major junior hockey, and that he attracted worldwide attention for his scoring and playmaking prowess in the 1978 World Junior Championships in Montreal. His scoring statistics were off the charts, and he was being touted as a "can't miss" major leaguer. But he was so young. And, over the years, other young players had shown great potential and been tagged as "can't miss," only to disappoint as they got into their twenties.

Johnny Bassett, Jr., owner of the WHA Birmingham Bulls (formerly the Ottawa Nationals, then the Toronto Toros) and a real hockey maverick and free spirit, wanted to turn Gretzky professional with his team towards the end of the 1977–78 season. Considered a man's game with limited opportunity before the creation of the WHA, the NHL never signed a player to a professional contract until he was at least twenty years old. Nothing in hockey was sacred to Johnny. He thrived on controversy and became a thorn in the side of the NHL, shaking the traditional foundations of major-league hockey to its very core. Bassett and other WHA owner/managers were grabbing top teenage prospects before the NHL had a chance to draft them. Signing "underage" players became the latest battleground between the WHA and the NHL. As far as Bassett was concerned, the NHL had no right to keep these young hockey players from turning professional, and he was legally correct. He was using the younger players to coerce the NHL into merging with the WHA, which began to look like a super junior league as young players were attracted by the promise of big money.

By the summer of 1978, the Bulls were a Mecca for underaged players—so-called "Baby Bulls." Johnny wanted to sign Gretzky but couldn't afford him. So Johnny encouraged Nelson to sign him. Nelson was at the top of the WHA class as a risk-taker. His goal in the hockey business was to make money when the WHA merged with the NHL, if he could hang on until then. Meanwhile, his struggling Indianapolis Racers needed some sizzle for the upcoming season. Wayne Gretzky as a wonder-kid might just be the answer. Nelson asked me what I thought about trying to sign Wayne. I thought common sense suggested it would be a huge and expensive gamble. My observation was discarded like water off a duck, and with his pal Johnny Bassett prodding him, Nelson went after Wayne. Who would have known how it would turn out?

Nelson Skalbania did everything with panache. He invited the Gretzky family and Wayne's agent, Gus Badali, to his Vancouver home, and wined and dined them. The negotiation of Wayne's first contract was not a protracted affair, and it wasn't a standard WHA agreement. Nelson planned to sign Wayne for seven years to a personal-services contract worth about $1.7 million. It was huge money for any hockey player, particularly a seventeen-year-old rookie.

With the ink on Wayne's first professional hockey contract barely dry, Nelson whisked him to Edmonton to announce the signing to the hockey world—one day before the NHL annual draft. Wayne hadn't even known which team he would be playing for. Being a personal-services contract, a couple of teams would approach Nelson for Wayne's services. But Nelson decided he needed him more for his Racers who were deflating faster than a blowout on a motorcycle.

Wayne arrived in Indianapolis to great fanfare, but his impact on attendance was minimal. Nelson realized the Racers probably weren't going to make it and began to reduce his losses. He viewed Gretzky as an asset that could be relocated. The Edmonton Oilers and the Winnipeg Jets were interested, but Wayne's preference was Edmonton. Pocklington promised more money, Nelson went for it, and on December 15, 1978, the Indianapolis Racers became another fatality in the WHA graveyard. Gretzky went to play for Peter Pocklington.

It seemed to me that owning the Oilers meant more to Pocklington than money. I thought he was hooked on the status he got from owning the team, a status he couldn't get by selling cars or doing real estate deals, and that he would beg, borrow and do whatever he needed to do to keep it. Hockey wasn't just another business deal to Pocklington; it was *the* deal.

The Northlands job was a very good opportunity for me. I might make more money in real estate, but money wasn't my only concern in a job. If I worked for Northlands, I would work for the landlord instead of the tenant. And while I would definitely be out of the hockey business, I would still be on the periphery of it. It could be an interesting and rewarding career, and would give me an opportunity to use my previous management skills and experience.

I started at Northlands on March 1, 1979. It was my first really conventional job. I felt fortunate for the relatively smooth transition to my life after hockey, and I was optimistic that I'd finally found an ideal post-hockey career with a future.

Northlands was a huge complex in the northeast corner of Edmonton. It was set up as a volunteer-driven, not-for-profit community-services and agricultural association; its primary mandate was to provide agricultural trade and exhibit space for events and activities for Albertans north of Red Deer. (The Calgary Exhibition and Stampede Association serviced Alberta south of Red Deer.) Alberta's population was less than two million, and half the people lived in Edmonton or Calgary. The economy was based on agriculture and oil. Agriculture was the historical foundation of the economy, but oil was the fire that was driving it in the late 1970s. Alberta's was the hottest economy in Canada.

Before the Coliseum was built there was the Edmonton Gardens, part of the Northlands complex. The Gardens seated five thousand and could accommodate the major junior Edmonton Oil Kings, but it was not large enough for major-league hockey. In the early 1970s, Wild Bill Hunter promoted that Edmonton was ready for a major-league arena that would attract the WHA. When Edmonton was awarded the 1978 Commonwealth Games, government funding became available to help build an arena that would accommodate fifteen thousand. The logical place to build was at Northlands, which would manage and operate the new arena, called the Coliseum, help with its financing, and eventually own the facility as part of its complex.

One of my new responsibilities was to liaise between Northlands and the Oilers. The first urgent issue was the future of the WHA. The 1978–79 WHA regular season was close to an end, and even before the playoffs began, rumours and speculation were rampant about an imminent merger with the NHL. The WHA had started from nowhere in 1972, had defied financial gravity for seven seasons, and along the way created the opportunity for many players to play major-league hockey. The league also left behind a legacy of broken promises, and many of its owners and franchises collapsed along the way. By the end of the 1978–79 regular season, only six teams were left standing, or rather staggering: Edmonton Oilers, Winnipeg Jets, Quebec Nordiques, New England Whalers, Cincinnati Stingers and Birmingham Bulls.

In 1977, when I was still with the Indianapolis Racers, John Ziegler replaced Clarence Campbell as president of the NHL, the initial round of discussions about a merger began. They had continued behind the scenes ever since. The perfect solution for the NHL would be for the WHA to collapse and go away. But, against all odds, the WHA always managed to field enough teams for one more season. With its continual raiding of underaged players, the WHA was really hurting the NHL. They wanted to stop the bleeding and strike a deal.

Finally, in late March 1979, the NHL put an end to the seven-year war and agreed to let four WHA teams merge with them: Edmonton Oilers, Winnipeg Jets, Quebec Nordiques and New England Whalers. The Cincinnati Stingers and the Birmingham Bulls were indemnified and paid off so they wouldn't contest the merger. I've often wondered if the NHL knew how close the WHA was to collapsing at the end of the 1978–79 season. And if they had just waited a few more months, it was quite probable the WHA would not have been able to field enough teams to start an eighth season. In any event, for four teams that kept up the battle, they reached their goal. The WHA was about to fade away into professional hockey history.

But before the final curtain came down on the WHA, the last act remained: the playoffs for the final Avco Cup, the emblem of the WHA championship. Led by the young Wayne Gretzky, who played for two teams in his first season—the defunct Racers and the Oilers, the Oilers ended the regular season in first place overall. In the playoffs, the Oilers defeated the New England Whalers in an up-and-down series that went the full seven games. In the final between the

Oilers and the Winnipeg Jets, the Jets won three of the first five close games, giving them a three-to-two lead in the best-of-seven series. The next game was scheduled in Winnipeg on May 20, 1979. Out of the blue, I got a call from CBC Television Sports. At the last minute, the CBC had decided to cover what might be the last WHA game ever played. Was I available to do the colour commentary for the game with Don Wittman as the play-by-play announcer? I had done the colour commentary for the very first WHA game, and I was pleased to do it for the last one. It brought my WHA experience full circle.

It became obvious not far into the game that the Jets were going to win and that this really was going to be the last WHA game ever played. A lot of the broadcast was a nostalgic look back at the WHA's turbulent history. In spite of all the challenges and chaos it faced over the years, there was a lot of very good hockey played in the league. Teams like the Jets, Aeros and Nordiques were every bit as good as top NHL teams. But the WHA suffered from having the wrong three initials. NHL was considered the premium brand in North America for denoting hockey's best.

The Winnipeg Jets won the final game 7–3 and the series four games to two. As much as any team in the WHA, the Jets, with their blending of the Canadian and European styles, would affect the future pattern of play in the NHL. The final moments of the WHA were very emotional. But there was a silver lining for both teams: there would an exciting tomorrow for both of them as part of the NHL.

The WHA Oilers had been the prime licenced user of the Coliseum. Their forty-plus playing dates were a very important source of revenue for the building. When I crossed the street to work for the landlord, I quickly realized that hockey wasn't the only master Northlands served. Northlands needed other events and activities to generate funds to keep the facility financially viable. Meanwhile, part of my job was to liaise with the Oilers and maintain an amicable working relationship with the team. One issue that irritated the top brass at Northlands was the Oilers' attitude to the Coliseum: they acted as if they owned it, and they came and went as they saw fit. Northlands occasionally had to remind both Pocklington and Sather that Northlands owned and operated the Coliseum. While Northlands wanted to accommodate the Oilers wherever possible, some members of senior management and the board were not fond of Sather or Pocklington, and still coveted control of the franchise. I didn't anticipate Pocklington losing control of the team in the foreseeable future.

But the most visible friction between the two organizations centred on the logo on the ice. It was a real lightning rod. The Oilers wanted to see their logo at centre ice. It irked Pocklington immensely when he saw the Northlands logo there. It seemed that Peter wanted people to think his Oilers owned the Coliseum as well, and their logo at centre ice would be symbolic of that perceived ownership. But George Hughes was adamant: the Oilers were welcome to place their logo on the ice, but centre ice belonged to Northlands. This issue exemplified the constant friction between the two organizations the whole time I worked for Northlands.

My challenge was to make the relationship between Northlands and the Oilers work—every day. The two organizations finally came to a mutual understanding: Northlands wouldn't tell the Oilers how to run their hockey team, and the Oilers wouldn't tell Northlands how to run the Coliseum. Generally it worked.

An exception was the licence agreement for the use of the Coliseum, an open sore which festered. The original agreement went back to 1972, the Oilers' first year in the WHA. The league had no standard agreement, and each arena and team negotiated its own deal. Pocklington inherited the Oilers' original deal, which ran to the end of the 1983–84 season. It was very much a landlord's agreement, with a lot of limitations and restrictions; its terms and conditions favoured Northlands. The per-game financial consideration was calculated as a percentage of the gross gate receipts, a relatively simple formula, with some smaller percentages for program and merchandise sales. The percentages increased for playoff games. The season I was general manager of the Oilers, we paid Northlands $200,000 in game licence fees. By the end of the 1983–84 season, the Oilers were paying Northlands around $1.2 million. Under Pocklington, ticket prices had steadily risen. Northlands was making some serious money from the Oilers; the Oilers complained they were paying too much. This was a fairly normal landlord/tenant scenario.

The Oilers had no alternative but to play in the Coliseum, but Pocklington was pushing for a whole new deal. Northlands was reluctant to forego its landlord's leverage. Further, the Edmonton economy was in a slump, and Northlands counted on the Oilers' rent money.

With any new licence agreement, two basic questions had to be resolved: How much was the use of the Coliseum reasonably worth? And what was reasonable? Because I had experience on both sides of the debate, I was chosen as the ham in the sandwich as negotiations for a new agreement began. The goal was clearly defined; the path to agreement was very rocky.

By the 1983–84 season, the Oilers were established in the NHL and most games were sold out. But Pocklington still had his hands full trying to keep the Oilers afloat, particularly since he had signed Gretzky to a long-term big-dollar personal-services deal. Peter was always looking for ways to save money or make more. A rumour began that he was trying to raise capital by syndicating the ownership of the Oilers under a limited partnership in which he would retain control as general partner. (Such partnerships were common in the US.) There was one problem with the scheme: it was hard to sell shares in a team that had no guaranteed place to play. And to rub salt into a very open sore, Northlands reminded Pocklington of the deal he had inherited from his WHA predecessors: ownership of the Oilers couldn't be transferred without Northlands "prior written consent." The old agreement handcuffed his efforts to infuse new money into the Oilers. A small but influential group in Northlands still coveted ownership of the Oilers, and they waited for the team to sink under its financial burden. Negotiating the extended licence agreement for the use of the Coliseum was contentious and protracted.

Finally, after a lot of time spent on some eight drafts, Northlands and the Oilers agreed to a new licence agreement, with a term of five years, and they signed on September 15, 1984. It wasn't perfect, but the new contract made it much easier to understand the rights and obligations of each party. Pocklington wasn't satisfied with the new deal, as it was still strongly weighted in favour of the landlord. But he was compelled to sign. I was reasonably sure the Oilers would revisit the still contentious question of licence fees before the term was up.

In the interim, the two groups co-existed in relative peace, although the relationship between Northlands and the Oilers would remain strained and litigious for years to come.

Before the Oilers' first NHL season, I got a call from Ralph Mallenby, with Hockey Night in Canada. I had worked with Ralph on the 1972 Canada–Soviet Hockey Series. He was trying to set up a broadcast crew for the three new western NHL teams and wanted to know if I was interested in being a colour commentator. It would be part-time work, and I was already going to the Oilers' games anyways. Northlands had no objections, and it sounded like another great broadcasting opportunity to me. But when Ralph ran my name up the NHL flagpole, I was still persona non grata. Whether it was a hangover from my book in 1970, my commentary in 1972, the fact I was involved with the WHA, or there was someone they liked better for the job, Ralph was apologetic when he called me with the news. My hopes were dashed.

Regardless of all the behind-the-scene issues between Northlands and the Oilers, on the ice the team became the darlings of all Edmontonians. With entrance into the NHL, Edmonton was on the brink of one of the most exciting periods in the history of professional hockey. One of my responsibilities was to attend all their home games. My preference was to watch the game from the end with some elevation to be able to see the patterns of play develop as the teams went up and down the ice. I sat in the top row of the lower deck. I was ideally situated for some of the most exciting NHL hockey ever played.

By the end of his rookie year in the WHA, Wayne Gretzky had established himself as a coming force in major-league hockey. However, there were still naysayers who felt that even though he looked good in the WHA, now playing with the big boys in the NHL, he was going to be just another NHLer. And the league did everything to keep their new WHA partners at heel. Wayne and Marcel Dionne were tied for the scoring championship in Wayne's first NHL season, but the begrudging and small-minded NHL denied him his share of the honour. Wayne was also denied consideration for the rookie of the year honours because of his WHA participation.

However, it wouldn't deter Wayne in his quest that would see him go on to become the most prolific offensive player ever. The Oilers made an early exit in their first NHL playoff appearance, but it was evident to the hockey world that Sather was assembling a team that in a few seasons would be at the top of the NHL. During the 1980–81 season, Wayne racked up points at a staggering pace. To acknowledge his amazing on-ice accomplishments, when only eighteen, he was selected by the Canadian Press for the Lionel Conacher Award as Canada's Male Athlete of the Year. The award was named in honour of my father, and I presented it to Wayne at the Hockey Hall of Fame at Exhibition Place in Toronto.

The Oilers consistently made the playoffs but had to wait their turn behind the mighty New York Islanders, who won four consecutive Stanley Cup championships. The Oilers weren't there yet, but they were on the right track and getting closer. The breakthrough season was 1983–84. Gretzky had established himself as the dominant offensive player in the game and had a mature and experienced supporting cast (Messier, Coffey, Anderson, Lowe and others). They played free-spirited hockey with speed, finesse, skill and lots of scoring. Their transition game was so explosive, it sparked a "run and gun" offence like never seen before in the NHL. It was some of the most exciting offensive hockey ever played. And with exceptional goaltending from Andy Moog and Grant Fuhr, who repeatedly bailed them out after defensive lapses, the Oilers were on the brink of greatness.

It finally all came together for the Oilers in the spring of 1984, and who better to do it against than the Islanders? They won their first Stanley Cup championship in the fifth game of the final before a home-town crowd, and Edmontonians were delirious. It had taken a few years to get it right, but the wait was worth it!

I would watch Gretzky play some two hundred and fifty games during five and a half seasons. He mesmerized me with his play. Certainly he had developed his talent, but he was also incredibly gifted. When in the midst of the action, Wayne appeared to have a visual perception of it as if he were looking down from above, giving him this extraordinary view and perspective of the playing surface. And at ice level, he seemed to have three hundred and sixty degree peripheral vision of all the players around him. His ability to handle the puck in traffic was something to behold as he would navigate his way through the maze while conjuring up and delivering deft passes, some of which landed on teammates' sticks as softly as a marshmallow. It was sheer puck magic and a joy to watch.

Virtually every game, I would see him creatively do something that I'd never seen any hockey player do before. It would take my breath away and make my heart skip a beat just watching him. Undoubtedly Wayne had a great supporting cast, but he was the catalyst who made it all happen. The ice surface was his canvas on which he painted many a masterpiece. Gretzky's years in Edmonton were a very special time in the history of the game, as a hockey virtuoso came to the forefront like no other before him. I enjoyed every minute he was on the ice in those years.

—⟋Λ⟍—

One morning in the spring of 1981, while I was reading the national edition of the *Globe and Mail*, I noticed an interview on the upcoming Canada Cup, planned for the late summer. The interview was with Al Eagleson, executive director of the NHLPA, Canada's czar of international hockey, and a man I had known since he formed the NHLPA. In typical Al style, he was using the media to initiate negotiations with possible game locations across the country; he mentioned Edmonton. I showed the article to George Hughes, who suggested I give Al a call. Al agreed to come to Edmonton to talk.

After the 1972 Canada–Soviet Hockey Series, there were international hockey games in Canada and the US, and the NHL and the WHA had hosted and played in exhibition games, some of them in Edmonton. (The Oilers had interlocking league games with the Soviet Union, Czechoslovakia and Finland during the last WHA season.) So international hockey was nothing new in Edmonton, and Edmontonians had already proven their support. Northlands had a lot to offer; we could negotiate from strength and didn't need to go begging to get a few Canada Cup games, even against the aggressive Eagleson.

The concept for the Canada Cup tournament was an Eagleson initiative to capitalize on the growing interest in international hockey.

There hadn't been a tournament with all the top international teams and players since 1972. This Cup series would be played primarily in Canada. Eagleson wanted to field a team even stronger than the 1972 Team Canada; he wanted to stroke Canada's fragile ego and reconfirm our status as the best hockey nation in the world. The original plan was to hold a Canada Cup tournament every four years. (Five Canada Cup tournaments eventually evolved into the World Cup of Hockey starting in 1996.)

The first Canada Cup, in 1976, included Canada, the US, the Soviet Union, Czechoslovakia, Sweden and Finland; that year's Team Canada was one of the strongest ever iced. On two gimpy knees, Bobby Orr toughed it out in his long awaited (and only) chance to play for Canada against the Soviets, and, in the second game of a best-of-three final, Team Canada beat the Czechoslovakians in overtime when Darryl Sittler scored.

The Cup was a national event hosted by Canada, and Edmonton was a great city for hockey. George and I knew Al would be missing a great opportunity if he bypassed Edmonton.

We met in George's office. Eagleson's initial negotiating posture was that he wasn't interested in dragging the teams all the way out to Edmonton; he could keep his costs down if all the games were played near Toronto and Montreal or in the eastern US, and he already had relationships with arenas there. He was in Edmonton as a personal favour, because of his long relationship with me. Then he went into his classic yo-yo negotiating strategy: one second courting us in a voice so mild and low we had to strain to hear him; the next moment cursing us with a belligerent rant full of expletives. He reminded me of Nikita Khrushchev, banging his shoe on the podium at the United Nations in 1960. George and I weathered the verbal tirades and stayed focused on our objective: to get as many Canada Cup games in the Coliseum as we could.

When we got past the bluster, it became evident that Hockey Canada was pressuring Al to put some of the games in western Canada, and we began to negotiate legitimately for a number of games and the cost to use the Coliseum. The teams would be from the same six nations that participated in 1976. Al wanted the early games in

Edmonton and Winnipeg and the final games in Ottawa and Montreal. Harold Ballard, who ran Maple Leaf Gardens in Toronto, refused to host any Cup games because of his hatred for the Soviets.

Al wanted five games in Edmonton: US–Sweden, Canada–Finland, Czechoslovakia–Finland, Canada–US and Soviet Union–US. It was a good slate of games, but the schedule was tight: two games a day for two of the days. But the timing was good: the games would be around the Labour Day weekend, and we were optimistic that hockey fans would support all the games.

The biggest issue to resolve in the cost of the Coliseum was our relationship with the Oilers. Peter Pocklington and Glen Sather were not happy about Northlands hosting five international hockey games a few weeks before the start of the NHL season. Pre-season games were always a hard sell, and now fans were being offered the Canada Cup—maybe the best hockey Edmontonians would see until the NHL playoffs. When we told Al that Northlands wouldn't let him use the Coliseum for less than the Oilers paid, he went ballistic.

The situation needed a creative solution. George and I agreed to give Al a good deal on the licence fees for the five games. In return, Al agreed to donate $40,000 to Alberta Minor Hockey. This package added up to the average licence fee for an Oilers game. Northlands, in good faith, could tell the Oilers that Eagleson didn't get to use the Coliseum for less than they did. It was a deal.

All five games were well supported, especially the two Team Canada games. Canada romped over Finland 9–0; two days later, they broke open a 3–3 game with just over nine minutes left and beat the US 8–3. In the last of the five Edmonton games, the Soviets got some revenge for their loss to the US at the 1980 Olympic Winter Games by beating them 4–1.

From our point of view, everything went along very smoothly, except for one detail of our deal with Al Eagleson. I asked Chris Lang, keeper of the purse for the Canada Cup games, when Northlands could expect the $40,000 donation for Alberta Minor Hockey. I had known Chris since high school days and had introduced him to Father Bauer in the 1960s, when Canada's national team was in Winnipeg. Chris was Hockey Canada's treasurer, and Hockey Canada was Eagleson's partner in the Canada Cup. I wanted Eagleson and his Canada Cup gang to make the donation before they left town.

I discussed my concern with George Hughes, and we devised a plan. We invited representatives from Alberta Minor Hockey to attend the last Edmonton game. We set up a pre-game ceremony at centre ice at which Eagleson would present the $40,000 donation cheque—on live television. Eagleson was trapped. To his credit, he graciously fulfilled his obligation.

Northlands did another Canada Cup deal with Eagleson in 1984. It was a much easier deal to negotiate than the first one. There were again six nations, with West Germany replacing Finland. Edmonton would host five games in the Coliseum: Soviet Union–West Germany, Soviet Union–US, Soviet Union–Canada, Sweden–US (a semifinal) and Canada–Sweden (a playoff game). The final game would be in Calgary

Team Canada had something to prove after their humiliating 8–1 loss to the Soviet Union in Montreal in 1981. Glen Sather was at the helm of Team Canada, and his Oilers superstars were well represented. Team Canada avenged their loss to the Soviet Union with a 3–2 semifinal win in Calgary; then, in the best-of-three final, Team Canada defeated Sweden in two straight games to win its second Canada Cup.

Northlands produced and presented several major events every year, and I was responsible for marketing them. When I began my job, Northlands was in the midst of planning the Klondike Days Exposition, one of the major annual fairs on the Canadian circuit, along with the Calgary Stampede, the Canadian National Exhibition and the Royal Agricultural Winter Fair in Toronto, the Pacific National Exhibition in Vancouver and a few others across the country. Northlands also produced two major agricultural shows, one in early March, which featured a rodeo called Superodeo, and the other in November, called Farmfair, which featured the Canadian Finals Rodeo (CFR).

Northlands also licenced and rented the use of its many facilities for concerts, curling, trade and exhibit shows, social and community events and whatever else might prove suitable. And it managed and operated a racetrack. The Northlands complex was a vital community organization and entertainment centre, busy and active year round.

The Klondike Days Exposition was the biggest annual event on the calendar. A ten-day exposition and fair, it attracted around 600,000 patrons and was Northlands' biggest revenue generator. The whole organization worked on it, and my job was to co-ordinate all the different components into one successful event. It was exhausting, but it was the one I enjoyed most. The 1981 Klondike Days Exposition was selected as Major Fair of the Year by the Canadian Association of Exhibitions. So the effort was well worth it.

The Canadian Finals Rodeo brought together the top professional rodeo competitors in Canada for a year-end championship in the five primary disciplines: calf roping, steer wrestling, bareback riding, saddle-bronc riding and bull riding. Winners in each discipline qualified for the National Finals Rodeo in the US. There was a real grassroots cowboy culture in Alberta, and rodeo was a big business and a big attraction. Northlands held the rights to the CFR, and produced, staged and presented the event in conjunction with the Canadian Professional Rodeo Association who delivered the cowboys and the rodeo stock. I was strictly an event producer. I enjoyed dressing up and looking like a cowboy for a week, but I knew nothing about rodeo and was smart enough not to pretend to. For several years I sat on the CFR Commission to represent Northlands' interests. For one wild week, the cowboy culture took over the city.

In all the sports I've played and watched, pound for pound there is no tougher athlete than the rodeo cowboy, particularly those who compete in the bucking events. The most high profile of these is bull riding. If a cowboy draws an average animal it's almost impossible to win, even if he has a near perfect ride. And if he gets thrown in the dirt or trampled on, he just picks himself up, dusts himself off, licks his wounds and makes his way out of the arena. There's no griping or hot-dogging, just stoic acceptance until the next ride. Professional athletes in most of the major-league sports could learn something about real professionalism from the rodeo cowboy; they have my greatest respect as athletes. Rodeo is down-to-earth competition and entertainment and the personification of the cowboy way of life.

Concerts were another important revenue generator for Northlands. Before the Calgary Saddledome was built in 1983, the Coliseum was the only major-sized venue in Alberta. Major touring acts that played Los Angeles and San Francisco often ventured north to Vancouver; our challenge was to entice them to cross the Rockies and play Edmonton, which many people thought was in the middle of nowhere. But the Coliseum had good acoustics, delivered a well run venue and had more than fifteen thousand seats. After acts played the venue once, it was easy to get them back. The Coliseum hosted most of the top concert acts and celebrity performers in the late 1970s.

The major concert promoters in Canada at the time were Concert Productions International (Bill Ballard and Michael Cohl) out of Toronto, DKD (Donald Tarlton) out of Montreal and Perryscope (Norm Perry and Riley O'Connor) from Vancouver. While I was at Northlands, those three groups controlled most major concert tours in Canada. A few local and regional promoters also brought bands and acts to the Coliseum. It was a time when venue owners could make serious money. In fact, everyone made money (unlike today, when the performers walk out with their money in a wheelbarrow and the venue and the promoter have to fight over scraps). And in the process, Edmontonians were treated to some of the most popular entertainment available. I remember my first major concert at Northlands: ABBA started a North American tour in Edmonton. Rehearsals were closed. Naively, I wandered into the Coliseum during a rehearsal and sat about twenty rows back from the stage. Fortunately, I wasn't asked to leave. I enjoyed every second of the rehearsal and both sold-out performances.

Northlands had a long history with Stampede Wrestling, a regular event in the Edmonton Gardens on Saturday nights. Stu Hart of Calgary, patriarch of the first family of professional wrestling, controlled and ran wrestling in Alberta. Several of his sons, who started wrestling in places like Calgary, Red Deer and Edmonton, went on to stardom in the World Wrestling Federation (WWF). The most prominent was Bret "Hitman" Hart. Shortly after his father died, I met Bret and told how his dad and I used to sit together in the Gardens on many a Saturday night and settle up on the event after the show. Stu Hart and his sons were true legends in the professional wrestling world.

One of the most unusual attractions at Northlands was an amateur fight night, in conjunction with a boxing show in the Coliseum. Wannabe tough guys had a chance to see what they could do in the ring. It was generally pathetic. One guy was so inexperienced he got into the ring wearing contact lenses. No one knew it until he asked the referee to stop the fight while he adjusted them. The main attraction that filled the arena was a three-round exhibition bout between Dave Semenko, the Oilers' tough guy who protected Wayne Gretzky, and Muhammad Ali. Yes, Muhammad Ali! I met him in 1966 when he fought George Chuvalo in Maple Leaf Gardens. He watched one of our Leafs practices from the team bench, and every player wandered over at some point to say hello. In the mid-1980s, Ali was fighting in boxing exhibitions and somehow the promoter was able to get him to Edmonton. I was dumbfounded that such a respected boxer would agree to the event at Northlands. Semenko was a legitimate NHL tough guy, and had the physique to go with it. He handled himself very well and displayed real boxing skills—he even tried to take a few shots at Ali. He looked like the "great white hope" in the ring with the legendary Ali. It was a most entertaining three rounds, and Ali made sure everyone saw glimpses of his famous in-ring moves.

Edmonton was a terrific community and a good place to raise a family. After hockey, my life settled down. Working at Northlands had similarities to the hockey business, but I was out of the public eye. The regular work routine made me realize how much I had been missing in helping raise my son. Sean enjoyed sports, especially hockey. There was active minor hockey in Edmonton, and I was conscripted as an assistant coach for Sean's Riverbend teams at the mite, peewee and minor-bantam levels. In an effort to be fair to all the boys, I think I might have short-changed Sean. A kid once asked Sean if it was true his dad had once played in the NHL. Sean's classic response: "My dad played in the NHL so long ago, he played in black and white."

My approach as a coach was low key and low pressure. Everybody got on the ice when it was their turn, no matter the on-ice situation or the score. I made sure all the kids got to play, and emphasized having fun while they did it. Winning was not the primary goal; trying to win was. When kids are having fun playing the game, and with a little bit of structure, some discipline and a lot of encouragement, it's amazing how well they perform.

However, I can remember one occasion when my low-key approach maybe went a little too far. When the game started, I noticed there was a brown paper bag on top of our goal net. I didn't really think about it. That is, until the puck had been in the other team's end for some time, and then our opponents broke out of their end and were racing towards the Riverbend goal. I looked to see if our goalie was set for the attack. Not quite! Here he was right in the midst of the game, with his goalie gloves off and digging into the brown bag for a sandwich. How could you get mad at him?

Sean got an unexpected hockey treat on the Sunday evening of Thanksgiving weekend, when he was twelve or thirteen. Northlands held an exhibition tennis match that featured top professional players, including Bjorn Borg, Jimmy Connors and John McEnroe. Greg Thomlinson, the local ticket broker, called me at home early on Sunday, asking if I could help find an hour or so of available ice at a local rink for that evening. Bjorn Borg wanted to play hockey. A Swedish friend who was touring with him had played minor professional hockey in the Central Hockey League, and Bjorn had been an avid player as a youth. I helped Greg find the ice and thought that was the end of it.

Around dinnertime Greg called again. Would Sean and I like to join Bjorn, his friend, Greg and a few of his friends for a game of shinny at eight o'clock? So much for the Thanksgiving turkey! Sean had his hockey gear packed and was in the car before I had a chance to ask him if he wanted to go. Eight or ten players showed up. To our surprise, Bjorn was a very good hockey player, fit from his tennis, and he could skate like the wind. He was a sports superstar, but in the dressing room he was personable and friendly. We all enjoyed the experience, and Sean had an unbelievable story to tell his hockey pals at his next game.

—ᴍ—

In Edmonton, many neighbourhoods had their garages at the back of the house, with access from an alleyway. The garbage trucks also collected our garbage from the alley. One day, I picked up our garbage cans and noticed a tag on one of them—a ticket from the by-law enforcement department. Apparently, our garbage cans were not legal for use in Edmonton. This was a bit of red tape I'd never heard before.

More out of curiosity than anything, I contacted the by-law enforcement officer who issued the ticket and requested an on-site explanation of the violation. The next morning an officious-looking young man showed up in our alleyway. Our garbage cans had made several moves before travelling to Edmonton, and had handles that hung down when they were not in use. The young man said the handles were illegal; by-laws required handles that were fixed in position. If our garbage cans were not replaced before the next garbage pickup, there would be a substantial fine. Apparently, it was too difficult for the "sanitary engineers" to pick up garbage cans that didn't have the proper handles.

I headed off to work. Before he began work at Northlands, George Hughes had been high up in the City of Edmonton administration. I told him the story. We thought it was ridiculous and humorous. George called a contact at the newspaper who wrote a regular column on city issues. The reporter called me, we chatted briefly, and I suggested he contact Susan, who was miffed about the absurdity of the ticket and planned to fight it. He called Susan, and there was an article in the newspaper the next day. Susan pointed out that our garbage cans had been good enough in Ottawa, in Clinton, New York, in Indianapolis, Indiana and a few other places, and she couldn't understand why they weren't good enough for Edmonton: "I have the best cans in the alley!" In spite of the focus of the article being on how Edmonton had recently gone by-law berserk, Susan was kidded about her "best cans" quote until the day we left Edmonton. But the ticket was cancelled and the garbage cans deemed acceptable.

—m—

In early fall 1984, I was invited to visit the Royal Agricultural Winter Fair (Royal) in Toronto, which was held a few days after our Farmfair.

The Royal was the largest annual indoor agricultural and livestock fair in the world, and I wanted to get some ideas about how Northlands could improve its events.

As I was making my travel plans, I heard about a new major trade centre/arena under construction in Hamilton, Ontario. On the last day of my trip, I drove to Hamilton and toured the building site. Afterwards, John Crane, the city's project manager, took me to City Hall to meet Lou Sage, chief administrative officer for the City of Hamilton. Lou had lots of questions about the building, operations and management of the new facility. After the visit, I returned to Edmonton.

About a week later, Lou Sage called. The city already owned Hamilton Place Theatre and the Hamilton Convention Centre, both within a block of the new trade centre/arena. Each had a separate volunteer board of directors. Instead of creating a new board, the city planned to amalgamate the three complexes under one large organization called Hamilton Entertainment and Convention Facilities Inc., HECFI as it would become known. He wondered if I was interested in becoming HECFI's first managing director and chief executive officer.

I hadn't been thinking about leaving Edmonton. My family was well settled, and I liked working for Northlands. However, how many times would I get a chance to be part of a brand-new major arena project? Particularly in Canada? The position was a big step up the managerial ladder, and I didn't foresee a comparable opportunity on the horizon in Edmonton. Susan and I had mixed emotions about the offer. It was a rare opportunity and also very attractive financially. But we both liked Edmonton and our many friends there. After seven years, it was difficult to contemplate uprooting ourselves. One key factor in the decision was Sean's situation. He turned fourteen in the summer of 1984, and his schooling was a priority for us all. In the spring Sean had taken the entrance qualification exam for the private boys' school I had gone to in Toronto, Upper Canada College (UCC). He'd been accepted into Grade 9. As our only child, Susan and I had mixed feelings about Sean leaving home to go to a boarding school. However, I'd gone there, Susan's father and brothers had gone there, and my brothers and nephews had gone there. We let Sean decide if he wanted to go to UCC. At his age, moving was a very delicate issue, and not one Susan and I would push. If he wanted to go, fine; if he wanted to stay in Edmonton, even better. After about a month of silence on the issue, Sean announced he'd like to go to UCC.

And as fate would have it, only a few months later we were given an opportunity to reunite the Conacher family in the Toronto–Hamilton area. In December, I gave my notice to Northlands, to begin my life as a managing director and a chief executive officer at the beginning of January 1985. It was with real angst that I left Northlands. I had been there for five and a half years and enjoyed the people I worked with and the work we did. Without the experience I gained at Northlands, I would not have been qualified for the position in Hamilton. Susan and I bid a fond farewell to our friends, neighbours and colleagues. We keep in touch with many of them to this day.

Hamilton and the NHL

I STARTED my new job in Hamilton on January 2, 1985. Susan stayed in Edmonton, making plans to move once we found a place to live. In the interim, I stayed with my oldest brother, Lionel, who lived nearby. Susan joined me in our new house in early March; Sean was in boarding school at UCC.

The new facility in Hamilton was the fruition of a dream: in the early 1970s, Vic Copps, a former mayor, envisioned the major-league arena and pushed for it so Hamilton could get a WHA franchise. Without the arena, Hamilton lost out; the WHA franchise went to Ottawa. A decade later, Hamilton was getting its trade centre/arena complex.

The city thought it made good sense for one entity to oversee its three major entertainment and convention facilities. I agreed. Not everyone did: some people, including a few who had been on the volunteer boards, weren't pleased about the amalgamation into one "super board." And here I was the first managing director and chief executive officer of the Hamilton Entertainment and Convention Facilities Inc. (HECFI). I didn't inherit a job or take over from someone else. I had to create and define my job where none had existed before. It was a unique opportunity. But who was this former hockey player, and what qualifications did he have for the job? Good questions. I planned to answer the critics and skeptics by doing, not by talking. My primary mandate was to co-ordinate the operations of the three facilities and to look for ways to make the overall organization more effective and efficient for the benefit of the city. I rolled up my sleeves to tackle the new and exciting challenge, one that would test all my management skills.

David Braley, politically connected and a very successful local businessman, was appointed by the city as the first HECFI chairperson. New boys to the city committee structures, we struck up a good working relationship from day one. We were working in a politically charged environment that attracted a lot of local media attention, but David said he would chair HECFI as a businessman and not as a political animal or a pawn. And he was as good as his word. He supported me one-hundred percent in every decision I made, and successfully controlled his board and the politicians, insulating me from their interference during his entire two-year term.

Initially, I shared an office with John Crane, the project coordinator and general manager of the new trade centre/arena, which was still under construction. John worked closely with the architects, engineers and construction personnel and had set up a small staff to begin marketing events. The facility was scheduled to open in November 1985. That was just eleven months away, and there was a lot to do to be ready.

The best use of my time in the short term was to assist John in getting the project built, opened and operating. John had excellent operations skills, but limited experience in marketing the kinds of events that would take place in the new building. I focused in on planning for when the facility was open for business. It was the biggest project any of us had ever worked on, and every day we made many important decisions. It was very much a team approach.

One of the first issues we had to resolve was what to call the trade centre/arena. It didn't take long to decide. Vic Copps had been one of the most successful and long-serving mayors in the history of Hamilton. And he had been pushing for an arena since the early 1970s. Unfortunately his health did not allow him to participate in the building that would bear his name: the Victor K. Copps Trade Centre/Arena. Quite a mouthful. It needed a shorter and punchier working name. Many suggestions were made, and Copps Coliseum was chosen, the Coliseum, for short.

The broadcast team for the 1972 Canada-Soviet Hockey Series. It's a little-known fact that I did the colour commentary for the historic Series, alongside Foster Hewitt's play-by-play. I am in the centre of the back row, fourth from right with the glasses; Foster is in the front row centre, fifth from right .

The Mohawk Valley Comets, 1975-76. When I hung up my skates, I took the job of coach and general manager with the NAHL team based in Clinton, New York. Idealistic and full of ideas of how I wanted to run the team, I soon learned the harsh realities of life in the minor leagues. I'm in the front row, fourth from left.

The new General Manager on the cover of the
Mohawk Valley Comets program, December 30,
1975, edition. Not only did I have to coach and
manage the team, I also had to sell advertising in
the program, act as the team's collections agent,
and even drive the Zamboni.

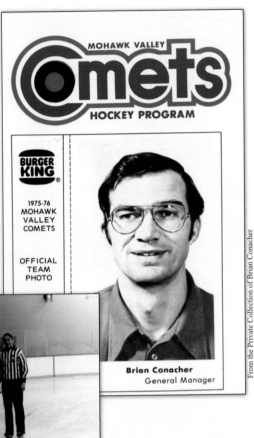

MOHAWK VALLEY

Comets

HOCKEY PROGRAM

BURGER KING®

1975-76
MOHAWK
VALLEY
COMETS

OFFICIAL
TEAM
PHOTO

Brian Conacher
General Manager

In the movies. In 1976, the movie *Slap Shot*—based on minor-
league life in the NAHL, and our rivals, the Johnstown Jets in
particular—was shot close by in the Syracuse Memorial Auditorium.
Recruiting any hockey talent they could find in the Mohawk Valley,
they cast me (centre) as an official, but I ended up on the cutting
room floor.

Paul Newman, who starred as player/
coach of the Charlestown Chiefs, Reggie
Dunlop, on the set of the *Slap Shot* movie
shoot, June 1976.

Farewell to the Mohawk Valley Comets, November 1976. Left to right: Brian, Sean Conacher, aged 6, Mike Dyer (fan club rep), Vic Ehre (head of the ownership group), Bill Shaut (game announcer), Kerry Bond.

At 1975 Indianapolis Racers training camp. Left to right: Ted McCaskill (coach of the Mohawk Valley Comets), Jacques Demers (coach of the Indianapolis Racers), Brian Conacher (Comets' general manager), Jim Browitt (general manager of the Racers).

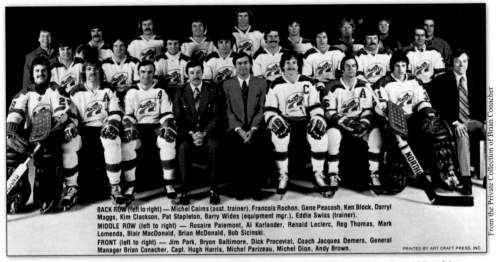

BACK ROW (left to right) — Michel Cairns (asst. trainer), Francois Rochon, Gene Peacosh, Ken Block, Darryl Maggs, Kim Clackson, Pat Stapleton, Barry Wides (equipment mgr.), Eddie Swiss (trainer).
MIDDLE ROW (left to right) — Rosaire Paiement, Al Karlander, Renald Leclerc, Reg Thomas, Mark Lomenda, Blair MacDonald, Brian McDonald, Bob Sicinski.
FRONT (left to right) — Jim Park, Bryon Baltimore, Dick Proceviat, Coach Jacques Demers, General Manager Brian Conacher, Capt. Hugh Harris, Michel Parizeau, Michel Dion, Andy Brown.

PRINTED BY ART CRAFT PRESS. INC.

The Indianapolis Racers, 1976-77. I was the team's general manager that year. I'm seated in the middle of the front row wearing the red jacket.

Doing colour commentary during the hockey broadcasts at the 1976 Olympic Winter Games in Innsbruck, Austria. Along with play-by-play announcer Curt Gowdy, I was part of the ABC Sports broadcast team. My brother-in-law took this photo of the actual picture on the TV back home.

The entire ABC broadcast team at the 1976 Olympic Winter Games in Innsbruck, Austria. I am way in the back row at right.

With Fred Walker (right) at the 1988 Olympic Winter Games, Calgary. Together we provided the hockey coverage for CBC's radio broadcasts of the Games.

In 1977 I joined the Edmonton Oilers, then of the WHA, as the team's general manager. The three suits in the middle of the front row are owner Peter Pocklington in the centre with Glen Sather (director of hockey/coach) on his left and me on his right.

As part of my life outside of hockey, I spent three years as CEO of the Royal Agricultural Winter Fair. At the 1991 gala, I had the pleasure of touring Sarah Ferguson, then The Duchess of York, around the fair. Left to right: A lady-in-waiting to The Duchess, Hilary Weston, my wife Susan, Galen Weston, The Duchess of York, Brian Conacher, Security.

In 1992 I became the vice-president of building operations for Maple Leaf Gardens, and managed the entire facility until 1998. At my farewell party in January 1998, pictured with the Board of Directors in the Director's Lounge of the Gardens. Left to right: Ted Nickolaou, Donald Crump, Larry Tanenbaum, Chris Dundas, Brian Bellmore, Terry Kelly, Brian Conacher, Susan Conacher, Steve Stavro, Claude Lamoureux.

The 1997-98 Varsity hockey team of Upper Canada College. I had been on UCC's varsity team myself in the late 1950s and I returned to help coach the team when my son Sean was at the school. I was an assistant coach, pictured in the second row, second from right. The 13 years I spent coaching high-school hockey were the happiest and most satisfying I spent in my 55 years in and around the game.

All of us involved with the Coliseum project worked flat out to get the facility ready to open. Everyone in Hamilton realized the Coliseum was going to be good for the city, and all supported the project. There were many tough decisions to make and many long days and sleepless nights for several months, but the adrenalin flowed and everyone knew we were part of making something happen in Hamilton that was very special and significant. We were all motivated to give the extra effort to achieve our common goal.

The Coliseum was not completely finished by opening day—some of the trade and exhibit spaces surrounding the arena were still under construction—but the arena itself was ready to open for business. After a formal official opening, at which Geraldine Copps represented her husband, the Coliseum hosted its first event: an NHL Oldtimers hockey game featuring former NHLers who had played for the major junior Hamilton Red Wings or the St. Catharines Black Hawks, followed by a reception and tours of the facility. We considered opening with a major concert, but there were huge risks in such a commitment, and we chose to have what is known as a "soft opening." The hockey game worked well, though at the last moment, the oldtimers were short a few players, and I ended up playing. It was a fun game, and a thrill to be one of the first people to skate on ice in an arena I had been a part of building.

Copps Coliseum opened on time and under budget (we spent approximately $40 million of the budgeted $42.7 million). I was determined to meet this first financial test in Hamilton. We kept the extra $2.7 million available for finishing the trade and exhibit space and to make any adjustments the new building needed.

Generally an excellent and functional facility, Copps Coliseum was quickly dubbed a "blue collar" arena by many in the major-league hockey business because it had a limited number of private suites and lacked some of the bells and whistles of other new arenas. The Coliseum was a single mid-concourse facility, with lower and upper deck seating. It could seat more than 17,000, so it qualified as a potential NHL arena. It also had the capability to expand its ice pad to the larger international ice size, approximately twelve feet wider.

The original plans had not included any private suites. The new generation of major-league hockey arenas in North America included as many private suites as possible, to attract corporate sponsorship and financing. I emphasized their importance in achieving the goal of attracting a NHL franchise and we were able to add ten suites to the original plan; they were between the goal lines at the top of the lower seating area. They were ideally located and excellent; there should have been many more of them, but we had no more room.

Another oversight I noticed the day I came to tour the facility in the fall of 1984. The sightlines from the lower seating area were as good as any I'd ever seen. But when I stood on the newly poured concrete platforms for the upper deck, I noticed that patrons on the sides might not be able to see all the hockey action. The pitch of the upper deck wasn't steep enough. And when the mandatory railings were installed in front of each row of seats, patrons had to lean forward to see the action near the boards on their side of the rink. And that was for a game using the standard-sized ice pad; what would the sightlines be like when the ice pad was expanded for international hockey? I pointed out this design concern, but it was too late to correct it. Generally the Coliseum had good sightlines, although not every spectator could easily see all the hockey action all the time. Compromises like this sometimes happen in a design when the mandate is to cram as many seats as possible into a building on a relatively small and limiting footprint, as was the case with the Coliseum.

The Coliseum was built as a multi-use sports, entertainment, trade and exhibit show venue, but the city wanted hockey to be one of its main uses. So it was a real coup when we negotiated to host the 1986 World Junior Hockey Championship as our first major event. It was a marketing and promotional opportunity to show the new Coliseum and Hamilton to Canada and the world.

Eight games of the tournament would be played in the Coliseum, the first on Boxing Day, 1985 and the last on January 4, 1986. The games played in the Coliseum were a huge success. The Championship gave hockey in the Coliseum an impressive start and was a great morale boost for Hamilton. It was the best attended and most financially successful World Junior Hockey Championship so far.

One of the main reasons I had been hired as managing director was my hockey background. And one of the main reasons for building the Coliseum was the hope the NHL would consider a franchise for Hamilton. Bob Morrow was the mayor, and one of his top priorities was to attract an NHL team. I was confidant Copps Coliseum and the city could be a viable host, given the opportunity. At my first HECFI board meeting, I circulated a memo for discussion on my recommended approach to negotiating with teams who might want to use the Coliseum. There was a steep learning curve for most on the HECFI board members, including the mayor, about what the NHL or one of its franchises would expect from a host city. Hamilton seemed prepared to promise anything to entice an NHL team; part of my job was to protect the city. Some didn't like what I had to say.

The first serious nibble came in mid-March. The mayor and I met Bill Ballard and Michael Cohl of Concert Productions International (CPI). Bill's father, Harold, ran Maple Leaf Gardens and the Leafs, and also owned the Hamilton Tiger Cats of the Canadian Football League (CFL). Bill and Michael ran a very successful concert-entertainment business, but also had aspirations to get into NHL hockey. There were rumours that the Pittsburgh Penguins might move after several years of heavy financial losses. They struggled in Pittsburgh and were looking not only to relocate, but wanted to bring in some fresh local money. Ballard and Cohl thought they might be able to get the franchise and transfer it to Hamilton—if they could get the right deal from the Coliseum.

Mayor Morrow excused himself, leaving me to discuss the possibility with Michael and Bill. My concept of a deal wasn't even considered before Michael made his counter-proposal. Michael Cohl is one of the sharpest people with numbers I have ever dealt with, and I listened in awe as he spun his financial picture of how the franchise would work. The city, HECFI and Copps Coliseum would relinquish control of most revenue sources—ticketing, food and beverage, souvenir and novelty merchandise, arena dasher boards, and scoreboard and clock display advertising. Also, CPI would hold the "exclusive" rights to provide concerts and other entertainments in the Coliseum. Bill seemed confident he could make a deal with his father so a Hamilton NHL team could encroach on the Leafs' territorial rights in southern Ontario.

On the surface, it looked like they just might be able to deliver. But at what price? Bill and Michael wanted control of all the revenue-generating areas in a facility they didn't own and for which they had paid nothing—Copps Coliseum was a public facility, built with public money—and they were prepared to share costs only while they used it. It was a sweetheart deal for them. In exchange, Hamilton would be able to say it had an NHL team.

Dialogue continued for about a month, and David Braley, chair of HECFI, joined me for the negotiations. By early June, both sides moved a bit, but it was evident that the city practically or politically couldn't give away use of the Coliseum, no matter how badly it wanted an NHL franchise. Hamilton had a $40 million building to pay for, and it needed paid use of the Coliseum to do so. At the same time, the city of Pittsburgh suddenly realized it could lose its Penguins, and rallied around the franchise and saved it.

HECFI entertained inquiries from a few other NHL franchises. I wasn't sure whether the NHL knew or approved of franchises threatening to relocate, but it certainly seemed to be a common happening at the time. For example, Dr. John McMullen, the principal owner of the New Jersey Devils, contacted Braley, and we prepared a proposal for him. The Devils were struggling with their landlord; when the locals realized they could lose their team, the Devils were able to negotiate a better deal at the Meadowlands. At least Dr. McMullen was honourable enough to admit he had used the Coliseum as a pawn in his efforts to get a better deal in New Jersey. And he said he'd vote for a franchise in Hamilton if it ever came before the NHL expansion committee.

Other inquiries came in over the months. Harry Ornest, originally from Edmonton, was the principal owner of the St. Louis Blues. Discussions with him never got serious because it was evident early on that Ornest was using the Coliseum as a pawn in his negotiations for a new lease. Unfortunately, Hamilton had to go along with being used as a pawn in someone else's game in the long-shot hope that one of these teams might move to Hamilton. Even the Winnipeg Jets explored the possibly of relocating to Hamilton, primarily because of the better facility. But one Canadian city taking another's NHL franchise was too politically charged, and the discussions with the Jets never were serious.

We hoped the success of the 1986 World Junior Hockey Championship would put the Coliseum and Hamilton on the NHL's radar screen as a potentially good Canadian hockey market. A lot of people thought the Toronto Maple Leafs would never let Hamilton have an NHL franchise. But our experience with Bill Ballard suggested otherwise. And I didn't think Harold Ballard would stand in the way of Hamilton getting a franchise. As the owner of the Hamilton Tiger Cats, he had a good relationship with the city and its officials. We felt his concerns could be solved with money. And a team in Hamilton wouldn't affect the Leafs—their games were always sold out. People in the Golden Horseshoe would provide the support for a new franchise.

I thought the main opposition to another NHL franchise in the area came from the Buffalo Sabres. Because the Leafs games were sold out, some three thousand Canadian fans in the Golden Horseshoe bought season-tickets for the Sabres' games. Without the Canadian fans, the Sabres would be in trouble. And television broadcast rights were and probably still are the biggest issue.

Hamilton had a young entrepreneurial hockey-enthusiast promoter named Russ Boychuck, who in 1986 arranged a pre-season game in the Coliseum between the Boston Bruins and the Washington Capitals. A huge crowd came to see the first NHL game played in Hamilton since 1925, when the Hamilton Tigers were part of the NHL. (In September 1988, Russ put together a second pre-season game between the Bruins and the New York Islanders. Again there was a very good crowd.) But the NHL continued to ignore Hamilton as a prospective franchise location.

After several futile efforts to get the NHL's attention, on October 15, 1986, I sent a letter to NHL president John Ziegler. I outlined a plan for the realignment of the NHL that would include Hamilton and that took into account the concerns of some American owners about Canadian teams that were "bad draws."

My proposed reconfigured league had two conferences: Canadian and American. The Canadian conference had eight teams: Quebec City, Montreal, Toronto, Hamilton, Winnipeg, Calgary, Edmonton and Vancouver. They would be divided into two divisions, determined by geography for travel considerations and team rivalries. The eastern division would include Quebec City, Montreal, Toronto and Hamilton. The western division would include Winnipeg, Calgary, Edmonton and Vancouver. The American conference would have sixteen teams and two or four divisions, again determined by geography for travel considerations and team rivalries.

The majority of games would be within a division, then within a conference, and then between different conferences. The playoff format would determine a winner from each of the Canadian and American conferences; these two teams would play each other for the Stanley Cup, the symbol of supremacy in North American professional hockey, which in reality is what it has become. In the scheme's ultimate progression, the Stanley Cup champions would play the winner of the European hockey championships for the real World Cup championship.

Ziegler responded on October 23, 1986. And what a response! I certainly got his attention. He was incensed that I was presumptuous enough to suggest how the NHL might be better set up. His letter began: "I am offended and disturbed by your letter of October 15, 1986." And it got worse from there. The primary purpose of my proposal was to get Hamilton included in the NHL; and it might still be a better set up than currently exists where several franchises continue to struggle to survive. Unfortunately, his response confirmed that Hamilton wasn't on the NHL's radar screen, and chances of being part of a future NHL seemed remote.

After I left HECFI, Hamilton supported another bid when the NHL expanded by two teams in 1990. Ron Joyce, the head of Tim Hortons, was one of the principals in the group; the bid looked promising. Hamilton was in competition with Ottawa for the Canadian location. Ottawa was prepared to pay the $50 million expansion fee all at once; Hamilton wanted terms as additional funds would be needed to pay Harold Ballard for infringement of his territorial rights. The NHL grabbed the full payment, and Ottawa dug itself into a deep financial hole from which it was not able to climb out of for years. Behind the scenes, it was inferred that Buffalo lobbied against Hamilton, and when Hamilton sought payment terms, it gave the NHL a way out. After the failed bid, it seemed that Hamilton got farther and farther away from ever getting an NHL franchise.

—∞—

Meanwhile, there was a very attractive second option. Major junior hockey was rapidly expanding across Canada, and the Ontario Hockey League (OHL) was always looking for good expansion cities. Hamilton had a strong history with major junior hockey, first with the Hamilton Red Wings and later with the Hamilton Fincups.

Under local ownership and management, the Hamilton Steelhawks made the Coliseum their home arena in early 1986. For the next couple of seasons, the Steelhawks played in the cavernous Coliseum, but it was a huge facility to fill. The team had decent crowds by major junior standards, but neither the Steehawks nor the Coliseum was making any money.

Most major junior hockey teams across Canada had one persistent problem: there was too much fighting and uncontrolled violence in the games. I attended a game with John Crane, and during a bench-clearing brawl on the ice, John ordered the lights turned off so officials and police could stop the on-ice craziness. It wasn't hockey; just a gang of rambunctious and undisciplined teens out of control. Hockey fans in Hamilton had seen the quality of play in Canada Cup games and weren't interested in the Steelhawks' violent style of play.

By early August 1988, in spite of a lot of political pressure to keep the Steelhawks in the Coliseum, they moved to Niagara Falls. Shortly after they left, I was approached by a local lawyer, Jack Pelech, who wanted to put another major junior franchise in the Coliseum. And to emphasize how small the hockey community really was, Jack and his group were negotiating with Harold Ballard, owner of the Toronto

Marlboros, my former major junior team. The Marlies had been in-operative for several years, and Jack and his group wanted to buy the franchise rights from Ballard and move the team to Hamilton. Discussion continued after I left HECFI and a deal was done. The Pelech group bought the franchise, but Ballard retained the rights to the names Marlboros and Marlies. They called the team the Hamilton Dukes and commenced play in the 1989–90 season. They too struggled in the Coliseum. It seemed Hamiltonians wanted the NHL or nothing.

—⁓—

Early in 1987, I received a call from Al Eagleson. There were plans for another Canada Cup tournament, with the same six teams as in 1984. Al was considering some games for the Coliseum. I thought, here we go again. The big advantage the HECFI/Copps Coliseum had in the negotiations was that Harold Ballard wouldn't let the tournament use Maple Leaf Gardens and Eagleson wanted to keep most of the games in Eastern Canada. I had experience with Al, so he knew what to expect. And the Coliseum was the ideal arena in the perfect location to expect good crowds.

The Coliseum would host nine games: two pre-tournament games, four round-robin games, one semi-final and the last two games of the best-of-three final. One key factor in the negotiations was to find the best game match-ups so all games would be well supported.

Generally, Canadian fans wanted only to watch games involving Team Canada, often ignoring many other of the necessary games that are required in an international tournament set up like the Canada Cup. In spite of many of these games being excellent hockey, the round-robin segment of a tournament was a hard sell. Eagleson put together a few different packages so fans who wanted to see more popular games had to buy tickets to less popular draws, as well. And if there were a Canada–Soviet final, we could probably sell 50,000 tickets. Unfortunately, Team Canada couldn't be in all the games.

I pointed out to Al that we could use the Coliseum's international-sized ice pad. Eagleson's reply: "No way!" He didn't want to give the international players an advantage on the larger ice surface, and (more important) he didn't want to sacrifice two rows of premium rinkside seats.

The first game of the tournament was scheduled for Sunday, August 30. At the end of the previous hockey season, the whole ice pad had been removed to repair several leaks in the under-ice plastic piping. When the ice pad was torn up, it was found that the plastic piping was defective, and we had to replace all of it. We were worried about getting the job finished in time, but as it turned out it was not a problem.

Then, early on Friday afternoon, two days before our first Canada Cup game, I got a call from the Coliseum's chief engineer, as Crane was not available. The refrigeration system for the ice was failing, and he hadn't yet found the cause. I was in a panic! The weather was hot and humid, so to keep a good sheet of ice in the Coliseum was already stressing the refrigeration system to the maximum, even when operating at top efficiency. We had to find the source of the problem, and quickly. The chief engineer called again to say he had found a leak in the refrigerant. Excessive frost build-up at a connection on the main header pipe caused a fitting to rupture. This was not just a little leak. There were many kilometres of plastic piping in the floor making up the refrigeration grid filled with thousands of litres of glycol (like the coolant in a car). Thousands of those litres had leaked into the header trench and gone down the drain. The system needed to be recharged as soon as possible, hopefully before the ice melted. We first needed to repair the pipe fitting, and then we needed several thousand litres of glycol—delivered immediately, late on a Friday, late in the summer. Time was of the essence; it was a race to get the system back on line, as the ice was literally melting before our eyes. And if it melted to the point where the ice markings started to run and the bond with the concrete floor was broken, we would have a major task to restore the sheet of ice in time for the first Canada Cup game that was less than forty-eight hours away. It was real crisis management.

After a very anxious and stressful weekend, the doors opened for the Coliseum's first tournament game of the 1987 Canada Cup; the hockey fans never knew how close the game came to being cancelled. The game started on time and ushered in probably the most exciting hockey ever played in the Coliseum.

Team Canada faced some roster challenges even before the tournament began. A few key players chose not to play and a few suffered injuries and were unable to play. Wayne Gretzky was a doubtful during the early summer, but finally committed. With Wayne and Mario Lemieux in their prime, with a good supporting cast backed by solid goaltending, Team Canada headed into the tournament confident of giving a good showing. But they were far from being favoured to repeat their 1984 victory. In the interim, several other national teams had made huge strides and were expected to give Team Canada all they could handle. Both the Soviets and Sweden looked strong; in fact, every team was competitive, and if not capable of winning, certainly able to cause an upset. It was going to be a close contest.

Team Canada had opened the tournament in Calgary on August 28 in a game against Czechoslovakia that ended in a 4–4 tie. It was a shaky start for Team Canada, who had been saved by the outstanding goaltending of Grant Fuhr.

Team Canada's first game in the Coliseum was against Finland. The modest crowd—9,000 —was a result of buyer resistance to Eagleson's ticket packages. Fans did not want to pay for games that didn't interest them. I discussed the ticket packages with Eagleson when advance sales were low; he decided to make available last-minute single-game tickets. My concern was that people who had bought a package could ask for refunds when they found out other patrons were buying single tickets at the last moment. Also, the Copps Coliseum box office was not set up to deal with a large walk-up crowd.

The Canada–Finland game was a wonderful opportunity to showcase the Coliseum for people who wouldn't normally make the trip to Hamilton. People from Toronto were duly impressed with the arena, particularly when they compared it to the much older Maple Leaf Gardens. And Team Canada jumped out to a quick 2–0 lead and went on to win handily 4–1.

At the gate, the tournament was off to a slow start: the next day, the US played Sweden, and there were fewer than 4,000 spectators.

Sweden had started the tournament in Calgary on August 29 with an impressive 5–3 win over the Soviets. The US handled Sweden easily, winning 5–2. I attended the game and realized it was shaping up to be a very close tournament.

Team Canada met the US on September 2. After two disappointing crowds, the Coliseum was sold out, a relief to both Eagleson and me. It was a hard-fought and closely contested game, but Canada hung on to win 3–2. Then, on September 6, Team Canada faced the Soviets before another sold-out crowd. Canada needed a third-period goal by Wayne Gretzky to earn a 3–3 tie. At the end of the round robin, Team Canada was in first place with three wins and two ties.

For the first game of the semifinals, the Soviets played Sweden in the Coliseum on September 8. To my amazement, only 7,000 fans attended, possibly because it was Labour Day. I enjoyed watching the game, which turned out to be an exceptional contest. And, to my surprise, seated directly in front of me was Father Bauer. I hadn't seen him for a while and the visit was as memorable as the game. The Soviets won 4–2, which gave them a place in the final. The other semifinal was in the Montreal Forum; Team Canada played Czechoslovakia. I watched it on television. The Czechoslovakians had a 2–0 lead in the first period, but Team Canada came back for a 5–3 victory and a berth in the final against their archrivals, the Soviets.

The final was a best-of-three series with the first game in Montreal and the second and third games (if needed) in Hamilton. The final series was to stir memories of the 1972 Canada–Soviet Hockey Series. It was a match-up of the top rivalry in international hockey, and a chance for the Soviets to redeem themselves after their loss in 1972. Everyone expected the series to be some of the best international hockey ever played. And they weren't disappointed!

Game One in Montreal set the tone. Team Canada was down 4–1 until late in the second period, when Ray Bourque scored on a power play. In the third period, three successive goals, the last by Wayne Gretzky, gave Team Canada a 5–4 lead with less than three minutes left in regulation time. But just thirty-two seconds later, the Soviets tied it up to send the game into sudden-death overtime. And five minutes into the overtime, the Soviets broke Team Canada's heart and stole the first game 6–5.

The teams headed to Hamilton to decide the 1987 Canada Cup winner. And as anticipated, the demand for tickets was overwhelming; I got calls from people I hadn't talked to for years. It was the hottest ticket in town. One call I was pleased to take was from Tom Berry, Jr., the former Indianapolis Racers owner. Susan and I had kept in touch with Tom and Maripat, and I was pleased to invite them to join us for the game.

Game Two had all the tension and suspense of the last games in 1972. The Coliseum was packed. Again, Team Canada had to win to stay alive. With several injured players, they had their backs to the wall against the Soviets, who were confident and relaxed. Backstopped by Grant Fuhr and with aggressive defensive play led by Mark Messier, Team Canada was up 3–1 at the end of the first period. At the end of the second period, Team Canada had a very fragile 4–3 lead. Gretzky and Lemieux were in an offensive zone and responded to every score by the Soviets. The game couldn't have been closer. Late in the third period, Canada couldn't hang on to a 5–4 lead and the Soviets tied the game to end regulation time.

For the second game in a row, Team Canada had let the Soviets force them into overtime. They were not only faced with overtime again, but the potential loss of the Canada Cup. In by now what was a hot and sweaty arena, the first twenty-minute overtime period decided nothing. It was after midnight, and the two teams still raced up and down the ice in desperate pursuit of that one last goal. And just past the halfway point of the second sudden-death overtime, Gretzky set up Lemieux for his third goal to give an exhausted but jubilant Team Canada 6–5 victory. The game had lasted four hours and fourteen minutes. After his five assists performance, Gretzky would remember it as one of his best games ever, and Lemieux was playing his best hockey.

One game to go. The first two games were dead-heats and decided nothing. On September 15, the Coliseum was again jammed to capacity for the final game between Team Canada and the Soviets. The drama rivaled the last game in Moscow in 1972. And we truly could have sold 50,000 tickets to the game, or even more.

When Team Canada took to the ice, the ovation was deafening, and it lasted until after the first faceoff. The fan support couldn't do anything but help the tired and depleted Team Canada roster. Everyone knew they were attending something special. But the Soviets scored and quickly had a commanding 3–0 lead. But a 3–0 lead is a dangerous one in hockey; it's difficult not to let the thought into your head that the game is over. And when Team Canada finally got going and made it 3–1, then 3–2, the momentum shift was difficult for the Soviets to stop. At the end of the first period the Soviets led 4–2, but everyone knew the game was a long way from over.

Team Canada dominated the second period, scoring three unanswered goals to give them their first lead in the game at 5–4. The third period was one of the most dramatic and memorable in Canadian hockey history. Team Canada protected a one-goal lead, but couldn't hang on and the Soviets tied the game at 5–5. Hard to believe, but Canada found itself in exactly the same position it had been in the previous two games. And then, with just over a minute and a half left in regulation time, Team Canada broke out of its zone and headed up ice. And who better to be leading the rush than Wayne Gretzky coming down the left side? He crossed the blue line with Mario Lemieux and Larry Murphy trailing. Murphy started to drive for the net to receive what would for most have been the logical play, but Gretzky held onto the puck momentarily before electing to make a drop pass to Mario coming late at the top of the face-off circle. With the coolness and poise of a surgeon, Lemieux aimed and fired a rocket into the top of the Soviet net, as possibly only he could have done. Gretzky knew! It was a goal that rivalled Paul Henderson's.

The Coliseum went crazy. But there was still a minute and a half remaining in regulation time. I'm sure every Team Canada player remembered what had happened twice before. However, not that night. The ecstatic crowd stood and counted down the final seconds, and Team Canada won 6–5. We had just witnessed some of the most nerve-wracking and exciting hockey imaginable, maybe the best three-game international series ever played. And coincidentally, all three games were settled at 6–5, the same as the final game of the 1972 Canada–Soviet Hockey Series.

There was sheer delirium as fans poured out of the Coliseum. You'd have thought Hamilton had just won the Canada Cup. Even people who weren't at the game but had seen it on television or heard it on the radio were on the streets or honking their car horns in celebration. A post-game party was held in the Hamilton Convention Centre for the team, tournament officials and as many people as could get in. Susan and I and the Berrys joined in the festivities. At the party, I noticed a young and very attractive young lady standing alone and somewhat at a loss as fans cheered their heroes. I recognized her from her 1984 role in *The Flamingo Kid*. Strikingly dressed in black leather was Janet Jones, the future Mrs. Gretzky. Her presence in Hamilton put truth to the rumours Wayne was seeing her.

Hosting nine games of the 1987 Canada Cup was a sports highlight for Hamilton, and although only the host city, the whole community felt good about itself. It had been hockey at its best. The games attracted more than 100,000 people, many of them visiting the Coliseum and Hamilton for the first time. It was the greatest promotion Hamilton could have hoped for.

A few months later, I received a call from CBC Radio Sports. The 1988 Olympic Winter Games would be held in Calgary from February 13 to 28. Was I available to do the colour commentary for their radio hockey coverage? Fred Walker was handling the play-by-play. I had done no sports broadcasting since the last WHA game in 1979, but I was interested: it would be my third Olympic Winter Games, and Canada was the host nation. I accepted and booked a couple of weeks' vacation.

I had never worked in radio, but I immediately liked it. Your words had to paint a verbal picture without any visual support. It was less complicated and less structured than television, and offered me more flexibility. And I knew I'd look better on radio. I was excited about the trip.

For the first time, the IIHF allowed professionals, including current NHLers, and there would be no retreat from that position as there had been in 1970. But the NHL was reluctant to release its top players or disrupt its schedule for the Olympics, so Team Canada was a hodgepodge of the best available players, mostly fringe NHLers and hopefuls. The Soviets, Finland and Sweden were the teams to beat for the medals. It was a shame that with hockey being such a high-profile sport and Canada as the host nation, that we weren't represented by the strongest team possible. But the NHL had yet to really buy into the Olympics as a premiere hockey showcase.

Live on the radio, Fred and I covered five games in the preliminary round. Team Canada got a real scare in their first game when they squeezed by the feisty Polish team by the slimmest of margins, 1–0. After the shaky start, the team improved its play and qualified for the medal round. They tied with Sweden and Finland for first place in their group.

The Soviets clobbered Team Canada 5–0 in the first game of the medal round, and even after an impressive 6–3 win over Czechoslovakia, Canada was behind the Soviets, Finland and Sweden in the overall points standings. We were out of the medals and had to settle for a disappointing and embarrassing fourth-place finish.

My most memorable interview of the hockey coverage was with Father Bauer, who still sat on the board of Hockey Canada and had attended some of the games. Alan Clark, head of CBC Radio Sports, became aware that Father Bauer was available, and knowing of my history with him was anxious for me to set up an interview. Because radio could be so informal, it was like a fireside chat. Father Bauer and I reminisced like old friends who hadn't seen each other for awhile. We talked about how far Canada's national hockey program had come since 1963, when he formed the first team. And the truth was, not very far. That year's Team Canada faced many of the issues and challenges the first team had struggled with. Hockey Canada, the CAHA and the NHL were still ambivalent, uncommitted and not united about how Canada should best be represented at the top level of international hockey.

During the sixteen days of the Games, I had a chance to see some other Olympic events. My nephew David Leuty was representing Canada in the bobsled. And I attended several figure skating competitions. As at the 1976 Olympic Winter Games in Innsbruck, I attended the final of the ladies' figure skating. It wasn't a gold-medal skate, but I'll never forget the pixie-like Elizabeth Manley giving the skate of her life and unexpectedly taking a glorious silver medal. Canada won only five medals in 1988, and no gold. Without much to cheer about, Elizabeth's performance was a real Canadian highlight.

The other lasting highlight for Calgary was that the Games made money, and left a legacy of excellent facilities and development funding for Canadian Olympic hopefuls.

—ᴍ—

Hockey was important to Copps Coliseum and HECFI, but it wasn't the only priority. Attracting concerts and other entertainment to the Coliseum was also important and a real challenge. Particularly after CPI was denied the exclusive rights they were after as part of their combined NHL/concert proposal in early 1985. CPI had exclusive rights in the Gardens in Toronto, but it was a privately owned facility. The Coliseum was publicly owned and couldn't deny local promoters access to use the building. Even I knew it would be political suicide for the mayor to permit exclusivity. General manager John Crane, booking manager Joe Tsao and I worked hard together to entice entertainers to the Coliseum. Hamilton was an unknown market for major events, and most promoters were hesitant. But after a few major successes, such as Kenny Rogers and Lionel Richie, the Coliseum's reputation as a good facility travelled quickly through the industry, and it was a lot less expensive to use than the Gardens in Toronto, the only other major arena venue in the area and our main competition.

I remember getting Lionel Richie to come to Hamilton. He was one of the most successful male artists of the 1980s. We heard he was going to play three concerts in Maple Leaf Gardens. Late on a Friday afternoon, I tracked down Michael Cohl of CPI and suggested that he move the third concert to the Coliseum, where it would be a guaranteed sell-out. He wasn't too warm to the idea as there were considerable costs to move out of the Gardens and down the road to Hamilton, and he was confident the third concert would also be sold out. But he said he would think about it. He asked me to call him back around nine that night.

As it turned out, Susan and I went to an event in Niagara-on-the-Lake that evening. In the middle of it, I excused myself and found a pay phone on the main street to call Michael. Fortunately, he answered. After several minutes of haggling, he agreed to let Lionel Richie come to Hamilton, but only after he played the third concert in Toronto. I was ecstatic! CPI was not easy to convince and were probably still a little miffed because we had rejected their proposal of an exclusive deal for the Coliseum. But both Cohl and Ballard were more interested in making money than holding a grudge. It was a real breakthrough with CPI. The tickets sold out in record time. And the concert was as good as anticipated, particularly when Lionel sang his current big hit "Dancing on the Ceiling," which featured several dancers suspended in the air, literally dancing on the ceiling.

And then there was the Grateful Dead. There was no venue in Toronto that could accommodate the large following of Deadheads who travelled from concert to concert all over North America. Our creative solution was to get the City Parks & Recreation Department to permit them to camp out on a nearby municipal golf course. Even the police co-operated: they turned a blind eye to the marijuana that came with the band and their concerts. The Dead played two back-to-back sold-out concerts, with no incidents. They acknowledged the Coliseum and the Hamilton set-up as one of the best they had ever played.

Once the Coliseum became known as a good and affordable facility, promoters began to bring us a wide variety of concerts, ice shows, circuses and other entertainment.

While David Braley was chair, our decisions were business oriented, and we always went after what was best for the three facilities and for the city. In the first couple of years, HECFI and particularly Copps Coliseum enjoyed good success. We demonstrated that if the HECFI facilities were offered only on a "user pay" basis and not given away free, they could be financially viable and not a burden on the city. At the same time they provided a diverse spectrum of cultural, entertainment, sports and business events for Hamilton's citizens to enjoy.

Unfortunately, Braley had other business commitments and stepped down as HECFI chair after two years. I watched him leave with real regret, as I enjoyed working under his pragmatic and businesslike leadership. I knew my life would take a turn for the worse with his departure. David acquired an interest for professional sports ownership during those years. He would later get involved as a pro sports franchise owner, first with the Hamilton Tiger Cats and then the BC Lions of the CFL.

Local politicians coveted a place on the HECFI board because of its success; it gave them a high profile in the community, particularly the aspiring ones wanting to advance their own political agendas. Working with the board members became like wrestling with an octopus. I'd get one arm under control and another one would up and grab me. I spent too much energy and time on a daily basis wrestling with the system. By 1989, the inmates were running the asylum. As I headed into my fifth year with HECFI, I realized it was a situation I could not change and that I had achieved all I was going to in Hamilton and with HECFI. Overall, I enjoyed my experiences in Hamilton, particularly having been part of the building and initial operations of Copps Coliseum, as well as the early successes of HECFI. But after a few stressful and exhausting years of wrestling with the political masters, it was time to move on.

On the Sidelines

IN EARLY 1989, Chris Lang, treasurer of Hockey Canada, contacted me. Chris was a friend of Galen Weston, head of Weston Foods and Loblaws. Galen was exploring the possibility he might build a new 18,000-seat major-league arena complex on company property in North York, just north of Toronto. It would be the potential home arena for a National Basketball League (NBA) franchise in Toronto, and possibly a second NHL franchise. He felt that Toronto, like New York, could support more than one team. The proposed facility would be part of Toronto's bid for the 1996 Olympic Summer Games.

Chris thought Galen's project could benefit from my experience with major-league arena complexes. In the meantime, Galen was part of the Royal Agricultural Winter Fair Association (RAWF) and in a year would be its president, a volunteer position. Was I interested in being chief executive officer (CEO) of the RAWF, and also helping with Galen's arena project?

I knew my time in Hamilton was up. The chance to be involved in another new facility, and the prospects of Toronto hosting the Olympics, were too good to resist. I was qualified for the job, and going to Toronto would be an easy sell: Susan always wanted to go back home.

I tendered my resignation to HECFI and left Hamilton at the end of February 1989, and became CEO of the RAWF at the beginning of March. The RAWF was a not-for-profit agricultural association, and its mandate was to produce and present an annual national agricultural and equestrian event, called the Royal, in early November on the grounds of Exhibition Place in Toronto. The Royal, first held in 1922, was the premiere event of its kind, where the best of the best in the agricultural world competed and showcased their livestock and products. Winning a red ribbon at the Royal was a coveted prize not unlike the Stanley Cup in hockey.

When I arrived, I found the RAWF in a state of financial crisis. The previous year's Royal had included a visit from Her Royal Highness Princess Anne, and expenses had got out of hand; the event had been a financial fiasco. My first task would be finance, but I also needed to determine what kind of management and operations team I had inherited. That assessment was a little more difficult.

When I left Edmonton and had gone into major facility management, I thought the fair business was behind me. But I found myself in it again as well as wrestling with another financial challenge. Coincidentally, three successive jobs were with facilities having Coliseums.

Both the organization (the RAWF) and the event (the Royal) were managed and operated by a large group of influential volunteers and a few paid employees. The volunteers were an invaluable resource, but occasionally some of the upper crust were pretty crummy towards the paid staff. Establishing mutual respect for each other's role became a key organizational objective. Management needed to earn the respect of the volunteers.

I realized that if the ship was to be righted there must be a change to the culture and work ethic at the RAWF, which when I got there was a country club atmosphere for volunteers and staff alike. The organization desperately needed more professional day-to-day management. My secretary, a kindly lady who had been with the RAWF for more than two decades, introduced herself by telling me she was not available on Wednesday afternoons, as that was when she got her hair done. Shortly afterwards, we had a nice retirement party for her. The hiring of her replacement sent a clear message that a new work attitude was expected. My goal was to transform the RAWF from a volunteer-led organization to one led by management. The RAWF needed to work on a business basis, or it would go out of business.

I rolled up my sleeves and tackled the work. In eight frantic months, the RAWF and Royal were reshaped and re-invented. Volunteers and staff worked together and put survival first and foremost: we were all saving the Royal from extinction. The result was impressive. The 1989 Royal was a huge success, both as an attraction and financially. When the bills were all paid, the RAWF was again on solid financial ground. The short-term success motivated us to continue moving the Royal forward.

For my second Royal, Galen Weston was president of the RAWF. He was happy to delegate the management and operations of the RAWF and the Royal to me, but was there whenever I needed help from him or his people. It was an ideal volunteer/management working relationship.

Galen and his wife, Hilary, had personal relationships with several members of the royal family, and Galen invited Her Royal Highness The Duchess of York to attend the 1991 Royal. She accepted. Sarah Ferguson's visit to the Royal was the highlight of the fair. She arrived in mid-morning with her entourage (security, secretaries and lady-in-waiting) and began a tour of the fair. The Duchess—"Fergie" as she was affectionately known—was swarmed by fairgoers who wanted to get close enough to shake her hand. No one could have been more accommodating, and she was a huge hit with the kids. Everyone who met her noticed that she was without airs or pretentions: she even let the llama give her a kiss on the cheek at the petting zoo. A person of the people, she gave a real sense of humanity to a family that often seemed removed from reality. I very much enjoyed the tour and my conversations with her.

Before her appearance at the Royal Horse Show, Susan accompanied me to a dinner in the Duchess's honour. Afterwards, we escorted the Duchess with only her security and lady-in-waiting to the area where a carriage would carry her into the show ring. It was a unique experience. Unfortunately, only a few weeks later, her royal life began to unravel. But on that day at the Royal, she certainly acted royally.

The 1989 Royal cost $2.5 million to produce; by 1991, the event cost close to $5 million and was self-sustaining under its new management and fiscal structures, and with the all-important support of the fairgoers.

The ship was righted, no longer rudderless, and a great Canadian tradition and heritage event was headed into an optimistic future.

—⚅—

While I was CEO of the RAWF, I was as far away from professional hockey as I could be. But Sean was playing high school hockey at UCC. The UCC rink was as cold and damp as any as I had ever been in, and I would shiver while I watched Sean play. At one game I introduced myself to the coaches.

The UCC hockey team had two co-coaches. Andrew Turner was a geography teacher and junior housemaster in Sean's boarding house on campus. Brent MacKay was the athletic therapist. I offered to help with the team, maybe as an assistant coach. I'm not sure if I forced myself on them, but I became part of a coaching triumvirate at UCC that lasted thirteen seasons. It was my most enjoyable and rewarding experience with the game of hockey at any level. It was good to get back to grassroots hockey, where kids played for the love of the game.

The primary objective of the hockey program at UCC was to make sure every young man who played on the team qualified to go on to college or university. It was a bonus when a few each year received scholarships to US schools. (Canada had no athletic scholarship opportunities.) One of my personal objectives was to help develop solid young men of character through the many lessons that can be learned in the context of playing hockey. One of those lessons was that along with privilege comes responsibility.

The young men who played on the UCC varsity team ranged in age from fourteen to nineteen. (The wide range of ages was one of the quirks of the high school hockey system.) There also was a wide range of talent levels. And many students also played for teams in the Greater Toronto Hockey League (GTHL). They had energy and infectious enthusiasm to spare. And they played full out: every player played as hard as he could every shift.

Andrew, Brent and I became a good coaching combination. With my background and experience, I had a credibility they might not have had, and I would need to be careful not to undermine their positions. Between us we provided a broad spectrum of coaching expertise. I focused on team building and instructing players one on one; I was kind of a team strategist and number-one cheerleader. It seemed to work.

My approach to coaching high school players was different from what it had been at the minor professional level. The UCC players were skilled enough to learn the fine points of the game, and they grew to learn the importance of team play, which is the basic difference between playing shinny hockey and real hockey.

I believe that players win games, and coaches can lose them. I'd seen a lot of over-coaching; I preferred understated coaching. I identified a few points that would benefit all the players and coaches whether on the ice, on the bench or in the dressing room:

- Players must demonstrate on-ice discipline in playing their positions, both offensively and defensively, and they must be two-way players at all times.
- Players must demonstrate self-control and composure at all times on and off the ice: no talking to the opposition; no foolish penalties; no talking to the officials; no outbursts of frustration. Just play hockey.
- The coach's role is to give the players direction as well as instruction.
- Coaches should encourage and support the players. There isn't a player on the ice who purposely makes a mistake. Hockey is a game full of mistakes, and the team that makes the fewest usually prevails.
- Coaching is a partnership between the players and the coaches.
- The team is the thing. Coaches and players together win as a team or lose as a team.

I have found that following the player–coach partnership generally produces more winning results than losing ones.

The UCC team played in two leagues: the Canadian Independent School Athletic Association (CISAA) and the Toronto District Colleges Athletic Association (TDCAA). There were about forty games between early November and mid-March, and the UCC team had some great rivalries in both leagues. In the CISAA, Nichols School in Buffalo had very strong teams, good coaching, talented and disciplined players, and was motivated to win. They were the standard to beat. In my first season, 1987–88, Sean's UCC team was also very strong. But when we played Nichols, some of our key players lacked discipline, self-control and composure. Between the testosterone and adrenaline, I was at a loss: coaching teenagers was something I had never faced in hockey. These young men needed to be kept on a short leash, and their explosive enthusiasm had to be focused on hockey. At times they had almost too much energy, some of it impulsive, undisciplined and uncontrolled. At times, it was like managing a time bomb. On the other side of the equation, they always came to play every shift of every game. The challenge for the coaching staff was to channel and focus the enthusiasm and effort. At the end of the 1988–89 season, the players defeated archrival Nichols in the playoffs to win the CISAA championship.

In the TDCAA, UCC played in the Catholic school league. Some of these games were real on-ice battles. Our opponents used a lot of intimidation tactics. In these games I emphasized discipline and composure. This was not an easy lesson for the players. But ever so slowly, UCC became known around the city as a team that could not and would not be intimidated. We had a game plan and stuck to it. We also had good power play units. When UCC started to win a high percentage of its games, the players began to realize that with discipline, self-control and composure on the ice they could win a lot of hockey games.

The games between St. Michael's College and UCC were always tough. Rivalry between the two schools had a long history, in football as well as hockey. The Basilian Fathers who ran St. Mike's teams strongly supported the high school hockey program. (My mentor, Father Bauer, had gone to St. Mike's, and had coached their major junior team, the St. Mike's Majors, when I played for the Toronto Marlies.) The irony was that I helped coach UCC to many wins over St. Mike's using coaching techniques, strategies and philosophies I learned from Father Bauer. The current St. Mike's teams often were uncontrolled and undisciplined, but they had some outstanding players. One year, a young Jason Spezza demonstrated the potential that would see him go on and excel in the NHL. St. Mike's teams proved that good players do not always a good team make.

In my thirteen seasons with UCC, the players won eleven TDCAA championships; they went on to win four gold medals, two silver medals and two bronze medals at the Ontario Federation of Secondary Schools Athletic Association (OFSAA) provincial hockey championship tournaments. In the CISAA league, UCC won the championship six times, five of them consecutively. In the 1997–1998 season, UCC won all three titles.

Tournaments were an important part of UCC's schedule. In 1956, when I was a student at UCC, I attended a memorable one in Lawrenceville, New Jersey, a few miles away from Princeton University, where they played some of their games. In the late 1980s I joined the team for another trip to Lawrenceville. The Lawrenceville tournament was important because most of the top US prep school teams attended, as did scouts who were recruiting for some of the top US colleges and universities. It was a showcase for the young men on the UCC team who hoped to go to a US school on a scholarship.

The tournament trips were about more than just hockey. They were about travelling and eating together as a team; camaraderie and fraternity; getting to know each other better; winning together and losing together; bouncing back after a loss; understanding and playing with real sportsmanship; shaking hands after a hard-fought game as a sign of respect for the opponent; making memories that lasted a lifetime, win or lose on the ice.

The OFSAA provincial championship tournaments were often struggles of attrition. It was not necessarily the best team with the best players that won. It was the team that played the best over a very intense weekend in late March. It was where a season's lessons needed to come together and be executed perfectly on every shift: totally disciplined and unselfish hockey, no energy wasted on foolish penalties, no talking to the officials, no getting frustrated or losing composure, just playing hockey and then going to the bench and resting for the next shift. And players needed to be prepared to do that for maybe three games in twenty-four hours and six games in one weekend to win the championship. It was a marathon, and a team had to keep winning to advance. Tournament hockey requires a different strategy and execution than normal playoff hockey.

An annual tradition at UCC was Hockey Night at the Gardens. They were keenly contested games, pitting youth against experience. UCC had a long connection with Maple Leaf Gardens and the Leafs. Conn Smythe, his son Stafford and his grandson Tommy, Harold Ballard, Foster Hewitt and his son Bill—all went to UCC. The night in Maple Leaf Gardens began the late 1940s when Leafs greats Syl Apps and Ted "Teeder" Kennedy helped coach the varsity team. I remember my first chance to play in the Gardens in the mid-1950s, when the varsity team played a team of former students. Forty years later I again attended Hockey Night at the Gardens, this time as a coach. UCC was playing a league game against one of their CISAA rivals. And they played with the intensity of the seventh game of a Stanley Cup final. It was exciting to be behind the bench at the Gardens. And the night was a real thrill for the players, because except for a rare few, it was the only time most of them would get a chance to play hockey in the Gardens.

Some schools had difficulty attracting the better players to their teams. But many players wanted to combine hockey with a conscientious school effort; each year the calibre of play got better. Parents were happy to have their kids opt out of the GTHL, where the schedules got longer and more demanding, and real values of the game were sacrificed to a winning-is-everything attitude. It's fun to win, but it's not everything. A lot of minor hockey has become modeled as a mini NHL.

UCC was fortunate to have some very talented young hockey players. Usually there were one or two players each season who demonstrated skills and talent well beyond their peers. Over the years I was assistant coach, several players went on to play professionally after great college careers, for example Mike McKee (NHL Quebec Nordiques), André Faust (NHL Philadelphia Flyers), Jason Cipolla and Syl Apps III (AHL St. John's Maple Leafs) and Daniel Tkaczuk (World Junior Championships, first-round draft pick with the NHL

Calgary Flames). A good hockey player can combine hockey excellence with education.

I think I got more out of my UCC coaching years than the players did. Being around bright and athletic youths gave me an insight into the challenges of being young—challenges I had forgotten. It's much more challenging to be a kid today than when I grew up. Children are exposed to so much more and at a much younger age, some good and some bad. The discipline the students learned through a team sport like hockey could last a lifetime. It really wasn't about winning, it was about trying to win, and the personal growth on and off the ice that came from that process. And hockey provided an environment to burn off an abundance of energy in a positive way. For many of the students I coached, participating in sport was important to personal well being. And it was often the pinnacle of their hockey careers, so the life skills they acquired in that experience were a lot more valuable than any championship wins or goals scored. The friends they made and the fraternity they shared with teammates and opponents alike were invaluable. When the goals, championships and game are but a memory, the friends remain for a lifetime.

When I was working for the Royal, I didn't pretend to know everything about the organization, agriculture, livestock and horse shows. I relied on the expertise of the many exhibitors who made up the Royal. We all had something to offer: they wanted to exhibit and compete; my job was to give them the opportunity to do so in a financially viable way. I had made a three-year commitment to the RAWF, and during the three events I oversaw, both sides of the people equation grew to understand and respect each other. I thoroughly enjoyed my three frantic and successful years, as well as the people I worked with and for. We were all part of a team success. But at the end of the three years, I felt that it was time to move on again.

Before I left the Royal, Toronto's bid for the 1996 Olympic Summer Games failed, and Galen Weston's plans for a new arena in North York seemed to slip off the table. Then, at one of my last RAWF board meetings, I had a casual conversation with Steve

Stavro, who was on the board. He was also, after Harold Ballard died in 1990, the apparent winner in the battle for control of the Ballard empire: Maple Leaf Gardens Limited (MLG), Maple Leaf Gardens (the Gardens) and the Toronto Maple Leafs hockey team. We talked informally about the possibility of my working for MLG. Steve suggested I contact Cliff Fletcher, recently hired as president and chief operating officer of MLG. The lure of managing another arena—especially the Gardens—was very attractive. I decided to explore the possibility.

Returning to Maple Leaf Gardens

I FIRST met Cliff Fletcher briefly in early 1992, at a Calgary Stampede reception, when I was with Northlands and he was the general manager of the Calgary Flames. Early in 1992, I geared myself up to phone him. Had Steve Stavro mentioned that I would call, or would Cliff think I was just another guy making a cold call looking for a hockey job?

When Cliff and I met, I told him my interest was in building management and operations, not the hockey team. The meeting went well, and early in February, Maple Leaf Gardens (MLG) hired me for a newly created position: vice-president of building operations. I would be responsible for the operations and management of the Gardens and for all non-pro hockey events. Many Canadians thought the Gardens was *the* hockey shrine. (Of course, Montreal Canadiens fans will argue for the Montreal Forum.) It certainly was a building with a lot of history, charisma and mystique.

As I walked through its doors in late winter 1992 for my first day on the job, memories flooded back. My family had a long history with the Gardens. Uncle Charlie scored the Leafs' first goal in the Gardens on opening night, November 12, 1931. The Leafs lost that first game 3–2 to the Chicago Black Hawks in "the house that Smythe built," but my uncle's goal marked the beginning of a legendary era in Leafs history. The "Kid Line" (Conacher, Primeau, Jackson), Syl Apps, Gordie Drillon, Red Horner, Hap Day—these were but a few who wore the blue and white in those early glory years. The Leafs were a real powerhouse in an eight-team NHL. (Montreal had the French-based Canadiens and the English-based Maroons, and New York had the Rangers and the Americans.)

I was a young boy in the late 1940s the first time I walked through the doors of the Gardens to watch the Leafs. My family had held season tickets since the day the Gardens opened, only a few seats away from the visiting team bench, in East Rails 69–70. I have vivid memories of sitting with my mother or father watching star players like Ted "Teeder" Kennedy, Todd Sloan, Max Bentley, Sid Smith, Harry Watson, Turk Broda and Harry Lumley and other memorable Leafs greats. I was a wide-eyed kid in awe of those hockey stars.

Hockey night was a dress-up affair in those days: shirt, tie and jacket. Our seats had no glass in front; I felt as if I was "in the game." I was told to watch intently, lest I get hit with a stray puck or an errant stick. My mother once forgot to pay attention and was cut by Maurice "Rocket" Richard's stick when he was checked along the boards. I remember Uncle Charlie coaching the Chicago Black Hawks in the 1952–53 season, and Uncle Roy playing for the Hawks; I remember the Leafs winning their third Stanley Cup in a row in 1949, and their fourth in five years in 1951, and so many more great memories.

My favourite visiting team was the Detroit Red Wings. I watched the semifinals of the 1956 Stanley Cup playoffs. In the previous game, in Detroit, one of the Leafs star players, Todd Sloan, was injured and was out of the series. Leafs fans were mad as hell and threatened to get even by taking out Ted Lindsay or Gordie Howe, two of the Red Wings' biggest stars. Threats circulated: if Lindsay and Howe showed up for the game, they'd be shot. Threats like that had to be taken seriously.

We were all searched as we entered the Gardens. Both Lindsay and Howe showed up. Well, there I was, only a few seats away from the Wings' bench, while we all waited nervously to see what would happen when Lindsay and Howe skated onto the ice.

It was a close game, and Lindsay was playing impressively—to thunderous boos from the crowd. Leafs fans loved to hate him. With regulation time running out, Lindsay tied the game for Detroit at 4–4. And then, to rub salt into a very open wound, at 4:22 of overtime, he scored the winning goal. The spectators sat in a state of shocked disbelief. You could have heard a pin drop in the Gardens.

When Lindsay was named the star of the game, he skated to centre ice and acknowledged the jeers and boos by putting his stick up to his shoulder like a rifle and mockingly shooting at the crowd. The Gardens fans went crazy as "Terrible Ted" skated off the ice with a wry and cocky smirk on his face. To this day, Ted Lindsay is one of my all-time favourite players. Pound for pound, he's the toughest hockey player I've ever seen. I love his grit.

In 2005, before the Hockey Hall of Fame induction ceremonies in Toronto, I had dinner with Ted and his wife, Joanne. I recalled that game, and so did Ted. He had been surprised that the Toronto fans were so mad at him and Gordie, because it was a check from defence-man Larry Hillman that injured Sloan. Ted and Gordie had some fun with their teammates as they readied for their game in Toronto. Gordie suggested that a young rookie, who spoke very limited English, wear #9 for the game. Even with a limited grasp of English, the offer was declined, an offer that on another occasion would have been a great honour. And as the team took to the ice for the pre-game warm up, several players asked Ted and Gordie not to skate too close to them—in case a crazed fan wasn't that good a shot.

My father died when I was twelve. On May 26, 1954, he was playing baseball on Parliament Hill, in a game between the press gallery and the parliamentarians. He was the Liberal member for Trinity riding in Toronto. Early in the game, he was hit on the side of the head by an errant pitch. After a brief delay, the game resumed, and my father continued to play. Later in the game, he stretched a single into a triple, but when he got to third base he slumped over and died, apparently from a heart attack. In reality, he had had an aneurysm, probably precipitated by the blow to the head. Cause of death was left as a heart attack, so no one would feel bad about the accident. And besides, a different cause of death wouldn't have changed the tragedy. And though it was premature, what better way for Canada's Athlete of the First Half Century (1900–1950) to die than the way he lived, trying to take that extra base, playing sports?

His sports career was over before 1941, when I was born. I knew my father was someone special because of his athletic achievements, but to me he was just my dad who was a federal member of Parliament. I never knew him as an athlete. I played many sports as I grew up, and loved them all. My dad encouraged me to participate, but he never pushed. Both my mother and father were adamant that all five children (I'm the youngest) get an education, and we were pushed to academics more than athletics when we were young; we were expected to go to university, and sports were always second.

At Upper Canada College (UCC), I played high school sports: football in the fall, hockey in the winter and track and field or cricket in the spring. I struggled academically because I loved sports and often spent too much time at them. (My two favourite classes were lunch and recess.) UCC had two outdoor artificial rinks, and I had ample opportunity to play hockey, but I never gave a moment's thought to the idea of playing professionally. As a high school athlete, I think I was probably better at football than hockey; I was a quarterback and running back, and like my brother Lionel Jr. before me, was touted as a top college football prospect.

When I was seventeen there were rumours that I was going to be put on the Detroit Red Wings protected list. My aunt Queen lived in Detroit and knew lots of the hockey crowd, and she said they were interested in anyone named Conacher. Then I was approached by the Toronto Marlboros (the Marlies) about playing for their OHL major junior team. If the Marlies didn't sign me before Detroit put me on their list, I would be permitted to play major junior only with Detroit's junior team in Hamilton. It was my first contact with the manipulative and controlling world of professional hockey.

My hockey playing at that point was strictly recreational; all I knew was that I had to finish high school and go to university. However, my mother had many discussions with Norm Sharpe, my hockey coach at UCC. They agreed that I could play for the Marlies as long as it didn't affect my schooling. And so in the 1958–59 season, I began going to the Gardens, not as a spectator, but to play for one of the Leafs' sponsored major junior teams. In the late 1950s, the Marlies and the other Leafs major junior affiliated team, the St. Michael's Majors, played their home games in the Gardens, mostly on Friday nights and Sunday afternoons.

Many of the Friday night games were between the Marlies and St. Mike's. There was an intense rivalry between the two teams. Players on both teams aspired to play professional hockey for a living, ideally for the Leafs. (Both were development teams for the Leafs organization at a time when major junior hockey was fully sponsored by NHL teams with the primary purpose of developing NHL prospects.)

The Leafs' home games were usually on Wednesdays and Saturdays (Saturday games were on Hockey Night in Canada.) Sometimes the Marlies practiced on Saturday morning after the Leafs had their morning skate. From noon on, everyone was kept off the ice until game time. The ice crew would scrape, flood and re-flood (all done by hand in the pre-Zamboni days), touch up the on-ice markings, touch up the dasher boards and clean the rinkside glass so the arena was ready to host the fabled Hockey Night in Canada. (The spit and polish tradition was a legacy of the Gardens' founder, Conn Smythe.) The Gardens hosted other events and activities, but there was no doubt that its raison d'être was to host the Leafs. Everything else came a distant second.

I played for the Marlies for four seasons (1958–62). I was one of only a few players who were still in school, and many people thought I was some private-school egghead or academic. It was far from the truth, but a hard image to shake. Most of the other players had quit school before they were eighteen, to follow the dream of achieving a professional hockey career. I never thought my next step after the Marlies would be professional hockey; my next step would be to go to university.

I struggled to get out of high school and qualify for university, so I was very fortunate and grateful for the opportunity to go to Huron College at the University of Western Ontario (UWO) in the fall of 1962. Between school and inter-collegiate football (for the UWO Mustangs), my hockey career was on the back burner.

In June 1963, Father David Bauer, former coach of the St. Mike's Majors, approached me about joining the new National Hockey Team program, which he had envisioned and was heading. One of the goals of the team was to restore Canada's supremacy in international hockey, but the primary objective was to demonstrate that good young hockey players didn't have to sacrifice their education to become top players, even NHLers. I was a young idealist, and I had great respect for Father Bauer as a coach, so I committed myself to Canada's first National Hockey Team (Nats), which would represent Canada at the 1964 Olympic Winter Games in Innsbruck, Austria. In the late fall of 1963, I next walked through the doors of the Gardens as a member of Canada's 1964 Olympic hockey team. I played in exhibition games against the Soviet and Czechoslovakian national teams as we all got ready to represent our countries at the Olympics.

In the fall of 1965, I left the Nats and turned professional with the Leafs organization. In my first season as a pro, I played for their American Hockey League (AHL) farm team, the Rochester Americans. By then I had completed two years of my three-year undergraduate degree, with graduation in sight. I was trying to exemplify the Father Bauer dream of combining education with hockey excellence. I wasn't there yet, but I was getting close. (I completed my schooling in three summer school sessions at the end of the hockey seasons.)

After a successful rookie pro year with Rochester—we won the AHL Calder Cup Championship—I cracked the Leafs' lineup and returned to the Gardens for the eventful 1966–67 season, in which the Leafs won their eleventh Stanley Cup championship. My second season with the Leafs was a turbulent one. After our Stanley Cup victory, the NHL doubled in size, expanding to twelve teams, and Al Eagleson formed the NHLPA. Punch Imlach was dead set against the NHLPA and disliked Eagleson intensely. Any Leafs player who chose to join the NHLPA was destined for Imlach's doghouse, which was not a place you wanted to be. Eagleson knew he needed the support of the Stanley Cup winners to get the NHLPA off the ground, so he recruited the Leafs aggressively. Many of the older players saw little to be gained from a players' association, and they didn't want to jeopardize their remaining years in the NHL by joining. Eagleson sought support from the younger players like me, Walton, Pappin, Stemkowski and Ellis, and from a few key players like Baun and Pulford.

Still an idealist, I thought there was a real need for better player representation, and with a handful of cautious but concerned Leafs, I supported Eagleson and the NHLPA. I knew my fate was cast when I became a founding member of the NHLPA. All that was left to be determined was how Imlach would get rid of me and the others who had taken the same bold step.

In the 1967–68 season, the Leafs went from winning the Stanley Cup to missing the playoffs. Imlach had the excuse he needed to get rid of all the players in his doghouse. I was one of them. In the spring of 1968 I was left unprotected, then drafted by the Detroit Red Wings. (Within eighteen months, Imlach got rid of some dozen players from that championship team, many of them founding members of the NHLPA. Coincidentally, the Leafs began their drift into hockey's wasteland, where they remain to this day. Ironically, ten players from the 1967 team have been inducted into the Hockey Hall of Fame.)

—⚊—

Thirty-five years after I first entered the Gardens, there I was walking through the doors to start my new role as MLG vice-president of building operations. I hadn't left a significant mark on the ice as a player, and it was my hope in my new job to leave a more significant mark off the ice.

When I began my job at the Gardens, Steve Stavro and his group were still wrestling for control of MLG, the fabled sports and entertainment company that housed the much coveted Leafs and the Gardens. After Harold Ballard died, people around him—Steve Stavro, Don Giffin, Ballard's children, particularly Bill—began fighting over the spoils of his estate. It was an intense and acrimonious power struggle. The previous summer, Don Giffin and Steve Stavro fought over who would head up MLG. The Leafs had acquired a legacy of turbulent and unsettled management before Ballard's death; Giffin and Stavro realized they needed a day-to-day, hands-on manager, and as soon as possible, as the 1991–92 season was not far away. During the chaos, Giffin hired Cliff Fletcher as president and chief operating officer (COO) of MLG and as general manager of the team. Fletcher hadn't been Stavro's first choice, but there was a real sense of urgency, and Fletcher was available immediately (he had just departed from the

Calgary Flames). With Al Eagleson as his agent, Fletcher negotiated a sweetheart deal. A key part of the deal, which was vital if Cliff was going to have any chance of rebuilding the Leafs into a contender, was his absolute and total control over all hockey decisions.

As president and COO of MLG, Fletcher had sweeping authority over the whole MLG organization, not just the Leafs. In previous jobs he had been primarily a hockey man, not an arena man. I believed I could really help Cliff by taking over the year-round operation and management of the Gardens, leaving him free to focus on the hockey business, which was his first love. He would be freed to devote his entire attention, around the clock, to rebuilding the Leafs. It could be a mutually beneficial arrangement.

Once Stavro got absolute control, he surrounded himself with a small group of pals and associates on "his" board, more for companionship than any specific expertise, except that they were hockey fans. Two exceptions were Donald Crump and Brian Bellmore. Crump and Stavro were executors of Ballard's estate, and he was the only board member with experience in running MLG. He had worked for Ballard for years, interrupted only by a brief stint as commissioner of the Canadian Football League. Crump was the guy who juggled the numbers and tried to keep MLG's financial house in order in the latter years of the Ballard era.

Apparently Bellmore had done some legal work for Stavro's chain of grocery stores, Knob Hill Farms. He developed a personal relationship with Steve and established himself as one of Stavro's main advisers, strategists and legal counsels. And he often acted as the public spokesperson for MLG, as Stavro was a very private person. During the litigious years to follow, Bellmore became a key member of Steve's small inner circle.

When Stavro first took control of MLG, it was a public company. And there were questions about how he emerged the winner of the Ballard sweepstakes. Ballard operated and controlled it as his own private enterprise, but it was accountable to its shareholders. Like Ballard, Stavro was strong-willed and autocratic, and he imposed his decisions upon the board members. One of his first initiatives was to make MLG a private company, so it could be managed and operated without public scrutiny; there were also questions about how he planned to do that. It was knock-down, drag-it-out, in-your-face legal confrontation on almost a daily basis. For MLG it was a period of corporate wheeling and dealing and legal maneuvering seldom seen in corporate Canada; the prize was the jewel of Canadian sport, the Leafs and the Gardens.

However, Stavro's domination over the hockey part of the organization was another matter. Fletcher had absolute control and authority over all decisions with respect to the Leafs. Diplomatically, he may have listened to suggestions and ideas from the board of hockey experts, but he wasn't bound to follow any of them; hockey operations were his exclusive domain. Because of the constant chaos surrounding MLG, Cliff needed autonomy if he was to get the Leafs back to winning ways.

Steve Stavro was a very proud man with a long background in sport. The pathetic state of the Leafs was a personal embarrassment to him, and something he desperately wanted to see changed. It was difficult to tell whether Ballard cared if the Leafs won; sometimes it seemed his sole interest in the "Carlton Street Cashbox" was to make money. Well, Stavro made it clear that he wanted Fletcher to build a winner and make the Leafs once again a top team in the NHL. And in a perfect world, Stavro's legacy would be a twelfth Stanley Cup championship for the Leafs. That was the only hockey direction the board gave Cliff Fletcher. He had a carte blanche to build a winner. The spotlight was clearly on the hockey department of MLG.

Quest for the Stanley Cup

SINCE THEIR last Stanley Cup championship in 1967, on paper at least, the Leafs had had their hands on enough good hockey players to win again. Instead, the whole Leafs organization, on and off the ice, plodded ineptly along, plagued by mismanagement, questionable coaching, suspect scouting, a dismal drafting record and a minor-league development system that failed to produce young prospects who could play for the team. (The Leafs seemed to devour their young upcoming players; it was a tough organization for a young player to develop in.) The management was reluctant to spend money to keep good players, and Harold Ballard kept interfering in their decisions. The Leafs were an embarrassment to themselves, their fans and the NHL.

Yet regardless of the on-ice futility over the years, Leafs fans lived in a perpetual state of hope and faithfully supported their team. Any other NHL franchise with the Leafs' record wouldn't have enough spectators in the arena for two tables of bridge. But Toronto was unique; the Gardens was always full. Many people thought the Leafs were never motivated to build a winner because the fans supported their miserable efforts, win or lose, so losing didn't hurt MLG financially. Cliff Fletcher, with Stavro's support, planned to restore the Leafs as one of the premiere teams in the NHL. He had a free hand to build a winner. But it was a double-edged sword; failure would not be tolerated.

Over the six and a half hockey seasons I worked for MLG, there were some exciting, interesting and intriguing games played in the Gardens. When Cliff took over in the summer of 1991, the team and the hockey department were in dire need of a major overhaul. By midway through the 1991–92 season, Cliff knew the players he inherited weren't good enough to be the winner everyone so desperately wanted. He planned to change. If the organization didn't have the raw talent to develop a winning team quickly, Cliff would go into the marketplace and buy a better team. Then he would rebuild the team's development system.

On January 2, 1992, Cliff made a blockbuster ten-player trade with his former team, the Calgary Flames. It was the largest trade in NHL history to date. The key acquisition for the Leafs was Doug Gilmour, who would join Wendel Clark. Together they would personify the new heart and soul of Cliff's Leafs. While the Leafs failed to make the playoffs that first season, Cliff had established himself in the minds of Toronto fans as a general manager who wasn't afraid to make deals or spend money to improve the team.

Cliff's next big move was to hire a new coach to replace Tom Watt. When Pat Burns resigned from the Montreal Canadiens, Cliff immediately signed him as the Leaf's twenty-second coach to guide the blue and white. With a new on-ice leader in Gilmour and a new off-ice leader in Burns, the team would have their coming-out party during the 1992–93 season.

Pat Burns was the right coach for the Leafs at the time. He was tough. He was intimidating. He was respected. He was fair. He demanded that all his players give their best every shift. He pushed the Leafs to be the best they could be. And they responded. The 1992–93 season was one to remember. The Leafs earned a team record 99 points in the regular season and went into the playoffs as a legitimate Stanley Cup contender. And they would have a playoff run second to none. The first round against the Detroit Red Wings went the full seven games, and included two overtime wins for the Leafs, one of them in the seventh game. Torontonians started to get really excited about the Leafs; after each win fans would spill out onto the streets and into the pubs celebrating each victory.

In the quarterfinals against the St. Louis Blues, Felix Potvin out-goaled Curtis Joseph decisively in the seventh game, shutting out the Blues 6–0, and the Leafs advanced to the conference semifinal. There was pandemonium in the streets of Toronto after each win: fans were starting to think it might be a Stanley Cup year. More important, the Leafs played like they believed it too.

The semifinal was against the Los Angeles Kings, led by Wayne Gretzky. With a chance to win the series in the sixth game in Los Angeles, one of hockey's worst non-penalties took place early in over-time. Gretzky cut Doug Gilmour with a high stick. Referee Kerry Fraser hesitated, and in that moment missed his chance to make the right call: the "Great One" deserved a major penalty. To compound his error, Fraser called no penalty at all. And instead of being in the penalty box Gretzky scored to force a seventh game. In game seven, in Toronto, it was too much Gretzky again and the Leafs' dream of advancing to the Stanley Cup final was shattered when they lost 5–4. The opportunity for another classic Stanley Cup final between the Leafs and the Montreal Canadiens was gone forever.

In the 1993–94 season the Leafs continued to develop under the direction of Pat Burns. Again they went to the conference final, and again Leafs fans got hyper excited at yet another chance to go to the final. But the bubble burst when the Vancouver Canucks lost the first game, then swept the Leafs away in four straight. Once again, Leafs fans would have to wait until next season. The Leafs twice narrowly missed chances to hold the coveted Stanley Cup. Cliff constantly pursued the missing parts which would get them there. The Leafs development system continued to fail, so Cliff didn't hesitate to go into the marketplace to acquire players.

On June 28, 1994, Cliff rocked the hockey world with another multi-player trade. And to many people's horror he traded his captain, Wendel Clark, to the Quebec Nordiques. Wendel Clark personified the true grit and spirit of the ultimate Leaf player, but his hurting body would no longer permit him to play the style of game that had made him so effective in his early years. In return, the Leafs got Matts Sundin; Cliff hoped he would be a franchise player and lead the team to the Holy Grail of hockey. It was a good trade for the Leafs, but many fans found it hard to swallow. No one was safe on the Leafs as Cliff relentlessly scoured the hockey world for players he felt would improve the Leafs in their quest for the elusive Stanley Cup.

In the 1994–95 season there was labour strife between the NHL owners and players. The collective bargaining agreement expired just before the season started, and without an acceptable agreement the owners locked out the players. NHL hockey was cast into a state of limbo as scheduled games started to be missed. By Christmas, fans worried that the whole season would be lost. (There had to be at least forty-eight regular-season games to legitimize qualification for the playoffs.) At the eleventh and a half hour in mid-January 1995, a deal was done. (The owners and players negotiated a last-minute collective bargaining agreement that sowed the seeds of an even more serious labour disruption to come ten years later.)

In spite of the abbreviated regular season and with several new faces in their lineup, the Leafs managed to make the playoffs for the third straight year, However, in the first round, the Chicago Black Hawks put them out in seven games. The Leafs were definitely better and more entertaining than they had been before Cliff arrived in 1991, but they still weren't a winning combination.

In 1995-96, Pat Burns had a dilemma: how could he get more out of his players? Pat was an intimidating coach, and his style of coaching had a relatively short shelf life, usually three to five years. It tended to consume coaches. He could only push so hard; he could only rant and rave so much; he could only threaten so many times; and then the players turned him off. By mid-season, it seemed Pat had hit the wall; he had taken his team as far as they could go under his direction. You can't push a rope.

On March 4, 1996, with a month to go in the regular season, Cliff abruptly fired Pat and appointed Nick Beverley to guide the team through the remainder of the season. Stavro and the board pressured Cliff to reacquire Wendel Clark, hoping he could reignite the team. It was the first sign Cliff was starting to lose his grip on total control over the team. The Leafs did make the playoffs, but disappointedly bowed out in six games in the first round against the St. Louis Blues.

By the start of the 1996–97 season, the Leafs appeared to stall after four seasons of promise. Cliff even seriously tried to get Wayne Gretzky into a Leafs uniform. Apparently, the deal was all but done, and Wayne seemed happy to end his illustrious career in Toronto, but Stavro and the board balked. Because of their takeover bid to make MLG a private company, Stavro and his new partners had huge financial obligations. Stavro still wanted a winner, but after five seasons he revoked Cliff's unrestricted privileges to achieve it. And like his predecessor, Stavro shifted his focus to the bottom-line of MLG.

Many might have questioned bringing Gretzky to Toronto. Was it a desperate act of a man to save his job? Stavro and the board probably thought the cost of signing wasn't worth the potential benefit, as there were no more seats to sell. But was there really any downside? Certainly, Gretzky was only a short-term solution. But his mere presence on the Leafs might have made that all-important difference, even though the best years of his career were behind him. And in Leafs' team jersey sales alone, MLG could have paid his salary. Every hockey fan in Canada, whether a Leafs fan or not, would have bought a Leafs sweater with "99" and "GRETZKY" on it. It was a gamble Stavro and the board weren't bold enough to take.

When Cliff took over in 1991, the Leafs' payroll was around $13 million. Within a year or so it was more than $20 million, and by the end of the 1995–96 season it was reportedly close to $40 million. The board had generously supported Cliff's spending habits, but by the spring of 1996 the money was spent but there was still no Stanley Cup. Stavro and his partners had to pay a lot more than they anticipated to turn MLG into a private company, and Stavro was growing impatient. Change was in the wind.

During the 1996–97 season, I began to see a familiar face in the directors' lounge. It was Ken Dryden. He and Larry Tanenbaum had gone to Cornell University at the same time, and were friends. Brian Bellmore also knew Ken. These informal visits were the start of Dryden's ambition to displace Cliff and become the head of the Leafs. Dryden was probably second-guessing every mistake on the ice; a small group on Stavro's board was quietly and methodically ambushing Cliff behind the scenes. Thus began a palace revolt that led to the eventual coup d'état.

With Dryden's supporters undermining Cliff behind his back, he was under more intense pressure to deliver a winner by the end of the season. Stavro still wanted to win, but no longer at any cost. Cliff was financially hand-cuffed. Despite the guidance of new coach Mike Murphy, the Leafs started to slide into a black hole. They finished dead last in their division and well out of the playoffs for the first time in five seasons. After a few promising seasons, the Leafs slipped back to where they had been in 1991.

At a board meeting shortly after the season, one of the final straws was when the board learned that MLG had some $11 million of payroll commitments for players who no longer played for the Leafs, and MLG had apparently paid some $800,000 of Larry Murphy's salary when he was a member of the Stanley Cup champion Detroit Red Wings. By the spring of 1997, after seventy or more player transactions over six years, including draft picks, future considerations and millions of dollars in player salaries and bonuses, Cliff had failed to build the Stanley Cup team the board and the fans so anxiously awaited. In 1993 and 1994 they came so close, but never got close again. The board had lost confidence in Fletcher. His time was up.

The curtain dropped on the Stavro–Fletcher chapter in Leafs history at the end of May 1997. Cliff Fletcher had never been Stavro's choice as general manager and was certainly not his preference for president and COO of MLG. (Stavro believed the positions should be filled by two people.) Stavro shrewdly gave Cliff enough rope to save himself, if the Leafs won, or hang himself, if they lost. They lost, and it cost him his job. Cliff was relieved of his position with a golden handshake; I think he might have traded a good portion of it for a Stanley Cup winner for Toronto.

Standing in the wings after Fletcher's dismissal was Ken Dryden. He was promoted as the next savior to lead the Leafs out of hockey's hinterland. Dryden, inexperienced and untried, was waiting for his big hockey opportunity. Shortly after Cliff was let go, Ken was hired as president and general manager of the Leafs, and interim head of MLG. Dryden had had a distinguished career as a player, but he had no apparent experience in senior management, particularly in professional sports. Many of the MLG staff thought his hiring was an act of frustration and desperation, and that the board of directors had lost its way in the world of NHL hockey. We all waited anxiously to see what Dryden would bring to the party.

Managing the Gardens

I PLUNGED into my new position as vice-president of building operations for the Gardens with great enthusiasm and optimism. But I wasn't at it very long before I realized that managing and operating the Gardens wasn't going to be like managing any normal business operation. It was obvious that the centre of attention for everyone who worked for MLG was the Leafs. Consequently, there was an unusual culture and work ethic in the Gardens, with two very distinct work groups: the hockey department and everyone else. The Gardens was a shrine of hockey in Canada and the home of the Leafs, but it was also a major entertainment venue in Toronto and Canada, and hosted a wide variety of activities: wrestling, boxing, basketball, indoor soccer, lacrosse, concerts, skating shows, circuses, religious meetings, political conventions, charitable events, corporate events, movies, TV commercials, opera and more.

Some of the staff and board members at the Gardens thought I was just another former Leafs player hired by the organization. I had to demonstrate that I was a qualified and capable facility manager. First, I set up an organizational structure for the building operations division. I made five departments: booking and events, box office, food and beverage, security and event staff, and building operations. Each had its own annual budget and dedicated staff: there were approximately 90 full-time employees, and as many as 550 part-time staff when the Gardens was in full event mode. When the building was used by the Leafs, or when there was a major event or concert, I was responsible for more than 600 staff. By 1992, when I was hired, the building operations team needed to be overhauled. While Cliff built a better on-ice team, I planned a better off-ice team.

There were always unionized employees working in the Gardens, going right back to when Conn Smythe built the place in 1931. Unfortunately, because Harold Ballard mistreated many of the building staff over the years, the Gardens was a high-profile and inviting target for further unionization when I arrived. In some areas, competing unions fought to establish jurisdictional rights in the mad scramble to certify as many departments as possible.

From a management and personal point of view, I had some concerns about the proliferation of unionization of Gardens staff. In the skilled trades—engineers, carpenters and electricians—I respected workers' acquired knowledge and had few problems. But I was concerned about the work ethic and attitude of many in the less skilled labour groups. It seemed that the union strategy was to take each task and divide it into as many parts as possible, to create more jobs, and then to be as inefficient as possible in doing the job. I didn't grow up in a union work culture; my attitude was, if there was a job to do you did what was needed to get it done on a timely basis. To me, the union work mentality did not fit with the demands and deadlines of the sports and entertainment business. Philosophically, I was at loggerheads with some of the unions.

Soon after I started, there were nine different collective agreements with seven different unions in the Gardens: Teamsters Local 847 (full-time and part-time labour and maintenance, part-time ushering, food and beverage); International Alliance of Theatrical Stage Employees Local 58 (IATSE); Theatrical Wardrobe Union Local 822; International Union of Operating Engineers Local 796; International Brotherhood of Electrical Workers Local 353; Carpenters and Allied Workers Local 27 (carpenters); Canadian Security Union/United Food and Commercial Workers (UFCW) Local 333 (full-time and part-time security, part-time alcohol security). With all of these in just one building, it was a jurisdictional jungle.

Most of the staff was unionized, and the union representatives constantly pushed for increased wages, better work conditions and fewer work requirements. Their objective was to create more employment opportunities for union members. Ironically, Cliff's generosity with his player contracts had a huge impact on my dealings with unionized staff. It was obvious that MLG had lots of money to spend on its hockey team, and the other staff (union and non-union) felt some of the liberal spending should also flow to them. It was hard to blame them. I wanted to be fair with the workers, but I didn't want to pay excessive wages for menial work. The battleground: what was fair and reasonable compensation for the work needed at the Gardens? It was a tough labour environment, and made my mandate—to manage and operate the Gardens as efficiently, effectively and economically as possible—more difficult.

I'm not sure Stavro, his board and even Cliff really appreciated the significant economic effect unionization had on the operating costs of the Gardens in the early 1990s. They seemed to look at union issues I struggled with on a daily basis as a nuisance rather than a financial issue. Without the board's understanding and support, I was negotiating with blanks in my gun. I remember going into a union negotiation one morning with the Teamsters. We were negotiating a $0.25 hourly increase. Before the meeting began, the union boss slid a copy of the *Toronto Sun* across the table. There on the front page in full colour was Doug Gilmour beaming about his new multi-million-dollar contract. How could I say MLG couldn't afford another $0.25 per hour? MLG appeared to be so reckless in the hockey department with player salaries, it made it difficult for me to be financially responsible in the building operations area. When I began at MLG, union negotiations were treated as nickel-and-dime issues, not real-dollar ones. The economics of operating the Gardens would change dramatically in the years after my arrival.

I had reasonable relationships with most of the unions, but with two I knocked heads from the day I arrived to the day I left. The Teamsters' boss was confident and cocky about the collective clout he had over MLG, and he made sure his members constantly pushed for more.

MLG was paying the price for all the years Ballard had treated them poorly. The Teamsters were definitely one of the most aggressive and belligerent bargaining units.

My other major union headache was the International Alliance of Theatrical Stage Employees (IATSE). Their local president, like the Teamsters' boss was old school. IATSE had been established in the Gardens for years—since the time when the Gardens was the only venue in the Toronto market—and they weren't going to let me change the good thing they had going there. The Gardens needed to price itself more affordably to attract business in an increasingly competitive and changing market. IATSE didn't care; they were determined to resist change. IATSE had the Gardens by the throat and wasn't going to loosen its grip. We had drawn the line in the sand; years of confrontation followed.

Some of the work conditions and demands made by IATSE were, in my opinion, out-and-out gouging of the event producers. And because the union agreements were with MLG, I felt it was my responsibility to represent the interests of my customers who paid the event staff. For example, the Gardens had no proper loading dock, so we were required to have a separate crew to unload equipment from trucks on the street and move it to the doors, sometimes a matter of only a few feet. Then, inside the door, another crew handled the equipment in the building. The procedure was reversed when equipment left. The effects of this type of gouging showed up clearly with the Stars on Ice show, which played both the Gardens and Copps Coliseum in Hamilton. Stars on Ice had to pay forty percent more in IATSE charges in the Gardens. Union costs were adding to the Gardens' difficulties in getting shows. The unions didn't care.

Another example: for years, the staging for concerts and other events was made up of wood riser boxes. Every time a stage was needed, Teamsters labourers would carry the riser boxes onto the arena floor; then the MLG union carpenters would assemble them; then the IATSE workers set up the sound and lighting equipment. I purchased a new staging system, which was state of the art and didn't need carpenters to assemble and set it up. So on the day the new stage system was delivered to the Gardens, I had three union stewards in my office filing grievances about jurisdictional rights. The Teamsters felt it was their work to carry the stage parts onto the arena floor and set them up; IATSE claimed it was their work, as it was part of the show equipment. The carpenters were riled because they no longer had anything to do. After some heated debate, we all agreed the Teamsters would carry the stage onto to the arena floor and set it up. One carpenter would assist as needed. And because the stage system was owned by MLG and not by the event producer, IATSE had no jurisdictional rights.

Unions had a silver bullet when negotiating with MLG: they all knew MLG would never let a labour issue threaten a Leafs game. As a result, my management group found itself in an awkward position and had to work by permission from the unions. Definitely the tail wagging the dog. Unions unilaterally accepted or rejected labour changes that were usually within the scope of management's rights. Any time the workers wanted something or didn't like something, the union representative would threaten MLG with work stoppage or strike, and the board would cave in. MLG sold the farm to its unions while I was there.

Except in the fall of 1994, when the NHL was in the midst of a lockout with its players. During the lockout, United Food and Commercial Workers (UFCW) Local 333 threatened to strike. There were no hockey games and there wasn't much activity in the Gardens, so MLG finally decided not to cave in. We let them strike. The strike got nasty. Several unions threatened not to cross the line, but relented when they realized the implications to their collective agreements. There was sympathetic picketing outside the Gardens during events. And one morning, when I left the underground garage of my condo, a couple of workers were picketing at the top of the ramp. In spite of this improper tactic and my complaint, the union received no reprimand.

And then, just when it looked like we might win a favourable new collective agreement, the NHL lockout ended. The Leafs would travel to Los Angeles early the next morning to get the shortened season started. When the equipment van went up the ramp to leave the Gardens on Wood Street, union pickets blocked the exit. The police would not intervene on MLG's behalf, even though the union's actions were inappropriate.

I contacted Cliff, who was agitated that, after several months of no hockey, some labour unrest could interfere with his Leafs getting into action. It all came down to money. How much was it going to cost MLG to settle the negotiations and clear the ramp so the Leafs could get back to work? A deal was done at the back door of the Gardens. The irony: The NHL was on strike against its players for three months to get a deal they felt they could live with, but when it came to the Gardens, the unions called the tune, and MLG danced to it.

From that early morning at the back door of the Gardens in January 1995, my effectiveness as a union negotiator for MLG was neutered. The unions knew that if they pushed hard enough, they would get what they wanted, no matter how unreasonable the demands. They all knew MLG would never sacrifice a hockey game. Their strategy worked.

Over my six years at MLG, I spent close to half my time dealing with union matters: collective agreement negotiations, meetings with the Labour Relations Board, grievances, jurisdictional disputes and so on. Most union workers were honest, decent and hardworking people just trying to do their jobs. Unfortunately and too often, it seemed, the scum, not the cream, rose to the top of union leadership. Some union representatives I dealt with used threats and intimidation not only to bully management, but also their own membership. It constantly made it difficult for MLG to manage its staff.

The booking and events department drove all the non-pro hockey event business in the Gardens. Until the early 1990s, if someone wanted to hold a major event or concert in Toronto, the Gardens was the only place to do it, and MLG had exploited the situation for years. MLG was an order taker. But by 1992, the concert business at the Gardens had slowed down considerably. And with the arrival of the SkyDome and later the Molson Amphitheatre, the Gardens faced serious competition. Bill Ballard and Michael Cohl of CPI, who had enjoyed exclusivity with the Gardens for years, began to look for the best deal. There were bidding wars for the concerts and events they promoted and produced. For the first time in its existence, MLG had to market the Gardens and compete for shows.

My office ran the booking and events department. The first thing I did was hire a young woman named Cindy Ross as my booking and events manager. Cindy had worked for CPI and was familiar with the event and concert business and its challenges. We worked very closely together (I had final approval on any deal that varied from our quoted rate card.) And as time passed, the rate card applied to producers and promoters who used the Gardens only occasionally. The regulars all wanted a deal. The Gardens was still the venue of choice for many events, but Cindy and I would have to work hard to attract the business. We wanted the Gardens to continue to be more than just the home of the Leafs.

One interesting event was the World Basketball Championships, held in the Gardens from August 4 to 11, 1994. John Bitove, Jr., had agreed to host some of the games in Toronto as part of his successful bid for a National Basketball Association (NBA) franchise, the Toronto Raptors. (Larry Tanenbaum lost with his bid for the franchise. In 1996 Tanenbaum would become a part owner of MLG and a member of the board.) There was personal friction between the Stavro and Bitove families, so I was instructed not to give John a special deal, even though the games came at a time when there was little activity in the Gardens, which did not have air conditioning. Normally, the Gardens was almost shut down during the summer.

The negotiations took several months. It reminded me of dealing with Eagleson for a Canada Cup tournament. Bitove and the NBA wanted to use the building for eleven days for next to nothing. And there were many logistical and operational issues to be resolved: the Gardens didn't have a basketball floor; the building needed temporary air conditioning, at least at floor level so the players wouldn't melt into pools of sweat; most of the MLG building staff were scheduled for vacations (which they had to take in the summer, because of the demands of the hockey season). The most difficult thing to achieve was to get Bitove or some other person with authority to sign the licence agreement with MLG. ·

The Gardens hosted twenty of the basketball games. Bitove and the NBA hoped the games would promote the arrival of the new Toronto Raptors. Two of the early games featured Team Canada, but the highest-profile games came as the playoff rounds began and involved Team USA. I remember standing near Shaq O'Neal when he took to the floor. He was a giant and was unmovable when he set up under the opponents' basket—an awesome display of power and skill!

During the NHL lockout in the fall of 1994, someone suggested we take the ice out of the Gardens, as maintaining it required a huge energy cost. I told Cliff that I thought it was a bad idea, as it would look like we were out of business. Instead, I initiated a casual ice rental program similar to one I had started in Copps Coliseum. The response was overwhelming. When one of the local newspapers mentioned the possibility that the Gardens would be available for adult recreational hockey teams, the switchboard was jammed. Within two hours of the news breaking, there were more than 220 inquiries.

At the unheard of rental rate of $700 for ninety minutes of ice time, teams from all over southern Ontario made the trek for the special opportunity to play in the Gardens, previously the exclusive space of an elite few. And after the teams had their picture taken at centre ice, we never heard a single complaint about the price. It was a very successful revenue generator for MLG.

In the mid-90s, heavy-metal and grunge bands played at the Gardens in increasing numbers. The notorious "mosh pit" phenomenon was in full swing. Bands like Nine Inch Nails, Smashing Pumpkins and Beastie Boys nearly blew the roof off the Gardens with what I called noise pollution—certainly not my idea of music. I had trouble getting ushering and event staff to work at some of the concerts because of the excessive noise and the unruly crowds. And after one concert I found all the pictures on my office walls askew because the noise had literally shaken the building. The Gardens needed the business, but it was tough business, and all the staff earned their money at those concerts.

A fun concert group was the Canadian band the Tragically Hip. Gord Downie, Paul Langlois, Bobby Baker, Gord Sinclair and Johnny

Fay were attending Queen's University in Kingston, Ontario, in the early 1980s when they started the band. Their first concert in the Gardens, on February 10, 1995, marked their arrival as a major rock band. They were all huge Leafs fans, and after their sound check before the concert, I took them into the Leafs dressing room and presented them all with team sweaters. And of course they wore them proudly on stage and brought the house down when they sang "Fifty Mission Cap," a song about Leafs' legend "Bashing Bill" Barilko.

During my years of booking events in the Gardens there were many memorable ones: I marvelled at the energy and athleticism of Michael Flatley in his production of Lord of the Dance; enjoyed the perfect symmetry and creativity on ice of Jane Torvill and Christopher Dean; I watched Kurt Browning ascend to the top of men's figure skating as a cast member of Stars on Ice; I listened to the inspirational oration of the charismatic Reverend Billy Graham; and I watched the shooting of a Campbell's Soup commercial with Nancy Kerrigan shortly after her incident with Tonya Harding, to name a few.

The box office was where most of the money came in to MLG. Because tickets to Leafs games and all other events were paid for by cash or cheque only, no credit cards, we needed proper financial and security procedures and controls for handling the large sums of money. In the later years of Ballard's life, the box office was pretty much left to run on its own. Without vigilant supervision, it was vulnerable to exploitation. And to many, box office operations were a mystery of accountability.

Season tickets to Leafs games were much coveted, but very limited. Some people wanted to control as many season tickets as possible, whether hockey fans or not (including scalpers and ticket brokers); they were a licence to print money and commanded premium prices. Many families passed on season tickets in their wills, a practice that was acceptable with proper documentation. Occasionally, upon the death of a season ticket holder, the family would notify MLG in writing of their desire to give up the tickets. MLG had a long list of people waiting to purchase or upgrade season tickets. Access to season ticket information was limited to a few senior box office and hockey department personnel.

Shortly after I arrived at the Gardens, I heard rumours of people playing games with Leafs season tickets. I was concerned. Many people believed Harold Ballard had manipulated season tickets. When he set up the Hot Stove Lounge in the Gardens as a private club, he used access to season tickets to sell memberships. He was the head of MLG, and he was sending a bad message to his employees, particularly in the box office.

A few weeks before the preseason games began in 1992, someone forwarded a telephone call to me. The caller wanted to know why he hadn't received his season tickets yet. I said I'd check and get back to him immediately. I was shocked by what I found out. Our records showed that the tickets in question were in the name of a season ticket holder who had died, and that the family had relinquished them to MLG. And yet here was someone else, asking about them. An alarm went off in my mind. The customer was dead but the tickets were still alive. What was going on?

With further investigation, I uncovered a scam run by an unscrupulous box office employee. He ignored the letter to MLG and kept the season tickets registered in the name of the deceased. Then he sold the tickets to my telephone inquirer. MLG received full payment for the tickets, which was probably why the scheme went undetected, and the employee pocketed a substantial premium from his client. I had to act swiftly.

I called the telephone inquirer, who said he'd given one cheque to MLG for the face value of the season tickets and another to his box office contact for, I believe, $8,000. I informed him that MLG would refund the money he'd paid them, but he'd have to deal with his contact for the rest. And needless to say, he wouldn't be getting any season tickets. The employee was encouraged to resign immediately (MLG preferred to deal with the matter internally).

I soon found out the problem was not confined to Leafs season tickets. There was evidence of ticket problems for some major concerts, where the demand for tickets was huge, especially for good seat locations. Some box office staff held onto concert tickets and sold them to their clients at a premium. MLG got the ticket price, and the box office person pocketed the premium. And some of their clients were ticket scalpers. Trusted employees scalping tickets to ticket scalpers! The majority of the box office personnel were honest and responsible, but there were a few opportunists who were at work while MLG drifted in the last years of the Ballard era when operations and administration accountability was lax. The whole department cried for a shake-up.

When I advised Cliff and the board of the transgressions I had discovered in the box office, all agreed that getting the department on solid and accountable operational ground was a priority, particularly with respect to Leafs season tickets. I hired a manager to revamp the whole box office organization and its procedures. Donna Henderson had several years of experience with the computerized ticket service provider TicketMaster and came highly recommended. And she was new and from outside. Donna took control and quickly got the box office department on track.

Ticketing for Gardens events was still all done manually, with paper tickets. At times, it was a nightmare to reconcile the ticket sales, particularly for concerts. The old manual system was flawed and obsolete. In the marketplace, there were several relatively new computerized ticketing systems whose biggest attraction was their ability to accurately monitor and control ticket inventory. This was something MLG definitely needed. It was time to step up to the future of ticketing. I negotiated a deal with TicketMaster. MLG would maintain control of all Leafs season tickets through the hockey department, while TicketMaster would provide services for all non-pro hockey events. It was a big step in improving the inventory control and accountability of ticketing at the Gardens.

Around 1993, rumours of a new Gardens swirled around the organization. I told Cliff and the board that if MLG was seriously thinking of building a new Gardens, we needed to get a better handle on who held season tickets. Obtaining accurate information about all registered Leafs season ticket subscribers was a first critical step, and one filled with many surprises. As an example, I remember contacting a senior executive at Imperial Oil, to confirm the couple of dozen season tickets registered in company and employee names. After a pause, the executive said Imperial Oil did not know it had that many Leafs season tickets. Over the years, the company had sponsored the Leafs and Hockey Night in Canada broadcasts, and several departments obtained tickets. Many were in the name of individuals. The company paid for the tickets, but the individuals used them for business and personally. And to further muddy the waters, some of these individuals had left Imperial Oil but still had tickets in their names.

MLG needed two pieces of information to accurately register a season ticket holder: the proper name of the person or company holding the tickets, and the actual mailing address of the person or company. We checked with every person and company noted in our records. Some season tickets were registered in a personal name at a certain company, but the person no longer worked at the company, and the address was a home address. Or even worse, the address belonged to a person to whom the original subscriber had sold the tickets. It was a real mess.

Donna and I decided we would give all Leafs season ticket subscribers a one-time opportunity to update their registration information with MLG; we would even effect transfers with proper approvals. For some of the transfer requests, there were real battles over who would be named as ticket holder of record with MLG. Slowly we revamped our records and procedures. We got our own house in order and were ready to go forward.

MLG accepted only cash and cheques as payment for tickets, and cheques were accepted only from known patrons. In 1992, I asked why MLG did not accept credit cards. The answer: Because MLG never had to. But ticket prices had escalated significantly; was it reasonable to expect ticket purchasers to show up at the box office with a couple of hundred dollars in their pockets? And was the cash-only requirement costing MLG some customers—particularly concert goers? Young people had little cash, but most had a credit card. After much persuasion, MLG finally agreed to accept a credit card as a form of payment for tickets. It's hard to believe that was a tough sell in 1992.

There were always issues to deal with in the box office department. Ticketing systems—both the computer systems and the people who ran them—had to be continually checked for security flaws. Unfortunately, the perfect system didn't exist; all were vulnerable to exploitation by the human factor. When dealing with money, there were always people out there looking for ways to beat the system. The best deterrent was constant vigilance.

—⁓—

The food and beverage department was another due for a major overhaul, both physically and operationally. The department ran the numerous concession stands located throughout the Gardens, which were old, tired and unattractive. The department also provided catering and other special services to the private suites and the directors' lounge. Food and beverage was a significant revenue generator for MLG, but I thought it could work a lot better.

The department manager and I agreed that we needed to improve all the concession stands and equipment, within the limitations of the Gardens. Many of the stands were crammed into small spaces that permitted limited access to electrical outlets and to water for sinks (the sinks were required by the health department). We began to upgrade every concession stand in the building, and we even expanded and added a few where precious space permitted. The objectives were to make them more appealing and attractive to the patron; to create more points of sale from which patrons could be served; to improve the signage and menu boards; and generally to better organize the product and its delivery. And instead of using outside consultants or contractors, we used the MLG carpenters and electricians, who could build or wire anything and knew the building's capabilities inside and out. They did a terrific job renovating and maximized every available bit of space.

During the concessions stand renovations, I noticed an interesting thing about the construction of the Gardens. To the casual observer, it looked fairly symmetrical on its east and west sides. However, the shape of the main supporting columns was slightly different on each side, as were some other basic design components. It made me think back to when Conn Smythe bought the property from the T. Eaton Co. in 1931 and built the arena in a remarkable six months right in the midst of the Depression for approximately $1.5 million. He used shares instead of cash as payment wherever possible. I imagined a horde of frantic workers busy on their section of the building, like ants, each creating their own piece of Maple Leaf Gardens. I also noticed that the original design in the prospectus showed the main seating areas on the south and north sides, and not on the east and west sides, where they ended up.

Once the stands were physically upgraded, we looked at the menu and equipment. We added new soft-drink fountain equipment to replace antiques and installed popcorn machines in several stands. (Before our renovations, popcorn was pre-popped and bagged, and it often didn't taste fresh.) The profit margin on popcorn was enormous, and the fresher it was the more it sold. Creating proper exhaust venting for the stands was impossible, which limited food items to hot dogs, popcorn, ice cream products, soft drinks and packaged snack foods.

The renos were done; it was up to the staff to sell. We hoped the transaction time for each sale would be reduced dramatically, so staff could serve more people during the short intermissions. Many of the part-time concessions staff had worked at the Gardens for years. The change to the way they did their jobs scared the life out of most of them; they were a part of the culture and work ethic I was trying to change. Generally, the transaction time was abysmal, and I'm sure many patrons didn't want to wait for most of an intermission to get served. And while there were also hawkers in the stands, their volume was minimal compared to what a concession stand could do. Getting good, conscientious and hard-working concessions staff was an ongoing struggle.

My focus shifted next to the all-important financial accountability. For years, financial settlements and inventory checks after each event were done on a "close is close enough" basis. Well, it was no longer good enough. Getting accurate financial and inventory counts was not easy, especially in the Gardens. None of the stands had cash registers (counter space was limited; electricity was not always available). It was an all-cash operation.

There were several food and beverage settlement and inventory systems in the marketplace. But most were tied to cash register systems. MLG needed a customized system that would combine manual and computerized input and calculation. The managers struggled to adjust to the new requirement for accurate numbers for each event. By the end of my first year at MLG, I felt it necessary to make changes at the top of the food and beverage department.

The Gardens had never had a liquor licence. The private suites could serve alcoholic beverages based on special-occasion permits, obtained for each Leafs game, but Harold Ballard had never applied for a licence to sell alcoholic beverages to the general patrons. Some felt it was long overdue and that MLG was missing out on a very profitable revenue stream. Others felt that Leafs games should remain dry. And some fans said the way the Leafs often played drove them to drink, and why not service the need?

Cliff and the board decided they wanted me to get the Gardens licenced for the sale of alcoholic beverages. Thus began a bureaucratic process that took months. The opportunity to sell alcoholic beverages at sporting events in Ontario was fairly new and confined to only a few venues; eventually the Gardens became one of them. When the licence was finally issued, alcoholic beverages were confined to beer and wine; hard spirits were allowed only in the private suites. To discourage over consumption, we had at least one "lite" beer on tap, and signs were posted with the message to "Drink Responsibly." All alcoholic beverage service at Leafs games stopped at the end of the second period. The licence was confined to professional sporting events, and alcoholic beverages were rarely permitted at other events.

The Gardens had no equipment for serving alcoholic beverages, and MLG had to buy portable stands, then set up pouring systems at designated concession stands and build refrigeration and storage areas for the products. The start-up cost was huge, but the payback flowed as soon as the first beer was sold. Alcohol presented its share of headaches, but it quickly became very profitable.

The liquor licencing body encouraged MLG to expand its menu in conjunction with the sale of alcoholic beverages. They wanted to see more substantial food choices, not just packaged snack foods. Pizza was our choice. When we started to make our popcorn fresh on-site at each concession stand, we freed up the room where the popcorn had been made. We did a deal with a major pizza company: we provided them with the space and they set up their own kitchen to make and supply fresh pizza to several designated concession stands. There were warmers to keep the pizza hot and fresh. It was a big initiative and strained both the Gardens and the pizza company staff, but the product was well received and a great addition to our menu.

Another area that needed revision was the service of food and beverages to the private suites. The Hot Stove Lounge prepared and delivered orders to the private suites, but the service was inadequate. I recommended that we contract an outside supplier to service the private suites for Leafs games and other events as required. I called for proposals and received a half a dozen of them. One was from J.J. Muggs Gourmet Catering. Not only was their proposal the best operationally and financially for MLG, they desperately wanted the contract. There was only one problem. Ted Nikolaou, the owner of J.J. Muggs, was a close friend of Stavro's and also on the MLG board. Definitely a conflict of interest. All the proposals were submitted to Cliff and the board, with management's recommendation to accept J.J. Muggs, who were approved. Nikolaou excused himself from the discussion and the decision. Accepting the proposal turned out to be a better solution than MLG could have hoped for. Manager Tony Palermo bent over backwards to make sure that J.J. Muggs complied with all the terms and conditions of the contract—or exceeded them. And they did.

Pricing was constantly monitored and reviewed. We regularly checked to see what our competitors were selling their products for. The venue we monitored the most was the SkyDome. When it opened, there was a lot of public outcry about the excessive prices charged for food and beverages at the SkyDome, particularly in their private suites. MLG's strategy was to keep our prices just below those at the SkyDome so we could stay below the radar and avoid criticism. Generally the strategy worked. But there was no question that most of the food and drink available at the Gardens was expensive.

The per-capita sales numbers for all food and beverage concessions sales steadily went up over the years, particularly for Leafs games, as we got better organized. There were always staffing issues to deal with, but generally the food and beverage department was a very successful and profitable area of the building operations division.

—∿—

The security and event staff department combined full-time and part-time security and was responsible for all security for the Gardens and part-time event ushering staff for all events.

Before Steve Stavro took over, the Gardens was protected only by a night watchman after hours. Because of all the comings and goings in Ballard's later years and Stavro's rocky start, the Gardens needed better surveillance and security. The goal was to protect the building and its property: there were many stories of how all sorts of things walked out of the Gardens. The doors were wide open. It was said Ballard tolerated pilfering because he never paid good wages, but every once in awhile he would catch someone and set an example, to remind everyone he knew what was going on. I planned to set up regulated access to and from the Gardens. First we would secure the exterior envelope, and then we would better secure the interior. We replaced all the exterior doors and installed new locks—a good first step, as it seemed everyone in the building had keys.

I hired a group of full-time and part-time security personnel to monitor all comings and goings from the building at all times. The next step was to install video surveillance equipment around the perimeter of the property and in the lobby, at main doors, and so on. The technology was rapidly improving, but it was expensive, and the cost benefit was questionable. Electronic monitoring didn't really deter theft and vandalism as expected. The best strategy was to discourage staff and outsiders from trying to exploit MLG property. The department had been unionized shortly after I arrived. When we tried to install more electronic security equipment, we faced a challenge. The union always pushed for people over equipment. Management pushed for what was best for MLG. The union never made any of management's decisions easy.

The other part of the department supervised the entire part-time event ushering staff. It was a huge logistical job. The need for ushering

at Leafs games was relatively easy: the games required a full comple-
ment. But not that easy! Only usherettes worked in the gold area of
seating. Why? Because it had always been that way. But by 1992, with
equal rights a big issue in the workplace, many of the male ushers
wanted the opportunity to work in the gold area.

Over the years, ushering staff were assigned regularly to the same
areas of seating, so they became familiar with their area and got to know
many of the regular hockey fans. The disadvantage was they seldom did
any ushering; the regulars all knew where their seats were. When I first
arrived, most of the ushering staff were more interested in watching the
games than in fulfilling their ushering duties. Many of them admitted
they only took the job so they could watch the games. This was definitely
a part of the culture and work ethic that needed to change!

The department manager moved the staff to different seating areas
and told them to escort patrons to seats and monitor their areas, especially after alcoholic beverages were allowed. They had a job to do,
and it didn't include watching games or events. There was some resistance to this strategy, but eventually the staff accepted the change.

Ushers and usherettes were recruited by Teamsters Local 847.
Once they were unionized, scheduling staff for Leafs games and other
events became a logistical nightmare. For events other than Leafs
games, ushering staff requirements were dictated by anticipated ticket
sales. There were minimum requirements for any event in the Gardens; union steward always pushed for more staff, and management
wanted the number required for safety. Events producers or promoters paid for ushering staff. MLG wasn't out of pocket if more staff
was used, so why did we care? We cared for several reasons. Event
producers always questioned the charges; we had no interest in gouging our very important customers; and in an increasingly tight and
competitive market, MLG had to keep costs as low as possible. The
department manager constantly struggled to convince unionized staff
that it was in everyone's best interest to keep costs down.

As rock concerts got louder and more raucous in the 1990s, it became increasingly difficult to get ushering staff to work them. Union
work is based on seniority, and many of the senior staff had the chance
to work almost every Leafs game or event. Some of them, particularly

usherettes, didn't like dealing with the rowdy concert crowd and chose not to work. Many didn't like the excessive noise—and I can't blame them for that. But management faced a scheduling nightmare for many concerts.

The alcoholic-beverages licence created a need for a whole new group of event staff. For a typical Leafs game, the alcohol security staff consisted of approximately thirty-six part-time unionized workers. They monitored the sale and consumption of alcoholic beverages, and they monitored the sellers. With the patrons, they focused on underage and excessive drinking. When they monitored the sellers and pourers, they watched for recycling of cups and other forms of cheating. Inventory control was based on the number of cups sold. Some sellers would refill a patron's used cup and pocket the money. This area needed constant vigilance as both groups were unionized and reluctant to snitch on each other.

The managers of the security and event staff had a stressful and demanding job. Their first responsibility was to make sure the Gardens was supervised, safe and secure, while producers wanted to spend the absolute minimum, and the union steward pushed for more, more, more. They generally performed their job well.

Early in 1997, a bomb exploded in the Gardens. Not an explosive, but a situation that ripped MLG and the Gardens apart with similar devastation. When the media broke a story of allegations of sordid and despicable acts of sexual abuse that supposedly took place in the Gardens, MLG and the Leafs jumped from the sports page to the front page. It would taint and tarnish forever the perception many had of the Gardens as a revered hockey shrine.

Apparently, a young man named Martin Kruze had confidentially approached MLG as early as 1992, alleging that when he was a young boy, he was sexually abused in the Gardens by a part-time MLG employee. In 1993, Kruze approached the police, and an extensive investigation followed.

And then, in early 1997, media attacked the story like sharks in a feeding frenzy. To them, the sordid story was better than following the colourless Leafs. Everyone wondered where it would lead. Naively, MLG had kept the 1992 meeting with Kruze confidential, probably not realizing that he later went to the police. Maybe they thought they had dealt with Kruze and that the unpleasant issue would quietly go away. After all, it had happened long before they were involved with MLG. They couldn't have been more wrong. Once the police were brought in, it was a serious criminal matter, and everyone at MLG was put under the microscope as the police tried to get at the truth.

Their investigation led the police to the early 1970s, to a part-time equipment manager named Gordon Stuckless, who was identified as the abuser by Kruze and some others who worked at the Gardens. During a three-year investigation, another part-time Gardens employee was identified as an abuser. John Paul Roby was a long-time usher at the Gardens and still part of the event staff while I was there. There was no evidence at the time that Roby did anything criminal in the Gardens, but he apparently used his job as usher to pursue his victims. I was shocked and distressed when this came to light.

My security and events staff manager and I met the police on several occasions in an effort to discover if there were other offenders currently working for MLG. It became evident that the Gardens was vulnerable to pedophiles, considered to be "the most devious of criminals," because the Gardens attracted young hockey fans and concertgoers. It was an ideal place for the sexual predator to prey on victims. Some members of the board aggressively and personally attacked me because I didn't know about Roby. He was one of some six hundred full-time and part-time staff working for me in the building operations division. We did some personal checking as part of a job application screening process, but privacy issues and personal rights made it very difficult to detect a sexual predator. And Roby had worked part-time at the Gardens for years, long before any such screening was done. One board member wanted me to guarantee that no such thing would ever happen again in the Gardens. I assured the board we would use all hiring precautions available to prevent a reoccurrence. But I couldn't guarantee it would never happen again. It seemed to turn into an internal witch hunt by the board looking for someone to blame.

At the end of my grilling by Stavro and key board members, I wondered whether some of them were more concerned about protecting themselves than protecting innocent victims in the Gardens. Board members were trying to get themselves off the hot seat—and the hot question was: why had MLG not dealt with Kruze differently in 1992? Their conduct compromised the integrity of all management.

Throughout this stressful period, Stavro and his board members stayed well undercover and made no public comment. They left Cliff to fend off the media all by himself. One day I found him in the front lobby of the Gardens, pinned up against the wall, microphones shoved in his face and questions flying at him from all directions. Cliff earned every penny he was paid that day. Eventually the MLG board had to face the media and explain their handling, or rather mishandling, of the biggest cover-up in MLG history. It was an awful time to be working at MLG.

Stuckless eventually pled guilty to twenty-four counts of sexual and indecent assault and after an appeal was sentenced to five years. Roby was designated a dangerous offender and incurable pedophile, and died of a heart attack in custody in 2001. A third suspect, George Hannah, died before charges could be laid. And tragically, Martin Kruze jumped to his death from the Bloor Street viaduct in Toronto shortly after Stuckless was convicted. The sex abuse scandal left an indelible stain on the Gardens and everyone who worked there.

The one department that operated year round was the building operations department. Whether for a Leafs game, event or concert, the building operated every day of the year. Just before I arrived, the building operations manager had retired. His replacement, Wayne Gillespie, had been head electrician, a unionized position, and this was his first non-union management position. Over the six years I worked with Wayne, I felt he was ambivalent about his role as a company manager and never really crossed over to management's side. He often tried to straddle the fence between unionized employees and the management team. It was an issue we wrestled with the whole time I was with MLG.

Wayne was dedicated to the Gardens. No one worked harder or longer hours to make sure the building was as functional as possible and always ready. In this aspect he was a very practical and effective manager. And he oversaw every Leafs game and every event while I was there, from the start of move-in until the last person had left the building on move-out, often into the middle of the night.

The only other non-union person in the department was the assistant building manager, Bernie Fournier. He had been Conn Smythe's chauffeur, and held the man in high regard. When I arrived at MLG, Bernie had been there for more than thirty years, and had done a variety of jobs around the Gardens. We developed a real friendship. There were two qualities he possessed that I greatly respected: he was intensely loyal to MLG and the Gardens, and he was honest. He was the perfect person to watch the back door of the Gardens on Wood Street. Once he was given procedures to follow and enough support, he guarded the back end of the Gardens like a hawk.

Bernie never threw away anything, and his office was like a museum of Gardens memorabilia. I always enjoyed my visits there; we would sit and reminisce about the "old days." Over the years, Bernie had seen it all. His adult life had been spent mostly at the Gardens, and he was intensely dedicated to its well-being. After forty-two years of loyal service, he retired when the Gardens closed in 1999, choosing not to move to the new Air Canada Centre.

The building operations department also oversaw the operating engineers, electricians, carpenters, sound technicians and all the building's labour and maintenance staff. The labour and maintenance staff were the toughest group to supervise, as all were members of the militant and aggressive Teamsters. Constantly prodded by their business agent and union stewards, they consistently questioned and challenged management's every effort to operate the Gardens as MLG thought best. Bernie determined the scheduling for labour and battled almost every day over who and how many people would work.

In addition to directing department staff, Wayne dealt with members of the IATSE union, who were called in for most events, particularly concerts. Dealing with IATSE's always excessive labour demands was probably the most difficult situation Wayne and I had to deal with in the Gardens.

—ɱ—

As vice-president of building operations, in the beginning I regularly attended board of directors' meetings to report on the operations of the Gardens. I sat through the whole meeting, waiting for my item to come up on the agenda. I was a spectator at discussions of legal issues and the status of the Leafs. By the time the board finally got to my report, they had often lost interest. However, I always came prepared and hoped that board members might read my report after the meeting. Most board members didn't pay much attention to building issues. After a few meetings, I waited to be called in when they got to my agenda items. I was never fully involved in board decision making.

As part of my overall monitoring of the Gardens during a Leafs game, I would generally drop in to the directors' lounge at the end of each period to check that everything was in order. Between periods, there was free booze and a lavish spread of food, and the directors always had guests and friends who wanted to be invited into the exclusive inner sanctum of the Gardens. Occasionally Stavro's assistant would call to say that Steve wanted me and Susan, if she was at the game, to go to the directors' lounge immediately to meet and greet with the guests. Steve spent most of his time in the directors' lounge either with family members or huddled in a corner in conversation with one of his inner circle of associates. He seldom worked the room or made people welcome.

Over the years, I met some interesting VIPs. On one occasion, a gentleman I instantly recognized was standing alone with his wife in the crowded room, ignored by all around him. It was Gene Hackman. I was a huge fan of his many movies, so I went up and introduced myself. He hadn't gone unrecognized, but many people were apprehensive about approaching many of the celebrities invited to the directors' lounge. Hackman and his wife lived in Santa Fe, New Mexico; he was in Toronto working on a movie. They were a very unassuming and personable couple.

There was some real commotion when Tom Cruise and his wife, Nicole Kidman, made an appearance. Everyone wanted to meet them. Tom grew up in Ottawa, and I'm sure he was knowledgeable about hockey. I was surprised at how short he was, particularly beside his statuesque and beautiful wife. The men were attracted to her like moths to a radiant light. I don't remember meeting Tom, but I sure do Nicole.

And there was Neil Young. He attended with his father, Scott, one of the sports writers who followed the Leafs back when I played. I had seen him periodically over the years and always had a great regard for his literary skills. Neil had launched his singing career at the Gardens. Canadian musicians who played at the Gardens had made it to the big leagues.

Most of the staff in the building operations division worked long and hard to make sure the Gardens was operated and managed efficiently and effectively. We made marked improvements in the building and installed better organization and greater accountability. However, our efforts went mostly unnoticed or unacknowledged by the executive, who didn't appreciate what was involved in keeping the building running.

Cliff and the board seemed always to be preoccupied: frustrated and disappointed with the Leafs, with Stavro's legal battles, with plans for a new arena, or with something as small as how many tickets they were going to get for an event. Generally, they had little interest in the day-to-day operations of the Gardens. And Stavro's interest in the building was focused on his pet projects. The people who worked for the building operations division felt ignored by the executive; we never felt as if we were an important part of the MLG team.

A New Gardens

ONE ISSUE that surfaced shortly after I arrived at MLG was the future of the Gardens. By the early 1990s, the Gardens was an old and tired building, and one of the few remaining NHL Original Six arenas. It had a lot of deficiencies; compared with the new generation of facilities being built by NHL teams, it lacked amenities. It was not air conditioned, which presented real operational issues at playoff time; its seating was tight and uncomfortable; it had a limited number of hodge-podge private suites; its electronic scoreboard-clock was obsolete and could not handle video replay; its food and beverage concessions were inadequate; and it seated only 16,000 patrons compared with the 18,000 to 20,000 the new arenas held. Plus, many of its operational systems were antiquated and obsolete.

Cliff had recently been involved in new arenas in Atlanta and Calgary. He was impressed with the history of the Gardens and its status in the hockey world, but he thought as a building it was a clunker. With his prodding, the idea of building a new Gardens somewhere in central Toronto was sown. While Cliff built his Stanley Cup championship team, I hoped I would be a part of building a new Gardens to accommodate it.

Most of the board had little apparent interest in how the building looked and operated. But, in spite of all the other issues he had to deal with, Steve Stavro had a real personal interest in the Gardens. The Leafs might have been Cliff's team, but the Gardens was Stavro's building. He was proud of its historical importance, and after some years of neglect he wanted it tidied up and put back into shape in a way that would have made Conn Smythe proud.

Cliff and some board members were interested in a new Gardens; Stavro was interested in renovating the existing Gardens. I was getting a mixed message. Stavro instructed me to focus only on fixing up and maintaining the current Gardens and not to worry about a new building. And so, with Stavro's prodding, I developed capital and operating budgets, and each year continued to pour money into upgrading, restoring, maintaining and improving the Gardens as best we could.

Stavro's personal interest and pride in the Gardens were a mixed blessing. It seemed that because he couldn't participate in the running of the Leafs, he became involved in the operations and management of the building. Along with his interest and support in building issues came a lot of dictatorial and impulsive orders, some of which made little economic sense and for which I had no budget.

The first major project Stavro announced was cleaning the exterior of the building. Back sometime in the 1970s, Harold Ballard had the bricks of the Gardens sandblasted. The yellow bricks had then lost their protective layer and begun to absorb pollution, and by 1992 they were dirtier and more stained than ever. The cleaning of the Gardens' exterior face was designed to show the public that there was a new landlord at MLG, one who cared about the well-being of the sacred Gardens. Stavro was shrewd and perceptive, and he knew that by doing something as visible as cleaning up the outside of the Gardens he could promote the image of himself as a benevolent trustee of this shrine of hockey.

It turned out to be a huge project, logistically, physically and financially. The cleaning method was a modern and acceptable chemical wash, no more abrasive and destructive sandblasting. The sidewalks around the Gardens were very narrow, so there were problems with scaffolding and there was limited work space. Also, most of the work had to be done in the evenings so as not to interrupt the daytime pedestrian traffic around the building. And people were concerned about the residue of the chemical wash going down the city drains.

In the midst of the project, I got a call from the contractor. He told me he wanted to see me right away on the front sidewalk. I rushed down immediately, fearing there had been an accident. He took me across Carlton Street and pointed out an obvious crack in the bricks that went from the bottom of the building to the top on each side of the main lobby doors. And there were two others in approximately the same locations on the Wood Street side. Had the building shifted over the years? What was the cause? Was it serious? What to do about it?

I immediately returned to my office and contacted MLG's consulting structural engineers. For a few days, while they were preparing their report, I was concerned that the Gardens might need major structural repair, repair that might not be practical. We might need a new arena sooner rather than later. However, after a thorough review of the cracks, the engineers concluded that they were not serious. In fact, the Gardens was made up of three separate structures enclosed by a brick facade. There was a square box with four large pillars that supported the domed roof; and there were two rectangular reinforced-concrete structures attached on each side, making up the main seating areas. When the structures were joined in 1931, the builders had not created proper expansion joints between the roof structure and the seating structures. The cracks we saw were just expansion cracks. And fortunately, all four of them were reasonably symmetrical, not too wide, and had only cracked the bricks from top to bottom. The contractor filled the cracks with caulking and moved on.

Most of the grime and dirt that had been washed away was carbon from exhaust fumes and other city air pollutants. When the job was finished the result was amazing. The yellow bricks were revitalized, and the building sparkled on the outside. The white dome roof had also been cleaned, and the old Gardens truly looked rejuvenated.

During this project I saw Stavro at work first hand. He was a tough negotiator. Ian Clarke, MLG's money man, and I had begun the negotiations with the contractor for a completed price. And then Stavro intervened and bullied the contractor into accepting his price. Fair and reasonable didn't seem to be part of the strategy. The contractor wanted the prestige of the job, and Stavro made him pay handsomely for it. It was the first of Stavro's many interventions into the building projects. No matter how good and fair a price Ian and I negotiated, it was only the starting price when Stavro got involved. It seemed that his price was the only price. I began to understand how he had made his Knob Hill Farms chain of grocery stores so successful. And I found out early that Stavro was a tough man to work for. You didn't work *with* him; it was strictly *for* him. There was Stavro's way, and there was Stavro's way.

Stavro worshipped the Gardens; it was his building. He knew that, physically and economically in the NHL of the 1990s, the Gardens was inadequate in many ways, but he wasn't pushing for a new home for the Leafs. Many in his court of advisers wanted at least 18,500 seats and at least 100 private suites, plus all the re-lated supporting amenities, but Stavro felt the Gardens could be restored and improved to meet NHL criteria. He was confident he could generate adequate ticket revenue out of the 16,000 seats in the Gardens. And thus began an unprecedented escalation of ticket prices, which continued dramatically each season. Many of us thought there would be buyer resistance, but Stavro realized that Leafs fans would pay top prices to see their team, win or lose. He wasn't convinced he needed a larger arena to make more money. He saw the home arena as basically a television studio, where he could produce the games before a relatively small and privileged "live" audience. The real audience would be the TV viewers. And why build a new hundred-million-dollar plus TV studio when the current one still worked? While his board and president dreamed of a new facility, Stavro was spending money in the Gardens as if he planned to stay there forever.

In the fall of 1992, MLG contracted a local architectural firm to in-vestigate ways in which the Gardens could be improved and upgraded. The company's real interest was in building a new arena. Stavro wasn't interested in their new arena proposal. I prepared a document outlin-ing short-term and long-term upgrading and renovation projects to improve the Gardens, and compared renovation to building a new building. After I submitted my information, I had very little input into the decision-making process, and I was never privy to what went on between Stavro, the board and Cliff.

All that came out of the architect's proposal was a plan to upgrade the lobby. The Gardens' lobby was shabby, dark and small. However, there was no way to expand it; all we could hope to do was dress it up and better organize it. After the upgrade, the lobby was much improved, particularly the box office ticket windows. Stavro realized the front lobby was the first impression of the inside of the Gardens a patron got, and it was important that impression be a favourable one.

Cliff also had projects he wanted done for his hockey department. First he wanted the whole hockey office completely renovated and expanded. The Leafs' dressing room had limited space, but he wanted it expanded as much as possible and totally renovated. Many people considered it the worst dressing room in the NHL. Discussions about a dressing room showed just how much hockey had changed since I played: now the players demanded a lounge area in which to relax, a weight and fitness room, whirlpool tubs and saunas. When it was completed, it was so cozy it seemed the players didn't want to go on the ice and play sometimes. A lot of good hockey players used the original Leafs' dressing room with great success, and it made me wonder if the current players were pampered too much.

From 1992 to 1996, the capital and operating projects I included in my yearly MLG business plans all made the assumption that there was no plan to move and build a new Gardens. While other people were determining the future of the Gardens, I plowed ahead to make it the best building it could be in the interim. We undertook to improve, upgrade and renovate the whole place: exterior cleaning, front lobby, washrooms, concession stands, hockey office, dressing rooms, private suites, box office. We replaced the exterior doors, then bought and renovated 70 Carlton Street for expanded administration offices. We painted throughout, replaced turnstiles, bought new staging equipment and an electronic-video security system, added a new exterior marquee and electronic message centres, purchased a new Zamboni, replaced the food and beverage refrigeration, bought new ice-refrigeration equipment, retrofitted the scoreboard clock, built tree planters on sidewalks around the building, and replaced all interior signage. And we did many more projects to improve the appearance and operations of the Gardens.

The Gardens was upgraded, improved and renovated to its practical maximum. Every square centimetre of space was being utilized and maximized. The upgrades cost close to $7 million and took almost six years, and after all that the same conspicuous deficiencies remained. The most notable was the absence of air conditioning. (There was no practical way to install air conditioning in the building.) There were other problems that couldn't be solved within the existing Gardens footprint and available space: the seating was still cramped and uncomfortable, the roof wouldn't support a new scoreboard-clock-video replay system, there was no room to add more private suites, and the food and beverage concession stands couldn't keep up with patron expectations. It was a good old building, but it was still an old building.

In the spring of 1996, Stavro was still the controlling shareholder, but his new partners in MLG started to push harder for a new Gardens. It was almost as if there were two companies within MLG: one to manage and operate the current Gardens, and one to work on developing a new building. Stavro felt the existing Gardens was adequate; Cliff and Stavro's partners thought it was time for a new, modern, state-of-the-art sports and entertainment venue for the Leafs. A whole new department was set up to explore this possibility and develop plans.

Meanwhile, across town, John Bitove, Jr., had won out over Larry Tanenbaum for Toronto's NBA franchise and had his Toronto Raptors operational. They were using the SkyDome as an interim venue, and even played a few regular-season games in the Gardens. Bitove and his partner, Allan Slaight, had plans ready to build their own brand-new arena on the site of the old post office at Bay Street and Lake Shore Boulevard.

What unfolded over the next year or so was the most ridiculous of scenarios. Steve Stavro and John Bitove, Sr., did not get along, even though they were related. They competed over who was most successful and influential in the Toronto Macedonian–Greek community. Stavro was adamant the Leafs would never be a tenant in someone else's building, particularly a building owned by a Bitove. While MLG was ambivalent and indecisive about whether to keep the Leafs in the

Gardens or build a new facility, Bitove and Slaight moved ahead with their own building.

So there were plans for two brand-new major arena and entertainment venues in downtown Toronto, one for the NBA Raptors and the other for the NHL Leafs. MLG's venue would be part of a renovated Union Station complex, a stone's throw from the Bitove–Slaight facility. The public thought this was inconceivable economic lunacy, and all because of the egos, arrogance and stubbornness of the two major-league franchise owners.

It seemed obvious that the first group with the shovel in the ground would be the winner in the building battle. And that was Bitove–Slaight with their Air Canada Centre. But massive ego and stubborn pride wouldn't let MLG's accept that they had lost the building race. And so the charade dragged on for months, like a soap opera. Finally, sanity prevailed, and MLG and Bitove–Slaight began to negotiate how both franchises would share one jointly owned facility. It was the obvious and only sensible solution.

And then there was a curve ball thrown into the bizarre scenario. In the ownership deal between Bitove and Slaight, there was a shotgun clause giving one party an ultimatum to buy out or sell to the other partner. Slaight was a reluctant principal investor, and didn't like the escalating costs of the Air Canada Centre or the daily chaos. He set a reasonable price for his exit, expecting Bitove to jump at the chance to own the Raptors franchise and the new building. To the shock of most and I'm sure Slaight, Bitove unexpectedly took Slaight's offer and cashed out. Slaight found himself the sole owner, not exactly what he wanted or imagined.

Bitove's departure from the ownership equation effectively cleared the way for MLG to make a bid to take over the Raptors and the Air Canada Centre and combine them with the Leafs and the Gardens into one big sports and entertainment conglomerate in Toronto. Slaight finally got his graceful exit and bid adieu to owning sports franchises or arenas.

MLG's plans to build their dream arena on the Union Station site disappeared in the blink of an eye. They got ownership of the Air Canada Centre early enough in the construction process so they could modify it to meet the Leafs' special needs. (The building had been designed primarily to accommodate a basketball team.) While an agonizing process, the end result was the obvious one to every sports fan in Toronto. When all was said and done, Stavro, Tanenbaum and their group had packaged two of the three major-league franchises in Toronto to play out of their new building, the Air Canada Centre. The newly formed Maple Leaf Sports and Entertainment Ltd. had approximately $500 million tied up in their new enterprise.

When plans to develop a new Gardens became serious, I made written submissions to the board and Cliff. I was involved in the building of Copps Coliseum and had some fifteen years' experience operating three major arena facilities in Canada; I thought I had something of value to offer. But it soon became apparent that I probably wasn't going to be involved in the planning, development and building of a new Gardens, as I had hoped. The sex scandal had cast a stigma of shame over the Gardens and everyone who worked there; perhaps the board planned to create a whole new organization when it moved, in an attempt to leave the Gardens' unsavoury baggage behind. It would be a sad epitaph for a building with such a long history.

—ɯ—

I had briefly been Ken Dryden's teammate with the Nats in 1969, but I was unable to connect with him when he became captain of the MLG management team. Within a few months of his hiring, it became obvious that my days with MLG were numbered. I thought my experience and background could be a real asset and complementary to him. But apparently he wasn't interested. Even without any experience, he was going to do it his way, and with his people. Somehow, he'd sold the board on his credentials, mostly theoretical, and the board, to the disbelief of most people at MLG, had turned control over to him. He was the organization's new guiding light. He would try to regenerate the Leafs as a winner, and he would micromanage the Gardens, right down to making sure there were better hot dogs in the concession stands. And so began another chapter in the MLG's, Gardens' and Leafs' long, illustrious and at times agonizing and epic saga.

I was confined to babysitting the Gardens until the Leafs left, at which point I would be responsible for turning out the lights and locking the doors on my way out. When you're on the outs, it's time to get out, and it was time for me to bow out of MLG and the facilities management business after some fifteen years. We negotiated a mutually agreeable severance package, and at the end of January 1998, I quietly left MLG and the Gardens and moved on to other things.

When I left MLG, the Leafs were no closer to winning their twelfth Stanley Cup than they'd been since 1967. Stavro had shown that in many respects he was not unlike his predecessor, which might explain their friendship and the disappointing performance of the Leafs over the years.

I left the Gardens with real sadness and regret. I had met and worked with many fine people, and I would miss them. And there had certainly never been a dull day on the job. But my biggest regret was that for the second time, first as a player and then as a facility manager, I had failed to leave much of a positive mark on the history of MLG or the Gardens.

On February 13, 1999, the Leafs played their last game in the Gardens. They played the Chicago Black Hawks, the same team the Leafs played to open the building in 1931. My uncle Charlie played in that first game, and there I was at the last game. He played on the first Leafs Stanley Cup team, and I played on the last one. And in 1999, just as in 1931, the Leafs lost. Between those losses, the Leafs won their share of games, but the loss may well have been prophetic as they readied to move to their new home arena. I didn't turn out the lights in the Gardens, but I was there when they were turned out. Along with about a hundred former and current Leafs players, from Red Horner to Matts Sundin, we gave the old Gardens an emotional send-off. The Conacher family had a long and varied history with the Gardens, from its first day to its last.

My last on-ice appearance as a former NHL hockey player took place during the 2000 NHL All-Star Weekend, held in Toronto. Leafs and Canadiens alumni played a game as part of the weekend activities, and I was invited to play. I was surprised to be asked, as there were many more notable players than me. I had had a short and inconspicuous NHL career, and I'd often said that the only problem with my career was that my first goal and my last goal were too close together. But the organizers of the weekend wanted all the Stanley Cup winners who could still skate and hadn't had heart bypass surgery, so I made the last cut. It was a really enjoyable night; we all had a chance to play in the new Air Canada Centre, and I knew I would never do that again. It was a memorable way to end a career. I took my skates off for the last time shortly after that game.

And my final NHL off-ice involvement began in the fall of 2002, when I became the president of the NHL Alumni Association (NHLAA). Since the inception of the NHL, only approximately 5,000 players have ever played a game in the league, and about 3,400 are still living. It is a very exclusive fraternity of which I'm proud to be a member. The NHLAA brings former NHL players together to support and participate in charitable causes, assists them in their transition to life after hockey, promotes the history and tradition of the game, and generally represents the interests of former players and preserves their contribution to the history of the game.

In the early fall of 2005, after almost three years as the president of the NHLAA, I stepped down and effectively left the hockey world—except as an ever hopeful Leafs fan. It marked the end of more than fifty-five years in and around the great game of hockey.

Post-Game Recap and Parting Shots

FOR MORE than half a century, I participated in Canada's longest-running soap opera, the game of hockey. I travelled in and around the world of hockey in many capacities on and off the ice. My journey has been quite different than most. As I look back, many observations and thoughts come to mind.

—⟋⟍—

On September 16, 2004, the game and business of major-league professional hockey came unglued, and the most acrimonious and lengthy labour disruption in professional sports history began. The NHL stopped when the owners locked out the players; the lockout seemed to symbolize many of the issues threatening the game and business of hockey at all levels. Yet another episode of the soap opera began.

At the time, I was president of the NHL Alumni Association (NHLAA) and a very interested observer. Over the years, I had been on both sides of the professional hockey table and certainly appreciated the positions of both players and management.

In early 1995 the league and NHLPA had negotiated a ten-year collective bargaining agreement (CBA); that CBA sowed the seeds of discontent that matured in the fall of 2004. As I saw it, several main factors caused the NHL to hit the financial wall.

Some NHL owners seemed to think future expansion opportunities were endless; and the expansion fees were a welcomed short-term shot in the-arm for many current franchises that constantly struggled with rapidly escalating salaries and operating costs. With an insatiable appetite for expansion dollars, some franchises were granted to questionable markets. Some owners probably thought the money-pie from expansion would just continue to grow. This proved to be a mistaken assumption.

For some thirty years, the NHL tried to force-feed television coverage of hockey to a generally apathetic American audience with only periodic and regional successes. The league had expected the NHL to be as popular as the NFL, MLB and the NBA, and anticipated the big money that comes from network coverage; it was supposed to be the financial foundation of the NHL empire. It hasn't happened and it's not going to happen. Hockey is a regional sport in the US, and the NHL will have to live with regional television coverage and the dramatically reduced dollars generated from this more limited exposure.

But it was the arbitration system used to resolve player contract disputes that had the biggest financial effect on the owners. The system allowed player salaries to explode between 1995 and 2004: average salaries skyrocketed from $500,000 to $1.8 million. Some marquee players were paid $10 million. A journeyman NHLer, the supporting cast, was just making too much money. Many players thought the owners were obliged to continue paying the astronomically high salaries. When the owners realized they were living beyond their means, they told the players, who did not believe it or refused to accept it. Every working stiff in North America got it, but it was a long, slow, acrimonious process for most of the players to get it.

To the NHLPA, the arbitration system and free agency were tools to preserve the open market the players definitely wanted to see continue. But the arbitration system as it operated between the NHLPA and the NHL was more a function of a union environment than a real open market. The NHLPA charts all player salaries. Based on statistics, age and status, each player is slotted within a salary range with his peers. Using this information, the goal of the NHLPA is to see player salaries steadily and collectively escalate. Under the direction of Bob Goodenow, the NHLPA successfully executed its strategy. Owners were driven by a desire to win; they wanted the best players they could get. Players' agents used the NHLPA salary chart to repeatedly exploit an obvious opportunity. It was a one-way street against the owners.

Because team owners and management seldom thought or acted collectively, the tactic was to divide (or isolate) and conquer. If owners protested salaries, more times than not the arbitrators awarded players huge increases.

By the end of the ten-year sweetheart deal for the players, most NHL owners had had enough. Everyone wanted more than the system could generate, particularly the players. More than half a team's operating costs went into players' salaries, and many teams were not successful on the ice or at the box office. Owners came to a business conclusion: they could not continue on this basis, and some teams would lose less money if they stopped operating. The financial platform of ice upon which the NHL planned to support itself was melting away as many owners struggled to stay afloat in a sea of red ink. The NHL owners decided that if they couldn't operate on a financially viable basis with some reasonable degree of "cost certainty," then they would not operate at all. To go forward, a new deal was needed.

The players generally blamed the owners for the situation and accused them of mismanagement. But it was the players who had benefited. Both parties agreed that the NHL was broken on and off the ice and had to be fixed. But the players were determined that a solution not affect their pocketbooks. The NHLPA and its players began a game of negotiation chicken with the owners.

The NHLPA totally misread the resolve of the owners, and they just didn't get the economic reality of the situation. The players didn't trust the owners; nor did they understand the normal employer–employee relationship. The NHLPA had a one-issue inflexible position: no salary cap. Negotiations were nasty and protracted; it didn't help that the lead negotiators, the NHL's Gary Bettman and the NHLPA's Bob Goodenow, were like oil and water at the negotiating table. It's a classic business case study of how a business could not manage its success. It began a journey of self-destruction and diminishing returns.

In 1967 I was a founding member of the NHLPA, which was set up to represent the interests of players in the NHL. I supported the NHLPA then and I support it today. The membership at large (some 750) relies on its designated leaders to define, articulate and achieve the players' collective goals. However, I realize that collectively the players are inexperienced and naïve; and the process and ability to communicate and understand are far from perfect. During the lock-out, because the NHLPA had such a strong-willed and focused leader in Bob Goodenow, it was often difficult to determine whose agenda was being pushed in the negotiations.

On the other side of the table, Gary Bettman was the mouthpiece for the thirty owners. The hockey owner (individual, group or corpo-ration) is a strange animal in the business world. Owners are driven by many different factors: too much money, boredom with their day jobs, greed, vanity, arrogance, ego, desire to win (sometimes at any financial cost), adulation of athletes, questionable decision-making, and I'm sure there are others. If some of these owners used the same business judgement and decision-making process in the business they earned their money in, they wouldn't have enough money to buy a hockey team. At work they are astute, shrewd and sometimes ruthless; when they buy a team, they become impulsive, arrogant, frivolous, reckless and irresponsible. And in the pursuit of winning, owners make ques-tionable decisions and often demonstrate a lack of common sense. What is it about professional sports ownership that changes otherwise successful businessmen into Economics 101 dropouts? Are there some good and responsible owners in the NHL? Probably, but we need many more. But in 2004, for one of the first times, the owners were more focused and unified than their counterparts. After 310 days of stalemate, the players had to eat humble pie to go back to work.

Like many hockey fans, I followed the work stoppage. The NHLPA and the players repeatedly said they didn't trust the NHL's financial numbers and that the NHL had mismanaged the operation of their partnership. I'm not suggesting the NHL is blameless for the situation. However, it's interesting that during almost a year of negotiations, I don't remember anyone asking a basic question of the NHLPA and its players: if they were so dissatisfied with their NHL partner, why didn't they set up their own Players Hockey League? In their league, they could have no salary cap, more free agency, any arbitration system they wanted, they could set up whatever franchises they wanted, they could build or rent arenas, they could negotiate their own TV deals, and they could make up all their own operating and playing rules.

And by the way, the players could finance their league with their own money. In the history of the NHL, there probably isn't a player who didn't want to make more money or think he was worth more. Quite natural. But every player makes nothing but money over his career. Yes, a player invests his time and body into the game, but he never has to invest money. If the players set up their own league and had to put their own money into it, I'd bet the lineup to participate would be very, very short.

Who won and who lost the NHL work stoppage? Everyone lost: the NHL, the players, the many people who work in and around the game, the fans and the game itself. How much irreparable damage was done? Only time will tell. How do the NHL and the NHLPA go forward? Together as real partners. They must develop mutual trust and an acceptable working relationship if they want to enjoy future success. They are opposite sides of the same coin; they must learn to co-exist, work and grow together. It's the only way. The NHL finally went back to work at the start of the 2005–2006 season.

The 1972 Canada–Soviet Hockey Series was a watershed in hockey history. Many of the issues and challenges that became apparent during those twenty-seven days in September are still not resolved, even after the longest work stoppage in professional sports history. The Series stands as the hockey series of the twentieth century, and an all-time classic sporting event. On the TV broadcasts, to this day, I'm the "mystery voice" in the shadow of the legendary Foster Hewitt.

It wasn't until Phil Esposito overflowed with his awkward emotional outburst in Vancouver and the team had been to Stockholm that the players started to gel as a team and play the way their talent suggested they could.

The Canadian fans who made the trip were a real part of Team Canada's success in Moscow. Their uninhibited and totally committed support was like having an extra player on the ice. Fans in the stands may never have meant more to a team than in Moscow in September 1972. The Soviets had never seen a crowd like them before, and probably haven't seen one like them since.

Game Six was pivotal. When the Soviets couldn't close out the Series in that game, the momentum started to swing towards Team Canada for the first time, and never swung back. Team Canada became confident they could win, and that they were going to win. Their passion to win rose, and the Soviets had never played at such an emotional level. They couldn't contain Team Canada.

The Clarke–Kharlamov incident is the only blemish on Team Canada's incredible win. Clarke's vicious and intentional attack on Kharlamov leaves a bad taste in my mouth to this day. Team Canada felt that to win the Series, Kharlamov had to be stopped. Clarke took it literally! It demonstrated the absolute desperation of Team Canada to win. Possibly Team Canada was more afraid of losing than the Soviets?

The Soviets had many exceptionally skilled and talented individual players, but each player functioned only as part of a team unit. Individualism was stifled by their system and way of life. The Soviets could only succeed as a team. When the team concept was not quite enough for Team Canada, inspired individual efforts ultimately made the difference. The Soviets had a truly great team; Team Canada had a more inspired one.

The Series wasn't won or lost by goaltending. Tretiak was certainly better than most people expected, but he didn't make the difference for the Soviets. The Ken Dryden–Tony Esposito tandem was good but not great, and didn't make the difference for Team Canada. All three goalies struggled at times. It was a goal scorer's Series, not a goaltender's.

Extraordinary individual efforts by Phil Esposito, Paul Henderson, Peter Mahovlich and a few others made the winning difference. Team Canada's individual stars were ultimately better than their Soviet counterparts. Canadian individualism, long a trademark of Canadian hockey, determined the outcome of the Series.

Phil Esposito repeatedly carried Team Canada on his back and gave them a chance to win. He was the heart, soul and inspirational leader of the team. Along with Paul Henderson, they made a pair the Soviets couldn't contain. Especially in Moscow on the big ice surface, Paul with his explosive speed and hot stick was an inspired man on a mission, evidenced by his timely goal in Game Eight and the other six he scored in the Series. The Soviets weren't able to contain Phil right from the start of the Series. He was the tireless workhorse who just wouldn't quit, and he had incredible determination and focus. He set up and scored goals whenever they were desperately needed. Paul was the chosen one to score the glory goals, but without Phil's preceding goals and set-ups at critical times, Paul wouldn't have been able to score three game-winning goals in the last three games. Phil was in on the last three goals in Game Eight, including the set-up for Paul's historic goal. Quite a combination!

However, had it not been for an uncharacteristically errant and disastrous clearing attempt by Soviet defenceman Valery Vasiliev with just over a minute to play in Game Eight, the outcome of the Series would probably have been different. Had Vasiliev hung onto the puck, as his training and discipline dictated, and taken it to the corner for a faceoff, the Soviets would probably have held on for a tie, which was all they felt they needed to win the Series. Vasiliev panicked and tried to clear the puck out of his zone, which instead went to Cournoyer at the point, and the rest is history. Maybe the Soviet hockey mistake of the century? How different things might have been.

Most Canadians think Paul Henderson's last goal is the most significant event in Canadian hockey history. It may well be the most dramatic and exciting goal in Canadian hockey history, but I'm not sure it's the most important event. I believe that occurred at the end of Game One, when the game of hockey in Canada, the NHL and the rest of the hockey world, changed forever. By the end of Game One, the myth of NHL supremacy and invincibility was dispelled forever, and a new era and order in hockey began. Paul's goal temporarily saved Canada's pride, naively supporting a false sense of security that Canada was still the undisputed supreme hockey nation. But after that first game in the Montreal Forum on

September 2, 1972, nothing in the hockey world was ever the same. It was the watershed for all that would follow, bigger, more far-reaching and more important even than Henderson's goal.

The Series started in one place in the hockey chronology and ended in a very different one. Seven games, fifty-nine minutes and twenty-six seconds after the opening faceoff, Henderson's electrifying goal in Game Eight made us all forget how the Series began. The euphoria of the dramatic win clouded the reality of the event. Most people thought Canada was again the top hockey nation. I thought that was a strange reaction to the win. For a Series where most predicted the Soviets would be lucky to win a game, I'm amazed that we gloat over "our victory," Canada's greatest moment in sports history, a victory won by a generous dose of good luck and the slimmest of margins. In the long run, it might have been better for Canadian hockey development had Team Canada lost.

Many players thought participating in the Series was the definitive hockey experience of their careers—even more than winning a Stanley Cup. It was the most courageous comeback in hockey history, and against outrageous odds. They became "our team" only after some serious doubts. They overcame those doubts and went on to win for Canada, and they unified the country like never before.

It's ironic that the visiting team provided all the surprises. In Canada, the Soviet team shocked Canadians with their superb level of play; in Moscow Team Canada left the Soviets devastated and bewildered as they snatched the Series with their last-minute heroics.

After 1972, the Canadian hockey establishment continued to live in the illusion all was well with the Canadian hockey system. Yet the Series revealed problems with the development of our game of hockey, and many of those problems are unresolved to this day. Canadian hockey was on the brink of decline. The Soviets and other European nations were ascending.

The Russians, eastern European countries and western European nations have in recent years, through their skills-based systems of player development, influenced and changed the hockey world—even the NHL—far more than Canada has. Our hockey system has become more like theirs, which in my opinion is a good thing. In spite of Don

Cherry's bluster and bravado over the years, Canada is still struggling to establish itself as the great hockey nation in the world. And we will only eventually achieve this goal if we build our game on—and continue to emphasize—basic skills development.

—⚬⚬⚬—

Some thirty-five years after the Series, Canadian hockey still faces many challenges that threaten the future of the game. Minor hockey provides an example. The primary goal of minor hockey shouldn't be winning, but rather learning the skills of the game, trying to win— and having fun while doing it. When winning is the only goal, the most important goal of minor hockey sometimes is lost: the development of properly educated and responsible young people. It's not the kids playing the game who are the problem. It's the people who are coaching and managing who manipulate the players and the leagues they play in for their egos, self-interest and greed. Too many coaches and parents are involved in hockey for their own gratification, rather than for the young players' well-being and development. Young people can learn life skills in the context of the game of hockey, and those skills are transferable to real life. This is primarily what the game should be doing for our youth.

Parents, coaches and organizers: stop living your disappointing lives, failed dreams and lost hopes through the kids and get on with your lives. Parents should support, encourage, create opportunity, but not push their kids to be what the parents want them to be. Not everyone is destined to be a professional hockey player, and the sooner parents realize that, the more enjoyment the kids can have from the recreational benefits of playing the game. Too many young, impressionable players are treated as marketable commodities. In this distorted environment, fewer and fewer young people will want to play hockey at all; they'll choose less violent sports with greater longevity.

The original slogan for Minor Hockey Week in Canada was: "Take your kid to the rink, don't send him." However, with the bad behaviour of some out-of-control parents at rinks in recent years, kids might be better off with a new slogan: "Send your kid to the rink, don't take him." Kids won't change their style of play until their role models do.

Parents, coaches and the NHL have to set a better example of how the game should be played. And remember, it's only a game. Just let 'em play and have fun!

Minor hockey shouldn't be set up as a mini-NHL hockey factory to develop professional hockey players. Professionals should be a by-product of the process, not its raison d'être. There's nothing wrong with young hockey players aspiring to play in the NHL; it's good to have dreams and goals. But young people shouldn't sacrifice their education and the opportunities it can create in the process of getting there. In life, what's between your ears has to carry you a lot longer and farther than your skating legs and playing talents. And unfortunately, because the school system in Canada isn't yet generally compatible with hockey, some of our best young talent goes to US schools, which offer scholarships. Most of these young people never play professionally—and many never return to Canada. What a tragic loss.

The Canadian Hockey League (CHL) oversees major junior hockey in Canada. Even going back to when I played for the Toronto Marlies in the late 1950s, the primary goals of team owners and management was developing professional-calibre hockey players, winning and making a profit. And for some strange reason, because the young players were paid only a modest stipend to play, they retained their amateur status. These days the objectives of major junior teams remain the same as they always have been. Plain and simple, it's a business. And while I would credit some coaches and managers with looking out for the educational interests of their players, the CHL is in fact Canada's primary minor professional hockey league. Operating under the guise of "amateur" is and always has been a sham.

Professional hockey (specifically the CHL and NHL) are reaching back almost into the cradle in their continuous and relentless search for future talent. Kids of thirteen and fourteen are too young to deal with the world of professional hockey, even if they possess exceptional physical skills. And beware of people who suggest they are, and who would like to represent them.

One of the key factors threatening the growth of hockey in North America is the increasing cost to play the game: equipment, ice rental, travel, time. For many parents, hockey is not an affordable option for their kids. And the cost to attend to watch an NHL game has also sky-rocketed, making it prohibitive for many. Purchasing tickets is often reserved for a corporate clientele; the average hockey fan has to watch on TV. The high prices to play and watch hockey could affect the NHL's ability to attract the next generation of hockey players and fans.

—ɷ—

At the NHL level, there is a new deal between the owners and players, and some signs of changes to improve the game. But there is room for more improvement. The style of play during the 1990s disrupted the natural rhythm, flow and speed of the game. Aggressive and violent play was common; teams had restrictive defensive strategies. The game was pulled down to the lowest common denominator, defensive hockey that was neither fluid nor entertaining to watch. Checking is not a natural skill; it's an acquired skill. A coach can teach any player to check. The real beauty in the game is in the offensive creativity of players, not in the mechanical discipline of defensive hockey. During the height of the "defensive trap" years, even Wayne Gretzky in his prime would have been hard pressed to score more than thirty goals in a season.

The new NHL introduced several new rules to improve the game for players and fans: they took out the red line, adjusted on-ice markings and introduced a game-deciding shootout. Many of the other so-called new rules have been in the rule book for years.

Penalties for hooking, slashing, high-sticking, cross-checking, reckless use of the stick, hitting from behind, board checking and interference have always been in the rule book. In the years just before the new NHL, too many players were literally clutching, holding and hanging on to their careers. The NHL failed to give their officiating staff the support to enforce the rules. Owners, general managers and coaches too often had players of limited talent; the league wanted to appeal to the less sophisticated American audience. So the rules were manipulated. It didn't work.

NHL great Jean Beliveau said the hockey stick is a tool of the game, not a weapon. For years less skilled players used it as a weapon of intimidation. In the new NHL, the stick is back on the ice, where it belongs. There are severe penalties for hooking, slashing, high-sticking and cross-checking. I hope the example of the new NHL filters down to the youngest levels of the game.

If the NHL really wants to improve the level, excitement and entertainment value of play, there's an even better way to do it. Go back to the time when a penalty was really a penalty. Make every player who takes a penalty sit out the full penalty time. No more coincidental or off-setting penalties. No erasing the remainder of a penalty if a team scores on a power play when short-handed. There would be many benefits on the ice and for the fans if real bite was put back into penalties.

If every penalty was served for its full time, coaches and players might think seriously about their conduct on the ice. All of a sudden, a hooking penalty would give the opponents a two-minute advantage. Enforcing penalty times could lead to 5 on 4, 4 on 4, 4 on 3 and 3 on 3 situations, giving the skill players more chances to play the game the way it should be played. It would make a penalty truly a penalty instead of what they are today: two players fight, they each get five-minute majors, they go to the penalty box, the game resumes with neither team short-handed—where's the penalty? Most times it gets players off the ice who shouldn't be there to begin with, but the team pays no real penalty.

If the league enforced penalty times, coaches would have to recruit and develop skill players; they couldn't afford the luxury of goons to intimidate their opponents with their fists and sticks. The benefits would be a better, more wide open and exciting game for players and fans, increased scoring chances and room for the more skilled players. Eventually players would incur fewer penalties, as it's often the lesser skilled players who take most of them. The performance level of hockey would get better and games would be more appealing. Does the NHL have the courage to make it a better, more exciting and entertaining game for players and fans alike?

And there could be another benefit from having all penalties served in full. As players have gotten bigger and faster over the years, the ice surface seems smaller and smaller, at times like a postage stamp with today's players whizzing around. The NHL missed an opportunity to introduce larger ice surfaces when numerous new arenas were built in the late 1980s and 1990s. But if all penalties were served in full, there would be times when fewer players would be on the ice, effectively creating more space for those who are.

The NHL should always be looking for ways to speed up the playing time of games. Yet an obvious way has been continually ignored. Here's a simple way to do it: on an obvious icing play, blow the whistle. Don't waste time making the player skate the length of the ice to touch the puck. Talk about wasting playing time. Wouldn't that time be better spent with real hockey for the fans? If it's a close or questionable call, the official has the discretion to wave off the call and keep the puck in play. Or is the NHL waiting for a player to break his neck or worse on some of these icing calls? Maybe the league is resisting the automatic whistle because it's an international rule, and the NHL is too proud or too stubborn to acknowledge that someone else had a better idea.

Has the time come to remove fighting from the game? Why is fighting permitted? There is a penalty for it, but generally players who fight are not ejected from the game. Hockey is a contact sport, as it has always been and should be. It takes grit to be an effective player. But for too long, the NHL-style game featured aggression and violence, hacking and whacking, hooking and holding, clutching and grabbing, blatant interference, late hits, hits from behind, hits to hurt, brawling and fighting, all combining to obstruct the flow, rhythm, speed, grace, beauty, skill and excitement of the game. And most of the infractions are committed by marginally talented players whose goal is to neutralize skill players. Goons reduce hockey to a sports spectacle, like roller derby or wrestling. Hockey is too great a game to be derailed by the goon mentality.

What precipitated the goon approach is a noticeable lack of respect between players. Too many players tried to hurt each other, and at times displayed real mean-spiritedness and dangerous hockey, so they could continue earning the large salaries. A player shouldn't have to risk his health or his life, or potentially have to fight every time he steps on the ice.

The NHL is the only major sports league in North America that permits fighting. In the NBA, the players are certainly big and strong enough, but basketball is a skill-based game, and fighting isn't a part of it. NFL players are also big and strong, and football is certainly a physical and sometimes violent game, but fighting is not allowed. Football players who fight are automatically ejected. In major-league baseball, tempers flare on occasion, but ejection is automatic no matter how many players have been in the fight. And then there's the NHL, which thinks that fighting is a necessary and inherent part of the game and that it adds to the appeal. Nonsense! It doesn't make the game any better. It's an unnecessary sideshow.

If a fight erupts, the participants should be ejected from the game. Or if this is too extreme a measure, eject the instigator and give the other combatant a five-minute major or ten-minute misconduct penalty. This remedy would stop goons from going after skill players. A player shouldn't have to be pugilist to be able to play and excel at the highest level. The time has come to stop fighting as a part of the game of hockey. Fighting is condoned in hockey because the NHL hasn't yet shown the courage to put a stop to it.

Where will the great game of hockey go in the future? Who is going to look out for the best interests of the game? Who will shape and guide the sport? Who are the keepers and trustees of the game? Who is going to save the game from the avaricious goals of the NHL owners and players? The fans? The CHA? Corporate sponsors? Aspiring players looking for new and different role models? You? Me? All of us?

Canadian hockey leaders are slow learners. Some thirty-five years after the Soviets demonstrated their skill-based game to the NHL in September 1972, Canadian hockey teachers and leaders are still supporting a game that promotes strength and aggression over skill and finesse.

Neither the NHL at the top of the hockey ladder, nor the CHA at the bottom of it, has demonstrated enough vision, leadership or courage to make sure the game stays on the road to success in Canada. Greed is driving hockey at every level right up to the NHL. Sadly, hockey has long since passed from a game built on skill and fun to a business. It's all about money.

Hockey is a troubled and struggling sport from top to bottom. I say from top to bottom because the NHL, at the top of the hockey hierarchy, has an intrusive and pervasive influence on all Canadian hockey players, right down to beginners, and on all Canadians. (One way or another, the game of hockey affects all Canadians.) So when I see the sports page starting to read like the front page, I know something is wrong. If hockey is to continue to enjoy broad popularity, changes are needed at all levels of the game.

Today's gladiators of the ice will go the way of their Roman predecessors if the game continues down the road it's on. Prospective players will turn their backs on the game, and fans will find other sports or activities to play and support, and the great game of hockey as we know it could disappear.

And so the puck continues to turn and the soap opera plays on. In retrospect, I achieved minimal success and was a misfit on and off the ice in the professional hockey world. But the road I travelled made for an incredibly interesting, fascinating, challenging and at times bizarre journey. It was a trip of a lifetime, and I'm grateful for having had the chance to take it. I love hockey—not the business or politics of it, but the game itself. The enjoyment and satisfaction come from striving for success. For me, it's been more the journey than the destination…and we aren't there yet.

Index